Canada and the Crisis in Central America

CANADA AND THE CRISIS IN CENTRAL AMERICA

Jonathan Lemco

PRAEGER

New York
Westport, Connecticut
London

Library of Congress Cataloging-in-Publication Data

Lemco, Jonathan.
  Canada and the crisis in Central America / Jonathan Lemco.
    p.   cm.
  Appendices (p.   ) : Excerpts from the draft Contadora treaty and
The Esquipulas II agreement.
  Includes bibliographical references and index.
  ISBN 0-275-93718-6
  1. Central America—Relations—Canada. 2. Canada—Relations—
Central America. 3. Canada—Foreign relations—1945- 4. Central
America—Foreign relations—1979- 5. Procedure to Establish Steady
and Long-Standing Peace in Central America (1987)   I. Title.
F1436.8.C2L46   1991
327.710728—dc20   90-43134

British Library Cataloguing in Publication Data is available.

Library of Congress Catalog Card Number: 90-43134
ISBN: 0-275-93718-6

First published in 1991

Praeger Publishers, One Madison Avenue, New York, NY 10010
An imprint of Greenwood Publishing Group, Inc.

Printed in the United States of America

The paper used in this book complies with the
Permanent Paper Standard issued by the National
Information Standards Organization (Z39.48-1984).

10 9 8 7 6 5 4 3 2 1

Contents

Tables

Acknowledgments

I am indebted to several people and I would like to thank them for all of their help.

Professor Bruce Bagley of the Graduate School of International Studies at the University of Miami first piqued my interest in Canada's role in Central America. Richard St. Martin of the Canadian Department of External Affairs provided me with a wealth of government documents and speeches that proved invaluable sources of information.

The many diplomats and politicians who agreed to be interviewed were a major resource. My colleagues at The Johns Hopkins University Paul H. Nitze School of Advanced International Studies (SAIS) and the National Planning Association provided friendly criticism and advice.

My family, and particularly my wife, Judy, were an ongoing source of love and support. Finally, whenever I grew too serious about this project, my daughter, Alexandra, insisted that I place myself in her world of play and laughter.

Canada
and the Crisis
in Central America

Introduction

Canada and Central America: The Transition from Ignorance to Concern

Until quite recently, Canada's interest in Central America was confined largely to occasional commercial transactions, missionary appeals, and development aid. Unlike their American counterparts, Canadian policy-makers paid little attention to the Central American region. It occupied the lowest rung on Canada's foreign policy agenda. The Department of External Affairs regarded it as an American area of concern, and Canadian politicians, the press, and the public preferred to direct their attention to the United States or Western Europe as areas where they might enjoy a sphere of influence.[1] In the early 1960s, the countries of the Pacific Rim and the island nations of the Caribbean also became the subject of some Canadian attention. Central America, however, was perceived as little more than a region composed of banana republics.

Further, Canadians felt little common identity with the area, and close personal ties there were largely absent. Historical circumstances were different as the Canadian development process was predominantly evolutionary and the Central American one revolutionary in character. Few serious academic studies of the region were undertaken by Canadian scholars, and a limited number of stories were filed by Canadian journalists. Also, few Canadians spoke Spanish (a majority of Canadians do not even speak French, Canada's second official language) and immigration from Canada to Central America had always been minimal. Ultimately, the Canadian attitude toward Central America was cautious, and knowledge of the area was limited. To the extent that Canada took an interest in Central America at all, it was often in an effort to safeguard British investments there. (Indeed, until 1926 Canada's relations with the region were handled by Great Britain.) For example, in El Salvador in 1932, the Canadian navy sent two warships to protect British railways and plantations during the "Farabundo Marti" uprising. At that time the Salvadorean army killed 30,000 people.[2]

Canadian contacts with the region were largely through short-term trade missions or through the work of Catholic missionaries. Business contacts were few because of a pervasive sense that Central America was dominated by the United States due to a special relationship built on long-term trade and security arrangements. Indeed, a sizeable number of Canadian firms, as subsidiaries of American companies, were not permitted to export to Latin America so as to avoid competition with their U.S. parent companies. This precedent was established as early as 1916 when a group of Winnipeg entrepreneurs initiated the construction of a railway in Nicaragua, but representatives of the U.S. Marines, who would permit only American financing and construction of transportation facilities in Central America, did not permit them to continue.

This is not to say that Canada had no economic interests in the region. A few Canadians owned tobacco, orange, and other fruit plantations in Nicaragua. Some of the major banks, utilities, and insurance companies owned branches in the region. Two large Canadian-owned mines were opened: Inco opened one in Guatemala (but closed it in the early 1980s due to diminishing profits) and Noranda purchased a gold mine in Nicaragua (which was expropriated later by the Sandinistas).

With an eye toward expanding trade possibilities, Canada opened a small trade commission in San Jose, Costa Rica, in 1946. In 1961 this mission was upgraded to embassy status (with a nonresident ambassador). This post was designed to serve Honduras, El Salvador, and Nicaragua as well.   Guatemala was handled by the Canadian embassy in Mexico. Throughout the 1960s, critics complained about the quality and quantity of Canada's representatives in the region. Economic and political ties remained minimal, however, until Pierre Trudeau was elected prime minister in 1968.[3]

Trudeau recognized the potential economic and political weight of Central America in hemispheric and global affairs. He focused on North-South issues throughout his 1968-1984 tenure as prime minister and announced:

We have to take greater account of ties which bind us to other nations in this hemisphere--in the Caribbean, Latin America--and of their economic needs. We have to explore new avenues of increasing our political and economic relations with Latin America where more than 400 million people will live by the turn of the century and where we have substantial interests.

This view was reinforced in 1970 by his government's booklet *Foreign Policy for Canadians*, which acknowledged that Latin America was becoming a "force in the world." Further, closer Canadian-Central American relations could be expected to enhance Canadian sovereignty and independence through trade and investment.

Soon after Trudeau's election to office, a high-level government mission including five cabinet ministers visited Latin America and delivered an encouraging report concerning the economic role that Canada might play in the region.[4] In 1971, Canada joined the Inter-American Development Bank (IDB) and within a few years a number of European nations and Japan followed Canada's lead. In the first two years of Canadian membership in the IDB, Ottawa's aid to the Central American region doubled to $13.07 million (Canadian).[5]

In the years to follow, Canada's ties to the region grew slowly. Central America remained a relatively low priority for the external affairs ministry, and the Canadian journalistic and academic communities, with few exceptions, virtually ignored the region.

However, in 1983 two major reports by the Parliamentary Subcommittee on Relations with Latin America and the Caribbean were published. Included in the reports was a broad overview of Canada's relations with Latin America during the 1970s and policy recommendations for the 1980s. The reports, responding to the deteriorating human rights situation in El Salvador and increasing public interest in Central America, urged the Department of External Affairs to pay more attention to problems in that region. Attention was devoted to the appalling human rights violations, poverty, large-scale displacement from homes, and the overall decline in the quality of life for many of its people. The Subcommittee reports also discussed strategic, political and economic issues, including the difficulties associated with encouraging moderate forces to emerge in such a polarized atmosphere, the growth of East-West competition, the struggle to promote economic modernization, and the effort to encourage investor confidence and stem the flight of capital. The reports emphasized Canada's extensive Central American aid program and recommended increased aid to Nicaragua and Costa Rica. They also discussed Canada's leadership role in the acceptance of refugees, and considered Canada's willingness eventually to oversee elections in the region. These subcommittee reports, which attracted considerable public attention, exhibited the clearest evidence of Canada's interest in supporting the interests of peace in Central America and in recognizing Central America as a priority region for Canadian foreign policy concerns.

Opinion is mixed, however, as to whether the Subcommittee reports actually influenced the direction of Canadian government policy. They did help to convince the government that, although there were flaws in the Salvadorean election program, the process should be supported. In addition, the Subcommittee felt that an agenda for negotiations was needed to encourage both political and economic reform as well as to foster mutual respect between countries. They were instrumental in persuading Canadian policymakers to support regional dialogue, which contributed, in turn, to the government's eventual decision to endorse the Contadora peace process.

On the other hand, the federal government stopped far short of accepting all of its recommendations, for the Subcommittee also called for a conference of the representatives of all countries in the hemisphere to discuss Central American security issues. Ostensibly Canada would help to organize such a conference and thereby become much more involved in the region than it had ever been before. The Canadian government rejected this suggestion out of hand. It did not want to be enmeshed in the difficult problems of the region, nor did it wish to be placed in a position whereby it might be forced to take a position different from one taken by the United States. Furthermore, it was arguable whether Canada had the diplomatic resources and expertise for such an endeavor.

The subcommittee also recommended the elimination of all forms of external military assistance; but this was regarded with some suspicion by the Canadian government. It should be acknowledged that despite the insistence that Canada would not alter its aid programs for political or ideological reasons, Canadian ambitions in the region were not wholly altruistic. In fact, Canadian aid was designed to bolster sales of military equipment and to promote political motives. For example, in 1983, the same month that Ottawa cosponsored a United Nations resolution condemning human rights violations by the Guatemalan military regime,[6] Canadian embassy officials in Guatemala City were discussing the sale of helicopters by de Havilland Aircraft Company of Toronto (a Canadian crown corporation) to that country's air force, which was known to use its equipment to strafe Indian villages. Interest groups represented by the Task Force on the Churches and Corporate Responsibility criticized the granting of an export permit for this sale on the grounds that such aircraft had been used by the military in the past to make war on its own citizens. The Canadian government granted the permit, however, and argued that the aircraft were not suited to military use. At about this time, the Canadian government's Export Development Corporation (EDC) also extended a $7.5 million loan to the Guatemalan regime for the purchase of locomotives from Bombardier Inc., a Montreal-based firm.

Furthermore, Canadian government officials approached Honduras, Canada's largest economic aid recipient in Central America, with offers to sell military hardware, despite Canadian church and labor opposition.[7]

External Affairs Minister Allan MacEachen responded to critics by noting that Canadian economic aid "is not designed as a tool to reward or punish foreign governments." This attitude met, and continues to meet, strong opposition from certain religious, labor and political (e.g., the New Democratic party) groups in Canada. The reality is that the federal government does tie its aid policy to political considerations, from time to time, though not necessarily for ideological reasons. For example, in September of 1983, the secretary of state for external affairs indicated that economic assistance to Central America would increase once some degree of reconciliation had been achieved and the area could absorb assistance more easily. The Canadian government also temporarily suspended development assistance to both El Salvador and Guatemala because of its concern over massive human rights violations there, and its concern for the safety of Canadian aid personnel in the light of the precarious internal security situation in both countries. On the other hand, aid was allowed to continue in Nicaragua, Costa Rica and Honduras.[8] Perhaps it would be most accurate to say that development assistance is rarely offered on the basis of politics, although it may well be withdrawn in response to gross abuse of human rights. Clearly, however, the recommendations of the parliamentary subcommittee were only partially implemented by the Canadian government.

In March 1984, following the release of the subcommittee reports and increased attention to Canadian aid and refugee policy in Central America from the media, MacEachen indicated that Canada would "be available for consultation with respect to the social, economic and security commissions which had been set up by [the] Contadora [peace process]."[9]

He also offered a rather benign perception of the Sandinistas when he said: "We have to acknowledge that required changes have taken place in Nicaragua . . . that improvements have taken place."[10]

This view had been shared by Prime Minister Trudeau when he indicated that

states have the right to follow whatever ideological path their peoples decide. When a country chooses a socialist or even a Marxist path, it does not necessarily buy a "package" which automatically inject [sic] it into the Soviet orbit. The internal policies adopted by the countries of Latin America and the Caribbean . . . do not in themselves pose a security threat to this hemisphere.[11]

Nonetheless, Trudeau would not go so far as to explicitly condemn U.S. influence in the region. Canada had and continues to have too much at stake in its relationship with the United States to humiliate its chief ally.

In late November 1987, External Affairs Minister Joe Clark visited Central America, further underscoring Canada's growing interest. At about this time his government announced that Canada would set up field offices in Nicaragua, Honduras, and El Salvador, where it did not have embassies. Canada also resumed aid to Guatemala, suspended since 1981 in response to the Guatemalan government's human rights abuses.

Collectively, the moves suggested that Canada was preparing to act more forcefully in the region. Canada had admitted thousands of refugees from the area, sent millions in foreign aid through a host of non-governmental organizations, and regularly criticized violations of human rights.

Clark toured Nicaragua, Costa Rica, Guatemala, Honduras, and El Salvador. He visited aid projects, refugee camps, and local church leaders, with the aim of assessing the impact of Canada's economic and political assistance. The external affairs minister's trip was a vehicle for gathering facts and, more symbolically, determining if this was an opportune time for Canada to increase its role as a regional power. As one observer noted, "There may be an opening for real changes. Clark will want to decide if Canada is more willing to assert leadership."[12]

It should be noted that Joe Clark's offer of support was likely more symbol than substance, however. There has been little concrete action to back Canada's supportive rhetoric. Canada will not act unless it is formally asked to do so by all the relevant countries, but it will venture very cautiously, to avoid embarrassing the United States. In addition, some suggest that whatever influence Canada has comes less from political expression than from the scores of aid projects undertaken by the Canadian International Development Agency (CIDA). Between 1982 and 1987 Canada gave more than $105 million in bilateral aid to Central America, tripling its assistance to the region. It also donated more than $50 million through nongovernmental organizations and multilateral bodies. The government remains fairly committed to providing technical and administrative support for its aid programs, and perhaps this is where the bulk of Canada's real influence may lie.

Clark's trip was regarded by many as something less than a great success. It was clear that he arrived in the region ill-prepared and had virtually no information about progress under the Arias peace plan. Indeed, there were frequent episodes during the trip in which Clark simply did not have the requisite knowledge available.

Furthermore, on the first day in the region Clark suggested that Canada might accept some contra refugees, to assist the peace effort. The idea was immediately rebuffed by Immigration Minister Benoit Bouchard, but not before the gaffe had been reported extensively in the national press. This was not Joe Clark's finest hour.

Since 1987 Canadian interest in Central America has continued to expand.[13] As will be discussed in Chapter 1, however, Canadian interests in the region will always be juxtaposed with Canada's bilateral relationship with the United States. In taking the policy stance that it does on Central America, Canada can assert a relatively costless independence from U.S. policy interests. This has been particularly relevant to its relationship with Nicaragua. On the other hand, Canada will never go so far as to publicly shame its most important ally.

It is because Canada had no interest in alienating the United States, and for other reasons, that Canada remained out of the Organization of American States (OAS), the largest hemispheric organization, until October 1989. This topic will be addressed in Chapter 2. Canada's business and investment ties in Central America are modest, but one factor motivating Canadian interest in the region is the profit incentive. An overview of Canada's commercial ties to the region will be presented in Chapter 3. Of far more importance is Canada's development assistance program in Central America. Indeed, Canada's most important contribution may be in the form of aid, an issue that takes on particular salience given the Canadian government's massive aid cutbacks in 1989. This will be discussed in Chapter 4.

The Central American peace process has offered great promise, and a few concrete results. An overview of the process and the prospects for peace will be addressed in Chapter 5. The Canadian government has offered technical suggestions, based on its peacekeeping experience, to the Central American presidents. Canadian government officials believe that Canada might realize a greater influence in the region by offering recommendations for monitoring the peace process and sending Canadian peacekeepers under the auspices of the United Nations. The nature and viability of such a contribution will be explored in Chapter 6. One obvious impact of the strife in Central America is the flow of refugee applicants to Canada. How generous is the Canadian government in this regard? How consistent is its immigration policy with its overall goals in Central America? What pressures does the Canadian government face from church groups, trade unions, and others to place human rights considerations above all others in its Central American policies? These are some of the questions to be addressed in Chapter 7.

The Canadian government devotes a substantial amount of its resources to Central America. It is not clear, however, if this attention is appreciated or even recognized by the relevant actors in the region. Nor should we be surprised by this. Rather, it will be argued throughout this study that many of Canada's foreign policy goals in the region are designed to appeal to domestic Canadian interests. Canada's policies are tied to such vital national concerns as its degree of foreign policy independence and its status as a "helpful fixer" on the world stage. Whether these are just perceptions without empirical support is less important than the fact that the public responds positively to government initiatives that promote these goals. As we shall see, then, whether Canada can truly contribute to Central America by offering advice, peacekeeping troops, investment or development assistance is no more important than whether the Canadian public perceives that Canada is making a difference.

NOTES

1.   For examples of Canadian acquiescence to U.S. interests in the region from the early part of the century until the early 1980s, see Peter MacFarlane, *Northern Shadows: Canadians and Central America* (Toronto: Between the Lines, 1989). Of particular relevance are pp. 94-100 for a discussion of the CIA-engineered coup in Guatemala in 1954, pp. 135-37 for an outline of Canada's position on the 1973 Chilean coup, and pp. 155-61 for an overview of Canadian policy interests and the Nicaraguan revolution of 1979.

2.   For a detailed study of this uprising, see Harvey Levenstein, "Canada and the Suppression of the Salvadorean Revolution of 1932," *Canadian Historical Review* 62 (1981), pp. 451-69.

3.   For a review of business ties, see Jonathan Lemco, "Canadian Foreign Policy Interests in Central America: Some Current Issues," *Journal of Inter-American Studies and World Affairs* 28:2 (Summer 1986), pp. 119-46.

4.   For a good overview of this mission, see J. A. Stiles, *Developing Canada's Relations Abroad* (Sackville, N.B.: Mount Allison University Press, 1980).

5.   Cecilio J. Morales, Jr., "A Canadian Role in Central America," *International Perspectives* (January/February 1985), pp. 12-15.

6.   The U.N. Resolution stated that its signatories expressed their "deep concern at continuing massive violations of human rights in Guatemala, particularly the violence against non-combatants, the wide-

spread repression, killing and massive displacement of rural and indigenous populations, which are recently reported to have increased."

7.   Traditionally, many of the actions initiated in support of human rights have been undertaken by the Catholic church, organized labor, and other ostensibly nongovernmental organizations (NGOs). For a discussion, see Steven Baranyi, "Canadian Foreign Policy Towards Central America, 1980-84: Independence, Limited Public Influence, and State Leadership," in the *Canadian Journal of Latin American and Caribbean Studies* 10:19 (1985), pp. 23-57.

8.   John Graham, "Canada and Contadora," speech delivered to the Canadian Institute of Strategic Studies (Toronto, November 9, 1985), p. 4.

9.   Ibid., p. 5.

10.   *Globe and Mail* (April 4, 1984), World News section.

11.   Prime Minister Pierre Trudeau, speech presented to the Commonwealth Western Hemisphere Meeting, St. Lucia, West Indies (February 26, 1983).

12.   Quote taken from Edgar Dosman, a Canadian-Latin American expert, *Financial Post* (November 23, 1987), p. 17.

13.   The Special Joint Committee on Canada's International Relations discovered that more Canadians wanted to talk about Central American issues than about concerns in any other region of the world. See their report entitled *Independence and Internationalism* (Ottawa: Supply and Services Canada, 1986), p. 111.

1 *Canadian Foreign Policy and Central America: Is There a Legitimate Role to Play?*

Currently, much attention is being paid by the Canadian press, a number of interest groups, and a small number of scholars to the role that Canada might play in Central America. It should be stressed that this is a new phenomenon, for as recently as ten years ago few Canadians knew or cared about that part of the world. One can suggest a number of reasons for this newfound interest, including: (1) a genuine Canadian concern for human rights in Central America, and the rights of Central American refugees in particular; (2) an opportunity to target Canadian aid where it can demonstrably improve living conditions; (3) modest opportunities for business investment in the region; (4) a desire to contribute to the peace process; and (5) a chance to distinguish Canadian foreign policy from U.S. interests and thereby contribute to national pride, increase the international perception of Canada as an international "good guy" and "helpful fixer," and realize certain electoral benefits as a result.

Undoubtedly, these and other reasons can help explain Canada's interest. Nevertheless, it remains to be seen if Canada can truly make a difference in a part of the world that was previously regarded, at least unofficially, as a U.S. sphere of concern.

The focus of this chapter will be the extent to which Canadian actions matter in the Central American region. Particular attention will be devoted to the following issues: To what extent is Canadian foreign policy in Central America similar to or different from U.S. policy there? To the extent that Canadian policy differs, does it matter? Does Canada run any risks, with regard to its bilateral relationship with the United States, in pursuing an independent policy?

As mentioned, until recently Canada's interest in Central America had been limited. Indeed, it was confined largely to occasional commercial transactions, missionary appeals, and development aid.

In the late 1970s, however, a number of factors emerged that focused Canadian interest on the Central American region. These included a series of development projects initiated by governmental and nongovernmental organizations, the participation of refugee organizations in the Canadian political arena, and the concerns of church-related groups about human rights violations. Of particular interest to Canadian Catholics was the assassination of Archbishop Oscar Romero and, later, the rape and murder of four nuns--all in El Salvador. Also, many Canadians had worked in the region and could now speak authoritatively about its problems. Furthermore, the Canadian media and the federal government[1] took a new interest, for reasons cited earlier, but also as a response to the Reagan administration's policies there. New Democratic party leader Ed Broadbent introduced the strife in El Salvador as a topic for debate in Parliament. This prompted the dispatch to El Salvador of two government officials, who subsequently reported hearing of abuses that had occurred there. Acting as a catalyst to these forces, however, was former Prime Minister Pierre Trudeau.[2] As a result of his preoccupation with North-South issues and related problems of development in Central America, unprecedented amounts of aid assistance flowed to the region. In turn, interest groups, particularly those affiliated with the Catholic church, organized relief agencies and pressured the federal government to devote more attention to the area. Nongovernmental organizations (NGOs) agreed to help, and mainstream newspapers began to cover the region more vigorously.

All this being said, however, one would be hard pressed to argue that Canadian government interest in Central America grew for purely selfless reasons. Canadian policymakers were also intent on pursuing a relatively independent, and heretofore costless, foreign policy vis-à-vis the United States. Indeed, Canadian interests in the region can be truly comprehended only insofar as they are understood in conjunction with relations between Canada and the United States.

By pursuing an apparently distinctive foreign policy in Central America, Canadian policymakers could enjoy a measure of international prestige by being seen as international "good guys" or "helpful fixers." This perception, in turn, could help federal politicians encourage national pride and unity.

To understand the growth of Canada's interest in Central America, one must understand something about Canadians' highly sensitive view of their complex and occasionally troubled relationship with the United States.[3] Canadians experience ambivalent feelings of superiority and insecurity simultaneously in their bilateral relationship. By superiority, it is meant that Canadians take great pride in their extensive social services, their clean cities, the relative lack of violence in Canada, the extremely good foreign press they receive, and the superior reputation that they enjoy around the world. In all these areas, a contrast is drawn, by some Canadians, to the apparent failings or weaknesses of the United States in these areas.

The Canadian sense of insecurity is fostered by the dynamic U.S. economy, the United States' superpower status, its vibrant cultural industry, and most important, the sheer dominance of North America that the United States enjoys by virtue of its military capacity, its economy, and its population base.

Canada's Central American initiatives, then, allow two goals to be reached. First, Canada can pursue a foreign policy that it truly believes is best for its own interests--and for political stability, economic development, and social justice in the Central American region. Indeed, Canadian policy there has been remarkably consistent for many years, and across partisan party lines. Also, Canada can use its position on Central America to assert its autonomy from the United States and thereby demonstrate its empathy for Third World nations. However realistic such a goal may be, the attempt to assert foreign policy distinctiveness cannot help but win support domestically. If Canadian government actions are perceived to be taken in Canada's best interests, and not automatically in concert with U.S. government actions, then public support will undoubtedly increase. A recent poll is only the latest to support this view. The *Globe and Mail* reported that 67 percent of Canadians think Canada should pursue a foreign policy independent of the United States.[4]

Canadian policymakers are not so short-sighted as to completely diverge from U.S. policy, of course. Canada is an ally with many shared interests, and will never go so far as to embarrass the United States. This has been evident throughout the history of the binational relationship. For example, during the Vietnam War Canadian government officials publicly chastised U.S. bombings of North Vietnam. This ended quickly, however, and Prime Minister Lester Pearson acknowledged that realpolitik dictated that Canada mute its criticism.

"Every small or middle country is in some way a satellite of a great power now," he said in 1967. "This is the kind of world in which we live. It's not a comforting thought . . . but when you have 60 percent of your trade with one country [this amount has since increased], you are in a position of considerable economic dependence."

A similar view was expressed by former Canadian Ambassador for Disarmament Douglas Roche to the *Globe and Mail* on October 28, 1989:

> I suppose the biggest shock that I got [on becoming ambassador] was to learn the influence, the pressure, that the U.S. government has on the Canadian government on the issues of disarmament and security . . . [U.S. influence] operates at every level, and it operates in varying degrees from subtlety . . . to crude threats.

It should also be acknowledged, however, that the United States has never penalized Canada for its foreign policies, particularly in Central America. Whether this is because Canada has never been perceived as a threat or an embarrassment, whether it is because there is a belief that Canadian policy does not matter and can be ignored in the region, or whether there is an honest sense in the United States that Canada is entitled to its own position--Canada has never been seriously chastised, stifled, or pressured by her neighbor over its foreign policy measures in Central America. The costs of Canadian divergence, then, have not been high.

It should also be acknowledged that the stakes in the region had, until recently, never been very high, either. Now, however, Canada is engaged in a free trade agreement with the United States. The Mulroney government would not take a foreign policy action different from the American one if there was a perceived risk to that deal. There has been no history of linkage on these or other such issues, however, and therefore Canada has reason to feel confident in pursuing a relatively independent foreign policy in Central America without American reprisal.

It is important to note that since there is no history of linkage, divergence from U.S. policy in Central America is not only costless but desirable as well. The free trade agreement promises to promote economic integration between the United States and Canada. To many Canadian nationalists, this is a terrifying risk to their nation's sovereignty. To assuage the fears of these people, the federal government in Ottawa will be striving to identify episodes of Canadian-U.S. divergence, to counterbalance the perceived threat. Central American policy differences provide an ideal opportunity for the federal government to argue that the free trade agreement will not make it an American "puppet."

It is also the case that Canada is loath to be perceived by the Central Americans merely as an extension of the United States and, to that end, has made a conscious effort to assert an independent position--this is reflected in its choice not to join the OAS until late 1989, and then only because it felt that it could take an independent stance within the largest hemispheric organization. At least the government's rhetoric tries to convey this impression. Furthermore, certain commentators argue that Canada harbors a sympathy for the countries of Central America, since it also must live in the shadow of the U.S. superpower.[5] So, for the past few years, Canada has gone out of its way to emphasize that priorities for peace in Central America must include a sustained effort to pursue economic growth and social reform, to discourage superpower intervention, and to reduce sales of military hardware. There is no strong evidence that this message has been received by the Latin American political actors, however. Some saw Canada's decision not to join the OAS as a sign of Canadian government acquiescence to U.S. foreign policy interests.

It should be noted, however, that the Canadian government's position on Central America, although consistent across governments, has not always been consistent internally. For example, in the early 1980s a gulf existed between the views of Prime Minister Trudeau and External Affairs Minister Mark MacGuigan. Trudeau focused upon North-South questions, while MacGuigan's primary interest was East-West tensions. Trudeau attributed most of the problems of the Central American region to indigenous causes, while MacGuigan's approach was internally inconsistent. At times his views corresponded to those of the prime minister. At other times his views mirrored the hawkish views of President Ronald Reagan's first secretary of state, Alexander M. Haig. When President Reagan visited Ottawa in March 1981 and several thousand demonstrators protested against the president's policies in El Salvador, MacGuigan declared that "there was no difference between the policies of our two governments."[6] It is no wonder that some critics called him "a Haig puppet."[7]

Further, in October 1982, then-Secretary of State for External Affairs Mark MacGuigan stated: "I am not aware that we have any serious obligations in that part of the world, in Central America, which is not an area of traditional Canadian interest. It is not an area in which we have any particular claim to knowledge of what is going on."[8]

At this point, MacGuigan interpreted political strife in Central America as a direct result of Soviet and Cuban expansionism in the area. He took a hard line on alleged Nicaraguan involvement in El Salvador and was supportive of U.S. policy in defense of "democracy" in the region. In 1981, he asserted that "I would certainly not condemn any decision the U.S. takes to send offensive arms there [El Salvador] . . . the U.S. can at least count on our quiet acquiescence."[9] The minister later claimed that he had been misquoted, and that he had meant to say "quiescence."[10] Nevertheless, the initial statement is instructive since Canadian officials, rather than criticizing American policy, frequently chose simply not to condone it. In the House of Commons, MacGuigan stated that he did not believe "that we should be leading a public crusade against the attitudes of the American administration which believes that it is acting in its own interests, and on the basis of information which it possesses and which it is beginning to share with its allies."[11]   At other times, however, MacGuigan spoke of the root causes of the Central American strife as being economic inequality and social injustice.[12]

Prime Minister Trudeau shared the views of the Western Europeans and Mexicans, who did not perceive the Soviet Union to be a direct threat in Central America. In a speech before the Commonwealth Western Hemisphere meeting in St. Lucia, Trudeau articulated his views: "For our part, we have consistently chosen to address hemispheric tensions from their economic and social causes, being equipped neither by ambition nor by the capacity to pursue military solutions or grand strategic designs."[13]

As a consequence, at that time, Canadian statements on East-West issues in general, and Central America in particular, were occasionally contradictory. In 1982, MacGuigan was replaced by a new minister of external affairs, Allan MacEachen, who was perceived as more experienced and progressive than his predecessor and whose views corresponded more closely and more consistently with those of the prime minister.

Perhaps the sharpest divergence between the United States and Canada on Central America concerns the roots of the conflict there. The influential Kissinger commission report of 1984[14] portrayed the conflict as an extension of the rivalry between East and West, Marxist vs. U.S. capitalist forces. Specifically, the Soviet Union, Cuba, and (until recently) Nicaragua represented catalysts to revolution in the region. By contrast, successive Canadian governments since that of Prime Minister Trudeau have viewed the conflict as the result of terrible poverty, uneven distribution of wealth, social injustice, and a failure to institute the economic and social reforms required to meet the people's needs.[15] Canadian officials argued that political instability is the inevitable consequence of this inequity. Intervention by major powers, then, only aggravates a dismal situation.

What was really in question, of course, were the motives of the Sandinista government. When the Reagan administration took office in January 1981, it warned against the contagion of a Communist takeover in Central America (like "falling dominoes"), it stepped up military aid against Salvadorean guerrillas, and it threatened the new leftist regime in Nicaragua. Prime Minister Trudeau's views differed from the president's in that he was willing to give the Sandinistas the benefit of the doubt that the expansion of their armed forces was for defensive rather than offensive purposes. Trudeau stated that "there are major divergences [from U.S. policy], beginning with the fact that we object to the interference in the internal affairs of other countries by any major power--even if that power is our friend." Trudeau tempered that statement later, however, by indicating that "we recognize that the United States has to be interested and intimately involved with the affairs of that part of the world."[16]

Nevertheless, from time to time Prime Minister Trudeau spoke out about his opposition to U.S. support for the contras in Nicaragua. External Affairs Minister MacEachen called the mining of Nicaraguan ports a violation of international law. Trudeau called it "an act of international terrorism."[17] Both stressed that although the Sandinistas might be Marxists, they were not totalitarian. This was at variance with the position of the Kissinger commission's members, particularly Jeane Kirkpatrick. To quote MacEachen:

> We are, however, concerned about the extent to which military aid is a major component of the Kissinger proposals. In keeping with Canada's position against third party intervention in Central America and the supply of armaments to opposing factions, we oppose continued military support for anti-Sandinista insurgents just as we oppose the promotion of, and support for, armed insurgency in El Salvador and Guatemala by outside powers.[18]

When MacEachen visited Central America in April 1984 his itinerary pointedly included Nicaragua and excluded El Salvador. This decision was made to emphasize Canadian recognition of the legitimacy of the Sandinista government. At the same time it underscored Canadian reservations about the credibility of recent Salvadorean elections. Trudeau also criticized the presence of U.S. troops in Honduras and of U.S. military advisers in El Salvador. Nevertheless, Stephen Baranyi argues convincingly that Canada's differences with the United States in Central America were not, and are not, expressed in a uniform way. For example, he maintains that, in general, Canada feels far more confident in diverging from U.S. policy in Nicaragua than it does regarding U.S. policy in El Salvador.[19] Indeed Canadian and U.S. policies in Guatemala, Honduras, Costa Rica, and El Salvador are not substantially different.

Prime Minister Trudeau supported the U.S. position that Soviet interference in Central America was deplorable. He believed that the Soviets were giving economic aid to friends in the region, and that they enjoyed seeing the Reagan administration publicly criticized, if not chastised. However, he discounted the president's alarm regarding Soviet military intentions. Trudeau was also distressed that the president paid mere lip service to the Contadora peace process. He lamented the Kissinger commission's recommendation that military forces should not be excluded as a bargaining tool with the Sandinistas. Trudeau spoke also of the necessity for diplomatic negotiations. Still, the prime minister's specific criticisms of U.S. policy were made quietly through diplomatic channels. It was not, and is not, in Canada's interest for the United States to lose face in any way. To protest too strongly would garner few positive results and only aggravate existing tensions.[20]

By 1985 Nicaraguan exports to Canada, notably beef products, rose despite the U.S. request for an allied trade embargo on the country. (They have since sharply decreased.) Canada's position was to abstain from the embargo and to regard the void left by the U.S. absence as a wonderful business opportunity. One official was quoted as saying that "the fact that the U.S. is out of the market means that there is room for everyone else."[21] External Affairs Minister Clark added that Canada was skeptical about U.S. policy and was concerned that it might achieve the opposite goals of those intended.[22]

With the imposition of the American embargo, Nicaragua's trade office was transferred from Miami to Toronto. Canadian shipments to and from Nicaragua through the United States were necessarily discontinued, and other outlets had been pursued, although Nicaragua's lack of foreign exchange was a major obstacle to greater trade. Canada had refused to oppose bank loans to the Sandinista government, however. It is not yet clear how it will respond to the Chamorro government, although it is likely that Canada will maintain a similar position for the time being.

In January of 1986 Canada endorsed the Caraballeda Declaration,[23] and in February External Affairs Minister Clark alluded to his government's apparent opposition to the U.S. contra support by emphasizing that countries should "refrain from committing acts that aggravate the present situation and are obstacles to the peace process . . . the Canadian Government opposes third party intervention in Central America."

Nevertheless, Prime Minister Mulroney visited Washington without seeking an opportunity to express Canadian opposition to Washington policies in Central America. By contrast, Presidents Raul Alfonsin of Argentina, Miguel de la Madrid of Mexico, and Francois Mitterrand of France all used their addresses to joint sessions of the U.S. Congress to express their countries' disapproval of the Reagan administration policies in the region.

Since 1984 two secretaries of state for external affairs have visited Nicaragua--Allan MacEachen in 1984, and Joe Clark in 1987. But Canada has yet to install an ambassador in Managua, relying still on its embassy in Costa Rica.[24] Reasons, or excuses, for this include the prohibitive costs involved, a distrust of the Sandinista government (until its electoral defeat), and the fact that Canada does not have an embassy in El Salvador either, although that country has double the population. Nor does it have one in Honduras, although it is a "core" country for Canadian development assistance. It is also the case, however, that here again Canada will not provoke the United States where there is a perceived possibility of hostility emerging.

On June 25, 1986, the U.S. House of Representatives allocated $100 million for contra aid. Joe Clark, speaking on behalf of the government, voiced his opposition to this action:

> The Congressional decision to provide additional aid to the Contras runs counter to our position. Canada has constantly emphasized its firm belief that the countries of Central America must be free to seek their own solutions without interference from any outside source.[25]

In November Canada applauded the World Court's judgment against the U.S. support of the contras and voted in favor of a U.N. motion calling on the United States to comply with the decision. In so doing it was the only North Atlantic Treaty Organization (NATO) ally that did not abstain on the vote. At the time of the U.N. vote, however, Canada attempted to soothe ruffled U.S. feelings by also criticizing the Sandinistas. Ambassador Stephen Lewis stated: "While supporting the resolution, we wish to express our concern that the resolution points only to the United States and fails to mention others, including Nicaragua, that are intervening in the internal affairs of other states in the region."[26]

Canada did abstain on a December 1986 U.N. vote condemning the commercial embargo of Nicaragua by the United States, however. It justified this inaction by stressing that the embargo did not violate the General Agreement on Tariffs and Trade (GATT). Clearly there are limits to Canadian divergence on an issue that does not have the backing of international law.

To reiterate, there is no doubt that Canada had been displeased by Nicaragua's ties to the Soviet bloc.[27] Some Canadian officials had expressed reservations about the presence of Cuban advisers in Nicaragua, although the Mulroney government remained willing to give the Sandinistas the benefit of the doubt. Furthermore, some suggested that Canada lent the Sandinista government a measure of legitimacy by taking such actions as witnessing talks between Sandinista representatives and those of the indigenous opposition group, Misurasata.

Canada's position on Nicaragua was vulnerable to attacks from both the left and right. If left-wing critics charged that Canada should use its privileged position to promote greater development aid and commercial ties with Nicaragua or to lambaste Reagan policy there, they would not be easily chastened by the government's cautious policies and interest in retaining warm relations with the United States. Critics on the right would stress that fighting communist subversion in Nicaragua must be the first priority. Therefore, Canada should lend whatever help it can to the U.S. effort to fight Marxist forces. Although left-wing critics were more numerous, mainstream Canadian politicians and public servants were still in the unenviable position of trying to accommodate these competing interests, and to responding to mixed signals from an ever more vocal public--all the while making every effort to be seen as not holding the United States up to ridicule. It was a very fine line to tread.[28]

One result, with particular relevance to Nicaragua, is that Canada would not be averse to taking public stands inconsistent with U.S. policy, while committing itself to little of substance. The rhetoric may have been that of an independent foreign policy actor willing to constructively support efforts at resolving regional conflict. The reality is that independent action has sharp limits, that support may be largely symbolic, that meaningful expressions of divergence--like Canada's U.N. vote to condemn contra funding--would emerge only if the costs of such action were perceived to be low and if a multinational organization like the United Nations could provide the required legitimacy necessary for such a move. This is not to dismiss the presence of real differences, then, but rather to shed light on the real constraints which exist. There are also, at times, internal inconsistencies. In July 1988 an all-party parliamentary committee studying Central American peace prospects recommended an end to the U.S. economic embargo of Nicaragua. A Cabinet spokesman responded by stating: "It's not up to Canada to protest every time the U.S. wants to do something."[29]

Other U.S.-Canadian differences pertain to strategies for economic recovery in Central America. The Kissinger commission report recommended that the private sector be the chief engineer of economic growth in Central America. Canadian policy, by contrast, emphasizes a combination of public and private sector involvement. This is consistent with Canada's historic reliance on the state to perform functions that are traditionally executed by the private sector in the United States.

It should be noted that although the differences between U.S. and Canadian policymakers are evident on certain issues concerning Central America, it is not clear that this is of grievous concern to U.S. officials. To cite one State Department spokesman: "Should we not supply the Contras because there are a few people from allied countries who side with the Sandinistas? "[30] This is not to say that U.S. spokesmen are not occasionally troubled by their inability to get Canada to support them more often. It is easy for Canadians to sit in their ivory tower and criticize our policy because they don't have to deal with the consequences if the policy doesn't work. . . . Canadians say the U.S. has no business interfering in Nicaragua. . . . they don't understand why the U.S. forces a moral commitment to the Nicaraguan people.[31]

Most U.S. officials, however, seem willing to let Canada maintain its own positions. They don't appear threatened or otherwise concerned by the existing differences, at least at the time of this writing.[32]

Nevertheless, Canadian officials recognize that there may be limits to Canadian divergence. If there is a U.S. government perception that Canada will diverge in a way that is deleterious and ultimately damaging to U.S. interests, the United States might be inclined to retaliate by canceling or hindering implementation of the free trade deal or sabotaging the bilateral effort to stop acid rain. So far there is no evidence of such linkage, but it is a risk that Canadian government officials might find unacceptable.

To sum up the discussion so far--Canada feels that the Central American countries themselves should safeguard security in the region. It is concerned that the United States is prepared to assume too great a military role. In this regard it regularly asserts its opposition to U.S. support of the contras, although it is also quick to criticize the (FMLN) guerrillas in El Salvador. Canadian officials stress that force should be a last resort, to be exercised only after diplomatic options are exhausted, on the grounds that the use of force poses a threat to the international order and puts all countries in danger.

Canada recognized the legitimacy of the Sandinista government and defended Nicaragua's right to self-determination and sovereignty. By contrast the United States did not acknowledge the legitimacy of the Nicaraguan government. Canada did not perceive Nicaragua to be a totalitarian state and applauded the democratic elections in February 1990. By contrast, the United States felt that "regimes created by the victory of Marxist-Leninist guerrillas become totalitarian and [considered] the democracy of Nicaragua to be a sham."[33]

Canada does not interpret conflicts in the area as an East-West issue so much as a North-South issue. It favors multilateral action, if necessary, in the form of United Nations involvement rather than major power incursion. Canada emphasizes pragmatism, not ideology, in its diplomatic efforts, although the protection of human rights is always a stated priority.

Canada and the United States also disagree on economic strategies for Central America. The Kissinger commission report advocated reliance on the private sector as the key to economic recovery in the area. By contrast, Canadian policymakers advocate a combination of government and private sector action to reverse decades of economic mismanagement in the region.

Finally, Canadian officials are not comfortable with the "march to democracy" theme advocated by the Kissinger commission and supported by the Reagan and Bush administrations. Some observers complain that "it conceals an ethnocentric bias which yields uncritical support for 'imperfect democracies' or authoritarian regimes."[34] They would suggest that the United States become more tolerant of ideological diversity in Central America.

Thus far, much attention has been paid to U.S.-Canadian points of departure. But this is misleading, for important lines of convergence exist as well, which force us to question how important the differences truly are.

First of all, Canada's interests necessarily are closely tied to those of the United States. Both countries have vital trade links and cooperate on economic programs. Both countries share liberal democratic traditions, fairly similar histories, and close political and cultural ties. There is an enormous degree of mutual dependence. As a result, in his first speech before the House of Commons concerning El Salvador, then-External Affairs Minister MacGuigan said, "In light of the full circumstances, we are prepared to contradict the U.S. policy of military aid but not to protest it; we are prepared to criticize it but not to condemn it."[35] One example of this, in 1981, occurred when Canada supported the United States in approving credit for El Salvador from the International Monetary Fund's compensatory finance facility, despite the refusal of IMF staff to recommend approval.

Later, MacGuigan said he was "pleased to supply our support for the general lines of approach which are emerging from the (Reagan) Administration, to the extent that I understand them."[36] One can make the argument, of course, that at times MacGuigan demonstrated strong sympathies for U.S. policy and might not have been a completely unbiased political actor. The parliamentary subcommittee on relations with Latin America and the Caribbean was a multiparty committee, however. Although expressing strong reservations with U.S. policy they still went on to say:

It should be clearly understood by all countries in the Caribbean and Central America that these regions are of strategic importance to the U.S. and to the Western Alliance of which Canada is a member. Any direct threat to vital U.S. and Western strategic interests will be resisted.[37]

Further, in 1983 Prime Minister Trudeau told the House of Commons that he saw no reason for the United States to end its military activities in the region as long as other external forces were similarly involved. Indeed, he stated that "what the United States does in Latin America is its own business because the Spanish-speaking world is one of its spheres of influence."[38]

Periodic assertions of Canadian unease over the "escalating military confrontation" in the area were increasingly accompanied by criticisms of the guerrilla movement in El Salvador and statements of "dismay" over "the increasing tendency toward authoritarianism" in Nicaragua.[39]

In fact, in April 1984 External Affairs Minister MacEachen asked the Nicaraguan foreign minister to tone down his government's criticisms of the United States.

Also, like the United States, Canada worried about the repression of civil liberties in Nicaragua and shared the American concern about the size of the Nicaraguan army and militia, as well as the apparent attempts of the Sandinista government to destabilize its neighbors. In 1987, Canada was so suspicious of Sandinista motives that it refused to send observers to monitor elections in Nicaragua. Liberal party external affairs critic Jean Chrétien suggested that Canada was simply acting out of deference to U.S. interests, since it had sent election observers to equally troubled El Salvador.

It is clear that both Canada and the United States share certain interests in the region. There is a common concern that political stability be pursued, that economic breakdown be prevented, and that civil war be avoided.

Both countries understand the importance of security interests in the region, although the United States is far more explicit in expressing its views on this matter than is Canada. Canada and the United States understand the necessity of retaining access to the Panama Canal and other sea lanes of communication. Both share certain apprehensions regarding the potential for Central American default on foreign debt, although this is not a substantial amount compared to some of the countries of South America. Both countries, as mentioned, are in substantial agreement concerning their support for the governments in El Salvador, Costa Rica, Guatemala, and Honduras. It is only with regard to Nicaragua that there was a meaningful difference.[40] Even this divergence must be qualified, for Canadian government officials, although not convinced that Nicaragua was a Communist state intent on overthrowing the governments of its neighbors, regarded the Sandinistas with suspicion. They would certainly not take any direct action to hamper American efforts there. Of course there is now no obvious difference between the positions of the United States and Canada after Violeta Chamorro's victory.

Ultimately, one is forced to acknowledge that although, at times, Canada and the United States will use different means to realize their objectives in Central America, their ends are essentially the same. Canada might diverge from the United States on grounds of principle, but it will not hamper U.S. actions because (1) it shares the same essential goals, and (2) the costs of active divergence are unknown and potentially great. As a middle power situated near a superpower, Canada can do little of substance.

Furthermore, in those instances where Canadian policy differs from U.S. policy in Central America, Canadian officials are most comfortable expressing their differences behind the scenes. As previously discussed, Canadian political leaders will speak out at times concerning their misgivings with U.S. policy, but in these cases they will bend over backward not to embarrass the Americans. Most often, diplomatic solutions to differences are expressed privately rather than in a confrontational and public manner. No recent prime minister has found himself in danger of being berated as was Prime Minister Lester Pearson by President Lyndon Johnson after Pearson had criticized the U.S. role in the Vietnam War. Lawrence Martin reported that Johnson picked Pearson up by his lapels and shook him.[41]

Since Mulroney's election as prime minister in 1984, his government has made every effort to present Canada's differences with the United States in Central America as dissimilarities between mature allies and friends. Disagreements do occur, but they are expressed in such a way as to not aggravate bilateral tensions. To quote the prime minister: "Good relations, super relations, with the United States will be the cornerstone of our foreign policy."

The most vociferous dissent from U.S. policy is kept behind closed doors. For example, External Affairs Minister Clark had frequently chastised the United States about its aid policy to the contra rebels. He or the prime minister would, often in mild terms, declare that third parties should not provide arms to any factions in the area.[42] While expressing Canadian disapproval, however, the government spokesperson would always insist on Canadian noninterference in U.S. actions and Canadian sensitivity to American strategic interests in the region.[43] This should not be surprising, of course. In fact, it might be unreasonable to expect Canada to play more of a direct role. Nevertheless, its lack of action weighs against Canada's playing much of a constructive function in the eyes of Central Americans.

To the extent that Canada does take more concrete action, such as its support of the United Nations resolution in November 1986 condemning contra funding, it does so under the umbrella of the world's largest multinational organization. Again, it is well and good that Canada acts under the auspices of a respected organization like the United Nations, but this won't convince the relevant political actors that Canada can make much of a difference. To quote External Affairs Minister Clark:

> The question really is whether it is the purpose of the foreign policy of a sovereign country to give lectures to others or to act within our own capacity to achieve results that we can achieve . . . we believe that it is our business to do our business and we are doing it.[44]

In that vein, Clark refrained from commenting on Washington's decision to send troops to Honduras in March 1988, for example.

Joe Clark has been criticized by prominent church and other religious groups and the New Democratic party for his reluctance to condemn U.S. policy more explicitly, but he maintains that Canadian policy would not be served by castigating the United States. As a result, the Mulroney government engaged in a number of actions that, some critics suggest, demonstrate quiet acquiescence to then-President Reagan's Central American policy. These included increased customs inspections and bureaucratic paperwork that periodically delayed aid to Nicaragua. A number of interest groups have charged Canada with indirectly assisting the U.S. trade embargo of Nicaragua in this way. Other examples include substantial quotas on Nicaraguan beef exports to Canada, Ottawa's refusal to grant special export credits to Nicaragua, occasional meetings between parliamentarians and contra fundraisers, and Canada's decision not to open an embassy in Nicaragua.

This last point is particularly salient to interested church and relief groups because, they argue, an embassy would promote trade, development aid, intelligence information, advisory services, and a visible Canadian presence. These are all debatable points, of course. (In November 1988 an "honorary consul" was appointed to Managua. This is a purely ceremonial post, however.)

What appears fairly clear, then, is that if Canada occasionally criticizes U.S. policy, it does so reluctantly. Furthermore, it has not demonstrated that it is willing to take direct action to support its rhetoric in the effort to bring peace to the region. Perhaps this lack of action is a realistic approach on the part of Canadian officials. They appear to believe that there is little of substance that Canada can do, short of providing development aid, peacekeeping advice, and a few peace observers. Certainly there is no strong evidence that Central American leaders recognize that Canada is making a substantial difference in the region, with the possible exceptions of aid policy and a Canadian advisory role to the peace process. It is unclear what Canada can do in terms of concrete action.

"Not-for-attribution" interviews with a number of Central American diplomats posted in Washington revealed that the diplomats were surprised, and a few a little bemused, to learn of the extent to which Canadian and U.S. policy diverged. All had assumed that the countries were very similar in their policy preferences.[45]

Statements about Canada's possible role in the region by Oscar Arias, Daniel Ortega, and other Central American political leaders have drawn attention in Canada. They suggest that Canada might have some role to play in a peace plan or in encouraging the United States to respect the World Court decision condemning American actions in the mining of Nicaraguan harbors and the attack on an oil facility. Nicaraguan diplomats in Washington, however, appeared unaware of Ortega's statements at the time.[46] If the Canadian government does aspire to a meaningful independent policy, the message apparently has not yet been received by all of the relevant political actors.[47]

Some have suggested that although little could be accomplished while Reagan was president, Canada could help to lay the foundation for peace in Central America when a less intransigent administration took office.[48] Certainly George Bush appears to be more pragmatic, if not more accommodating, than his predecessor. Accordingly, Canadian officials are cautiously optimistic that American and Canadian views on Central America, and particularly Nicaragua, will converge. To quote Joe Clark: "I think there's a genuine consensus in the United States to proceed on a more bipartisan basis (between Republicans and Democrats), and that might mean it will result in more agreement between Canada and the U.S. on the analysis of the problem."[49]

Of course, the differences are now all but non-existent following the Chamorro government's victory. A gulf between Canadian and American interests never did exist with regard to policy toward Nicaragua's neighbors, however, as evidenced by Canada's support of the U.S. invasion of Panama and the capture of General Manuel Noriega. On the morning of the invasion, President Bush phoned Prime Minister Mulroney to inform him of the impending incursion and to hear his thoughts. This simple courtesy was enormously important to Canadian government officials, for prior to the Grenada invasion Canada had not been consulted and, in a fit of pique, voiced opposition to the American action.

There is no evidence to suggest that had Mulroney expressed his misgivings, if any, to President Bush, the U.S. chief executive would have called off the operation. Nevertheless, the prime minister undoubtedly regarded the Bush phone call as a face-saving measure for the prime minister, and Mulroney immediately expressed his support for the attack. Mulroney called General Noriega "a drug-running thug and assassin who looted his own country."[50] The prime minister regretted, but understood, the American use of force in Panama, given the failure of diplomatic efforts to dislodge Noriega's "savage" regime.

Not all Canadians were pleased with Mulroney's solidarity with the United States, however. The opposition Liberal party, the New Democratic party, and many among the Canadian press and public opposed the U.S. action, charging that it set a precedent for an international order where force prevails.

Prime Minister Mulroney was unmoved by the criticism, however, and indicated that although his government regretted the use of violence, it did not rule out one country's right to intervene in the affairs of another in special circumstances. This was just such an occurrence. The argument that the United States acted out of self-defense was curious, since the American attack was premeditated and since diplomatic options might not have been exhausted. Various diplomats from the Soviet Union, Nicaragua, and other countries declared that Canada's immediate support for the invasion again demonstrated Canada's acquiescence to U.S. interests. A Soviet U.N. spokesman was quoted as stating: "It is to be expected. After all, Canada and the U.S. are so very close."[51]

Mulroney's defense of the U.S. invasion contrasted sharply with an earlier position in which he stated that "Canada does not approve of third-party intervention anywhere in Central America, whoever the third party may be, regardless of its legitimate interests in the area."

Nevertheless, Mulroney decided that it was in Canada's interest to give the United States the benefit of the doubt in this special circumstance. His decision was entirely in keeping with the policies of his predecessors.

CONCLUSION

Clearly, Canada has maintained an ambivalent stance in its response to U.S. policy in Central America. It has refused to support military interests there, sought political solutions to its regional conflicts, and refused to oppose bank loans to the Sandinista government of Nicaragua. On the other hand, Canada is wary of criticizing U.S. policy, is not averse to condemning Nicaraguan abuses of civil liberties or troop buildups, and understands that its first priority is to promote a generally accommodative tone to relations between the United States and Canada. To the extent that Canada has taken an independent stance, there has been no retaliation by the United States. Possible reasons for this have been suggested, but none are more persuasive than the fact that (1) there is not a clear perception held by Central American leaders that a distinctive Canadian policy, by itself, can make much of a difference in the region, and (2) the United States also needs Canada to be "on board" on a host of vital bilateral efforts. It can be concluded, however, that Canadian government politicians and bureaucrats are in a most unenviable position. On the one hand, there are a substantial number of interest groups and vocal members of the public who feel that Canada must do more to oppose American policy and present a strong and independent voice. They are not averse to pressuring government officials to act accordingly. On the other hand, there is a recognition that as a "middle power" there is only so much Canada can do without harming its far more vital bilateral relationship.

Canada can provide development aid, which is a tangible contribution. As we shall see subsequently, it can also offer less tangible, yet substantive comments to the peace process. Perhaps it is unreasonable to believe that Canada should do more, given its foreign policy constraints. Canada's Central American policy demonstrates the opportunities and responsibilities associated with being a middle power.

NOTES

1.   Some critics have suggested that one factor hampering a more substantial Canadian role in Central America was the embarrassingly low quality of Canada's diplomatic representation there until the 1980s. See Edgar Dosman, "Hemispheric Relations in the 1980s: A Perspective from Canada," *Journal of Canadian Studies* 19:4 (Winter 1984-85), p. 51.

2.   This is ironic given Trudeau's unpopularity in Canada at that time. Trudeau's economic and other domestic policies were anything but a success. Nevertheless, his views on foreign policy issues were still widely supported.

3.   For an overview of some of the tensions in the relationship, see Jonathan Lemco, "The Myth of Canadian-American Harmony," *Atlantic Community Quarterly* (Spring 1987), pp. 91-97.

4.   *Globe and Mail* (August 18, 1987).

5. For example, see Brian K. Murphy, "The Pan-American Game: Canada and Central America," *Canadian Forum* (February/March 1988), pp. 9-13.

6. For a more thorough discussion of this point, see Graham Mount and Edgar Mahant, "Review of Recent Literature on Canadian-Latin American Relations," *Journal of Inter-American Studies and World Affairs*, 27:2 (Summer 1985), pp. 127-51.

7. See, for example, *Globe and Mail* (June 10, 1982), p. A-5.

8. As quoted in Tim Draimin, "Canadian Policy Toward Central America," paper published by Canadian-Caribbean-Central America Policy Alternatives (February 1983).

9. *Globe and Mail* (February 5, 1981), World News Brief Section.

10. Ibid. (February 27, 1981), p.1.

11. *Debates*, House of Commons, vol. VII (February 19, 1981), p. 7459.

12. See, for example, Mark MacGuigan, "Central American and Canadian Foreign Policy," speech delivered to the University of Toronto Law Faculty by the secretary of state for external affairs, March 31, 1982.

13. Prime Minister Pierre Trudeau, speech presented to the Commonwealth Western Hemisphere Meeting, St. Lucia, West Indies (February 20, 1983).

14. The Kissinger commission report was officially titled *The Report of the National Bipartisan Commission on Central America* (January 1984).

15. For a discussion of this point, see Mark MacGuigan, "Central America and Canadian Foreign Policy."

16. *Globe and Mail* (April 23, 1984), p. 1.

17. *Toronto Star* (April 12, 1984), p. 1.

18. As quoted in "Notes for a toast on the occasion of the visit to Ottawa of the Foreign Minister of Columbia, H. E. Rodrigo Lloreda Caicedo" (Ottawa, February 20, 1984), p. 4.

19. Steven Baranyi, "Canadian Foreign Policy Towards Central America, 1980-84: Independence, Limited Public Influence and State Leadership," *Canadian Journal of Latin American and Caribbean Studies*, 10:19 (1985), pp. 23-25.

20. Part of this discussion is adapted from Jonathan Lemco, "Canadian Foreign Policy Interests in Central America: Some Current Issues," *Journal of Inter-American Studies and World Affairs*, 28:3 (Summer 1986), pp. 119-46.

21. As quoted in E. Bradford Burns, *At War in Nicaragua: The Reagan Doctrine and the Politics of Nostalgia* (New York: Harper and Row, 1987), p. 115.

22. *Los Angeles Times* (May 21, 1985).

23. The Caraballeda Declaration on January 13, 1986, called upon the countries of Central America to take specific measures to reduce tensions and to advance the Contadora peace process.

24. It should be mentioned that relations with Central America are now handled through the Division of Caribbean and Central American Relations of the Department of External Affairs.

25. As quoted in E. Bradford Burns, "Nicaragua: Paving a Separate Path," *In These Times* (September 10-16, 1986).

26. As quoted in *Globe and Mail* (November 4, 1986).

27. For a more substantial discussion of this point, see James Rochlin, "Aspects of Canadian Foreign Policy Towards Central America, 1979-1986," *Journal of Canadian Studies* 22:4 (Winter 1987-88), pp. 5-26.

28. Indeed, Rochlin reports that when policymakers at the Department of External Affairs formulate Canada's policy toward Central America, they consult two groups of their own experts. One group focuses on Canada's relations with the Central American countries, the other specializes in U.S. strategic interests in the hemisphere. Canadian officials understand that it is always important to balance these two interests. See James Rochlin, "Aspects of Canadian Foreign Policy Towards Central America, 1979-1986," *Journal of Canadian Studies* 23:4 (Winter 1987-88), p. 5.

29. Deborah Wilson, "MPs Urge U.S. to Drop Embargo on Nicaragua," *Globe and Mail* (July 7, 1988), p. A-10.

30. Marci MacDonald, "On the Road to a New Vietnam?" *Maclean's* (November 10, 1986).

31. Bob Hepburn, "Canada and U.S. Poles Apart on Nicaragua," *Toronto Star* (April 14, 1987).

32. To a point, of course, they need Canadian goodwill as well, and will not seek to embarrass their neighbor.

33. As quoted from the Kissinger commission report (1984), p. 105.

34. For an overview of this position, see Thomas Bruneau, "Canada and Latin America: Background," in *Canada, the United States, and Latin America: Independence and Accommodation* (a conference report), Washington, D.C. (Latin American Program, Woodrow Wilson International Center for Scholars, April 1984), pp. 1-11; or Edgar Dosman, "Hemispheric Relations in the 1980s: A Perspective from Canada," *Journal of Canadian Studies* 19:4 (Winter 1985), pp. 42-60.

35. *Debates*, House of Commons, vol. VII (February 19, 1981), p. 7459.

36. Canadian Press (CP), press release of August 9, 1983.

37. House of Commons Report on Canada's Relations with the Caribbean, by the Parliamentary Subcommittee (Ottawa: Queen's Printer, 1983).

38. As quoted in James F. Petras and Morris H. Morley, "The United States and Canada: Perspectives on Capital in Central America," in John Holmes and Colin Leys (eds.), *Frontyard/Backyard* (Toronto: Between the Lines, 1987), pp. 149-79.

39. Ibid., p. 173.

40. It is interesting to note that the Canadian position is not unlike the mainstream view of the U.S. Democratic party. Jimmy Carter, Walter Mondale, Michael Dukakis, Cyrus Vance, Sol Linowitz, and George Mitchell favor multilateral diplomacy, negotiation, democracy-building, and debt relief for Central America. They eschew military force or the threat of it, except as a last resort in cases where vital national interests are at stake.

41. This episode is recounted in depth by Lawrence Martin, *The Presidents and the Prime Ministers* (New York: Doubleday, 1982), chap. 13.

42. In addition, see the statement of the Canadian ambassador to the United States, *Ottawa Citizen* (March 15, 1986), p. A-16.

43. For example, see MacEachen's statement to that effect, *Calgary Herald* (July 23, 1983), p. A-4.

44. As quoted in "Clark Refuses to Rebuke U.S. for Arming Nicaraguan Rebels," *Ottawa Citizen* (January 29, 1986).

45. Central American diplomats in Ottawa were much more aware of Canada-U.S. policy divergence, but were not convinced that these different views would make much of a difference in policy terms. A few noted that if Canada wanted to pursue a meaningful and independent foreign policy in the region, then taking a leading role in the OAS might be one vehicle to achieve this goal. Canada joined the largest hemispheric organization in late 1989.

46. For example, see "Canada Should Enforce the Central American Peace Pact: Ortega," *Montreal Gazette* (November 25, 1987).

47. Political actors were not alone in lacking knowledge about Canada's peace efforts. During Joe Clark's eight-day visit to Central America in late fall 1987, his name was misspelled in the press and his presence virtually unknown by average citizens. For a discussion of these points, see Brian K. Murphy, "The Pan-American Game: Canada and Central America," *Canadian Forum* (February/March 1988), pp. 2-13.

48. See Tim Draimin's statement to that effect, reported in Robert Chodos, "Central Americans Look North: Can Canada be a Counterweight to the U.S.?" *This Magazine* (August/September 1987).

49.   "Clark Hopes U.S. Revises Contra View," *Toronto Star* (February 12, 1989).

50.   Canadian Press (CP), press release of December 20, 1989.

51.   Olivia Ward, "Canada Criticized for Backing U.S.," *Toronto Star* (December 23, 1989), p. A-16.

2 *Canada and the OAS*

The past decade has witnessed a new Canadian interest in the problems of Central America. Governmental and nongovernmental organizations have donated developmental aid to the region and provided sanctuary for some of the area's refugees. A Canadian effort to contribute to the peace process has begun with offers of advice to the architects of the Esquipulas II agreement. The deployment of Canadian peace observers or peacekeepers is ongoing. All this being said, however, there is no strong perception in Latin America that Canada has yet begun to make a meaningful difference in the region. Although this should not be surprising, given Canada's proximity to the U.S. superpower and its interests in not diverging too sharply from U.S. policy, many critics of Canadian foreign policy still maintain that Canada might have more of a presence in Central America. One remedy for the situation might be the Mulroney government's decision to become a full member of the Organization of American States (OAS), in October 1989, after forty-one years of choosing not to accept its "seat at the table."

The decision not to join the OAS until 1989 was not taken lightly. Successive Canadian governments since the beginning of the century maintained that joining would not be in Canada's national interest. Nevertheless, most governments recommended further study on the matter. In the eyes of many Latin American policymakers, however, the decision by Canada not to join the OAS was a clear indication of Canada's apparent subservience to U.S. foreign policy interests.

Canadian government officials would agree that the decision not to join the largest organization in the hemisphere was related, in part, to concerns associated with the enormously vital relationship with the United States. But they would also maintain that by not joining they were able to demonstrate, to the relevant Latin American nations, Canada's strength and not its weakness. They could make clear their foreign policy independence. They would also stress that while Canadian policy decisions would have implications for other nations, ultimately the federal government had to make decisions based on Canada's interests. Choosing to join the OAS until October 1989, then, had been in Canada's best political interests.

After a brief historical overview, the discussion here will focus upon the costs and benefits associated with Canada's OAS membership and the circumstances prompting the Mulroney government to change its policy.

One of the earliest reasons cited for not joining related to Canada's complex relationship with the United States. Indeed, when Canadian officials were asked just after World War I to join the OAS's predecessor, the Pan-American Union, they refused on two grounds. First, Canada's foreign policy was still largely dictated by Great Britain (Canada gained its full foreign policy powers only in 1962). Canada was perceived by OAS members to be a monarchy, and only republics were permitted to join. This did not stop Brazil and the English-speaking Caribbean nations from joining, however. Second, and more important, the federal government regarded the Pan-American Union as an affiliate of the U.S. State Department and American corporate interests.

In the 1920s the question of Canada's participation reemerged, but here again Canadian officials were wary and, equally important, U.S. officials, including President Calvin Coolidge, were reluctant to admit a member of the British Empire to the Pan-American Union. Clearly, the United States regarded Latin America as its bailiwick and was averse to permitting a potential rival to join.[1] Until the mid-1940s there was no general support in Canada for joining, and while the United States did not explicitly oppose Canada's entrance, it did not encourage it.

During World War II Canada expanded relations with Latin America. Canadian diplomatic missions were established in five countries between 1941 and 1944, and a number of Canadian government officials[2] and Cooperative Commonwealth Federation party (CCF) pressed for Canada's admittance to the Pan-American Union. Also, a few U.S. congressmen and State Department officials expressed an interest in Canadian participation, for they felt that Canada could contribute to the organization's budget and thereby reduce the economic burden of the United States. Most American experts worried about the possibility of British influence if Canada joined. Another concern was Canadian competition in South American markets. The Canadian government reserved judgment on the matter.

In 1947 a regional collective security system under the Inter-American Treaty of Reciprocal Assistance, the Rio Pact, was established. This pact reflected U.S. concern over the perceived Soviet threat and the resultant need to establish a zone within which the American states would be united for the defense of the continent. This agreement emphasized that all states, and not just the republics in the region, were welcome to join.[3]

In 1948, the OAS was created,[4] and it soon became clear that the United States would pay the predominant share of that organization's budget. In turn it would play a preponderant role in promoting the activities of the OAS in pursuit of its own security and ideological goals. The Latin American members resented the U.S. dominance, but they believed that the United States would always attach a priority to hemispheric interests, rather than to global or superpower concerns. Years later the U.S. support of the British during the Falklands/Malvinas crisis would come as a profound shock to most OAS members and dispel any myths about where American priorities truly lay. Of course, the invasion of Grenada and attempts to destabilize the Sandinista government in Nicaragua are just further evidence of this.

At the time of the founding of the OAS, the government of Prime Minister MacKenzie King of Canada was wary of joining an inter-American agreement. It argued then, as do some critics of government policy today, that joining an organization like the OAS might obligate Canada to join the Rio Pact and thus be forced to take up arms for hemispheric defense, should the situation present itself. (There is still a substantial difference of opinion on this issue, a point that will be discussed subsequently.) A few Latin American countries, anticipating the possible consequences of dealing with the U.S.-dominated organization, pressed Canada to join. Brazil, Colombia, Mexico, and Chile were particularly supportive of a Canadian presence. The United States kept a fairly low profile on the issue. On the one hand, it would welcome Canada's economic support. On the other hand, however, it feared that Canada's presence in the Commonwealth and its close ties to Great Britain might force its allegiances to lie outside the hemispheric alliance. The United States would not deny Canada's entrance to the OAS, however, and a neutral position was chosen. For their part, Canadian government officials reserved judgment on the matter until an unspecified later date.

It should also be noted that the large majority of the Canadian population was, and is, indifferent to the region, and therefore few electoral votes were to be gained by joining. Rather, Canada's U.N. participation, which was very popular, would be the priority. If the OAS was dominated by the United States, then it was within the United Nations that Canadians felt Canada could have its greatest impact.

In addition, Canada's defense needs would be met within the Permanent Joint Board on Defense and subsequently, NATO and the North

American Air Defense Command (NORAD). In 1949 Prime Minister Louis St. Laurent stated: "For the moment we consider it much more pressing to realize the North Atlantic Treaty Organization than to add one more vote to an organization that one can consider exclusively reserved to the Western Hemisphere."

Until the mid-1950s Canada remained largely indifferent to OAS involvement, although some Latin American countries continued to take an interest in Canadian participation. At the Inter-American Conference at Caracas, in 1954, a Brazilian draft resolution extended an invitation to Canada to join. Canada maintained that it was not ready, however.

In the late 1950s and early 1960s, a number of Canadian officials traveled to Latin America and returned home to recommend that Canada join the organization. On each occasion, the government deferred a decision to a later date. This was most evident in 1961 when President John F. Kennedy issued a direct invitation for Canada to join, during an address in the House of Commons.[5] The Canadian Cabinet was split, but ultimately it was decided that any final decision would be postponed. Reasons for this deferral included the perceived lack of advantage for the national defense, the potential for conflict with the United States on issues related to Latin America, and the lack of significance of Latin America for Canadian national interests. Prime Minister John Diefenbaker, for example, saw any Canadian OAS participation as inconsistent with the nation's U.N. obligations. He felt that regional organizations competed with the more important work of the United Nations and the more important issues associated with East-West interests. He was also suspicious of U.S. motives and knew that Washington usually got its way in the organization. Diefenbaker was also concerned that the United States saw the OAS as a bulwark against communism, rather than an instrument of development, which was the Canadian priority.

In 1970 the Trudeau government issued the most comprehensive foreign policy statement up to that time, *Foreign Policy for Canadians*. One portion of this document was devoted to Canada's Latin American interests, particularly Canada's possible membership in the OAS. Three options were presented, and the one adopted in 1972 called for Canadian government establishment of an observer/ambassador to the OAS and an upgrading of bilateral relations with specific countries in the region. Canadian representatives could now attend meetings of the Inter-American Economic and Social Council, for example. Canada's mission could act as a "listening post" for events in the region. There would be no formal Canadian entrance into the OAS, however. This was by no means a universally popular decision. Heath MacQuarrie, M.P., a perennial advocate of full membership, expressed his disappointment in the House of Commons on February 25, 1972: "We will join the ranks of Spain, Israel and Guyana in that regard. This is not, in my opinion, a tremendously courageous move." The Toronto *Globe and Mail* (February 1972) observed: "So into this incipiently moribund organization moves Canada, going in carefully by the back door so that it will not have to deal with the thorny issues that confront a genuine member. It is a stuffy, somewhat disgusting move." Support for Canada's decision came from those who felt that it was taking a necessarily modest step toward broadening ties with the nations of Latin America.

In 1982 a report of the subcommittee of the House Standing Committee on External Affairs and National Defense recommended (by a bare majority) that Canada pursue full membership in the OAS. The subcommittee members argued that if Canada were to join the OAS, it could contribute to and extend regional development programs. Also, it would strengthen the Inter-American Court and Commission of Human Rights. A full Canadian membership might encourage universal membership of American nation-states in the OAS, including Belize, Cuba, and Guyana. Finally, it was proposed that Canada might realize certain unspecified economic benefits from membership.

However, an earlier section of the report suggested that "the present effectiveness of the OAS is not sufficient to justify Canadian membership." The report was contradictory and confusing, and reflected the ambivalence that some committee members felt. Trudeau's government considered the proposal seriously, but ultimately rejected it.

Two years later an editorial in the July 7, 1984, edition of the *Globe and Mail* again urged Canada to join. At his first press conference, External Affairs Minister Joe Clark stated that the new Conservative government would "look very favorably upon joining it [the OAS]."

In a speech to the Canadian Bar Association on October 18, 1985, Joao Clemente Baena Soares, secretary-general of the OAS, called for Canada's entry into the inter-American organization. He stated:

The eventual incorporation of Canada as a member of our regional organization would be a landmark in the history of the inter-American system. On the one hand, the OAS would benefit with the participation of one of the great nations of the hemisphere. On the other hand, closer relations with the Latin American and Caribbean states through a well-established multilateral forum would enable Canada to increase its political, cultural and economic links with countries of the hemisphere.

The previous day at the University of Ottawa, Soares had said, "What Canada can do for the United Nations, Canada can do for the OAS." Nevertheless, in December of 1986 the Mulroney government announced that in the face of widespread financial cutbacks in the Department of External Affairs, there would no longer be a permanent observer to the OAS based in Washington. That responsibility would now be covered from Ottawa, on a more informal basis. Support for a Canadian role in the OAS had never been weaker.

There are several reasons often cited to explain Canada's decision not to join the OAS until October 1989. Some of these are more persuasive than others, but all have been presented by Canadian government officials or interested observers, and all merit some discussion.

Undoubtedly, one of the most cited reasons for not joining the OAS had to do with the Canadian government's ostensible fear that if it were to become a full member, there might be negative consequences for its bilateral relationship with the United States. That is, contentious issues might bring the two nations into harmful disagreement. Further, Canada might find itself in the no-win position of having to choose between the United States and Latin America. For example, so long as Canada remained outside of the OAS it could retain its independent foreign policy with regard to Cuba and Nicaragua. But full OAS membership might put it in direct confrontation with U.S. policy interests. This would be a particular irritation if Canada felt it had to oppose the U.S. position on a Latin American issue of lesser concern to its own interests. By not joining the OAS, therefore, Canadian policymakers could argue that they were less likely to be placed in such a difficult position.

Also, some Canadian officials argued that full OAS membership would draw Canada more closely into the American sphere of influence.[6] The OAS charter has a provision which makes binding upon its members any decision taken by a two-thirds majority. This provision could seriously restrict Canadian freedom of action. But note the inconsistency here. Some officials argued that joining the organization would force Canada into a more confrontational position with the United States. Others maintained that Canada would lose a measure of its independence. This divergence exemplifies a central theme of Canadian foreign policy, that is, the extent to which Canada can play a meaningful role on the world stage. It is discussed at length by scholars and politicians who debate whether Canada might become a principal power, a middle power, or a minor power.[7] The divergence reflects the widespread Canadian ambivalence about the nature and underlying goals of the relationship between the United States and Canada.

As a related argument, some have made the point that by not joining, Canada was implicitly accepting the validity of the Monroe Doctrine.[8] In this line of argument, Latin America had been part of the U.S. strategic domain. It was the responsibility of the United States alone to preserve its influence there and protect the region from outside intervention. Certainly a number of prime ministers, with MacKenzie King and Louis St. Laurent most notable among them, had made this point both explicitly and implicitly. The OAS headquarters are in Washington, half the organization's bills are paid by the United States, and the United States used to set the OAS's agenda. It utilized development loans as leverage to force the other members of the OAS to exclude Cuba from 1964 to 1975. President Johnson used the organization to sanctify his country's intervention in the Dominican Republic in 1965. As recently as 1988, the Reagan administration retaliated against Nicaragua's decision to expel U.S. embassy staff by forcing out Nicaragua's representative to the OAS.

The arguments that Canada would be wary of joining the OAS because of the fear of a confrontation, the concern about appearing subservient, or the willingness to allow the United States alone to influence matters in the region have been historically popular among some Canadian government officials and the majority in the scholarly and journalistic community. They are less persuasive to some of the most knowledgeable government officials today, however. These experts stress that Canada, to be a more mature power, must take foreign policy actions solely on the basis of Canada's best interests. Just as Canada votes its interests at the United Nations, within NATO, or as part of the United Nations Educational, Scientific and Cultural Organization (UNESCO), so must Canada's decision not to join the OAS be a result of careful examination of what is in the best interests of Canada. The possible negative reactions of the United States must not be allowed to be a major concern.[9]

Undoubtedly Canada must act in its own interests, but it would be hard to deny that these interests must also be weighed against American concerns. There is no history of linkage between Canadian actions and U.S. retribution; but since Latin America is not yet a vital policy concern of Canada, and since bilateral Canadian-U.S. issues are much more important, Canadian government officials would be foolhardy to ignore the implications their actions in Latin America could have on their relationship with the United States. The Department of External Affairs knows this, of course, and assigns specialists to investigate possible U.S. responses to any Canadian foreign policy endeavor. It should also be noted that when Canada officially joined the OAS in October 1989, the U.S. welcome was confined to a terse two-line statement. American officials appeared to be concerned that Canada might dilute U.S. dominance of the OAS.

This is not to say that a possible negative U.S. response would prevent Canada from supporting an independent position. Clearly, Canada's ongoing recognition of, and trade with, Cuba marks a distinct divergence from American policy preferences. Canadian policymakers decided that the costs of such recognition would be negligible and the political and economic gains substantial. In retrospect, of course, they were quite correct. One must acknowledge, however, that the decision to recognize the Cuban government was not made blindly. It was a delicate matter, and the possible consequences were evaluated carefully before the decision was reached. The relationship has produced admirable returns ever since.

There are other reasons cited for not joining the OAS that related to the vital U.S.-Canadian bilateral relationship. Of least consequence, I suspect, was the notion that many Canadians retained an emotional tie to Great Britain that interfered with their perception of Canada as having a separate national identity. Thus, joining the OAS, which implied closer identification with the United States, also implied a certain rejection of the mother country. Similarly, Canadian officials in the 1950s and 1960s would stress that Canada's OAS membership would conflict with its Commonwealth obligations. This argument is easily refuted, however, by the fact that certain Caribbean members of the OAS are also members of the Commonwealth, La Francophonie, and other international organizations. The argument is spurious.

In addition, some Canadian officials maintained that there were political gains to be derived from nonmembership. If Canada were to join the OAS, it was argued, those members of the Third World who view the OAS as a tool of the United States would then regard Canada's actions as a sign of acquiescence to American interests, a compromise of heretofore noble Canadian principles, and a disregard for the concerns of the emerging nations. This last position was held in the face of the OAS failure to protest human rights violations in Latin America, as well as the inevitable inclusion into the OAS of the ruling dictators of some of the member countries.

Of course, one should also acknowledge the other side of the coin. A few Latin American diplomats, particularly those from Brazil and Colombia, have stated that by not joining, Canada was responding to U.S. demands. That is, it was their sense that Canada did not join precisely because it was asked not to join by the United States, whose interest is to continue dominating the organization.

Other Latin American diplomats, however, who spoke strictly off the record, were pleased with Canada's absence because it meant one fewer non-Spanish-speaking country in the organization. With membership from language groups including Spanish, Portuguese, French, English, and native languages, they argued that the OAS had already lost much of its original linguistic flavor. A Canadian presence would only aggravate that situation. Of course, the perceived dominance of the OAS by the English-speaking United States effectively negates that argument.

Underlying the Canadian concern about the cost and benefits of joining the OAS and the resulting implications, if any, for Canadian-U.S. relations was the ongoing question of what domestic and foreign constraints exist for Canada, as a middle power. This point has been addressed earlier. Of course, questions concerning the extent of Canadian foreign policy independence also lend themselves to investigations of the depth of Canadian national unity. Ultimately, concerns of this scope and magnitude reveal an insecure country. This is not meant as a criticism, however, for any middle power neighboring a superpower must understand the limits of its power and influence.

Although bilateral relations were of prime concern in the Canadian-OAS debate, they were by no means the only considerations. Security interests also played a vital role. The first of these was not heard as frequently in the late 1980s as it was twenty years earlier, but it was still occasionally addressed.

There was a concern that Canada's NATO and NORAD obligations might interfere with its membership in the OAS. One question asked, for example, was whether there were provisions in the NATO or NORAD charters limiting Canada's freedom of action. In the monograph *Behind the Headlines*, published by the Canadian Institute of International Affairs in March 1970, John Holmes wrote:

> Before committing ourselves to the Organization of American States and full participation in inter-American security and economic agreements, it would be advisable to examine whether our NORAD and NATO obligations would in any way prejudice our freedom of action in considering inter-American security questions. What would be the American expectations of our behavior as a special kind of ally in this system?

As mentioned, this argument was recently heard less often, since there was a general consensus that the two organizations acted independently and incurred completely different responsibilities. More important, however, was the view that if Canada were to join the OAS it would then be required to join the Rio Pact, which binds its members in a collective security network. A number of parliamentarians had argued that Canada might then be burdened with a military role that would be incompatible with its other interests. For example, joining the Rio Pact might make it difficult for Canada to maintain an independent role should the United States decide to invade Nicaragua. Canada would prefer to judge the merits of the circumstance, rather than be automatically obliged to involve itself in a belligerent action. Related is the consideration of whether Canada could avoid taking sides regarding an open violation of the OAS charter. At the heart of these security considerations were questions concerning the degree of foreign policy independence that Canada could exercise if it were to join the hemispheric union.

An important caveat, however, is that the assertion that joining the OAS necessitates joining the Rio Pact is patently false, at least in a legal sense. The Bogota charter is quite explicit in stating that countries party to the OAS agreement would be bound by their already existing defense agreements in the future. Indeed, there are no provisions within the Bogota charter for the Rio Pact. The OAS agreement is clearly a political association concerned with social justice, human rights protection, etc. The Rio Pact is a security pact. Both may be necessary, but legal scholars and experienced Canadian diplomats concur that membership in one organization does not legally bind a nation to membership in the other. Furthermore, Article 20 of the Rio Pact specifies that "no state shall be required to use armed force without its consent." All this being said, some officials, including Ambassador Gorham, had suggested that there might be an understanding that a moral obligation exists for OAS members to join the Rio Pact, although this is in no sense binding, and although the prime minister has explicitly ruled out joining.[10]

The whole argument may be moot, however, in the wake of the Falklands/Malvinas crisis. If the United States and certain OAS partners were unwilling to support Argentina, then many Latin Americans are questioning the value of the collective security agreement altogether. Nevertheless, questions that arise include, "As Canada is entering the OAS, will it be forced to take a position on Argentina's dispute with Great Britain over the Falkland Islands?" or "What is the Mulroney government's position on the long-running battle over whether landlocked Bolivia should have an outlet to the sea?" It is not obvious what the Mulroney government's position on these issues would be, or if they have even considered the questions.

Other Canadian concerns are economic in nature. Most observers agreed that there are few real economic gains for Canada from OAS membership, although the economic costs would be a relatively low $6.6 million (Canadian) a year, less than the cost of two diplomatic missions. Many have attested to the fact, however, that Canada has gained comparable economic benefits without the costs, from its bilateral and multi-lateral arrangements with Latin American countries. Canada participates actively in at least six of the principal agencies of the OAS, including the Pan-American Health Organization, SECA (the OAS drug commission), the OAS Commission on Women's Rights, the Inter-American Institute for Cooperation in Agriculture, and the Inter-American Telecommunications Conference.   Canada also maintains membership in the Economic Commission for Latin America (ECLA) and the Inter-American Development Bank. When critics pointed out that only within the OAS could Canada play an important role in hemispheric affairs, Canadian officials could point to these and other hemispheric commitments.

Another argument might be that Canada already enjoyed sufficient membership in international organizations. That is, its resources would be overstretched and its alliances compromised. Canada is a member of NATO, NORAD, the British Commonwealth, La Francophonie, the United Nations, the G-7 countries, the Cairns Group, the World Bank, the Organization for Economic Cooperation and Development (OECD), the International Labor Organization (ILO), and several other organizations. Canadians are great joiners, but would their presence in the OAS make that much of a substantial difference for themselves or their hemispheric neighbors?

Another criticism of the pre-October 1989 Canadian government stance was that the federal government would be unwilling to donate the funds expected from the second most developed country in the region as a condition for joining. More specifically, while Canada's OAS costs would be low in the near term, there were expectations about the amount of Canadian aid that would be required in the ensuing years. Similarly, if aid would be increased in the years to come, could it not be done within the context of bilateral relations, rather than within the confines of the OAS? This question is rarely expressed explicitly, but there is no doubt that OAS membership would require expenditures that any Canadian government might rather see spent elsewhere. Also, by joining the OAS, Canada's Latin American aid programs might have to be channeled through the organization. This is particularly troublesome given the OAS administration's record of economic inefficiency. It is certainly true that the senior OAS work force consists not of economists, but predominantly of former diplomats, politicians, and others who hold patronage positions. There should be a legitimate Canadian fear, then, that a sizable portion of their aid budget for the region will be wasted within such an organization. Also, as within any large international organization, there are administrative costs that have to be borne by donor countries. Since the Canadian International Development Agency (CIDA) had been fairly effective in administrating programs on a bilateral and direct basis, CIDA's officials have to be convinced that they could work within the OAS structure.

It should be noted, however, that this did not hinder CIDA from occasionally donating funds to the OAS or its subsidiary organizations. For example, in 1988 CIDA approved a contribution of $1.3 million to the OAS to establish a fund for technical cooperation and development in the Americas.

Another reason cited for not joining was the evident lack of Canadian public interest in the matter. There were no important interest groups pressuring government officials to join, and the recent cutback of Canadian staff at the observer mission in Washington was a non-issue in Canadian political life. This lack of interest stemmed in part from

1. the lack of historical ties between Canada and Latin America;
2. the perception that Canada could not make much of a substantial difference in Latin American affairs;
3. the Canadian public's disapproval of the OAS's sanctions against Cuba, a country that enjoys good trading relations with Canada; and
4. evidence of disenchantment with the OAS on the part of many Latin Americans and of some of their governments who see the OAS as an instrument of United States policy that is located only at the margin of inter-American relations.[11]

According to Benjamin Rogers, who surveyed the Canadian press for evidence of public interest in the OAS, the few expressions of opinion on the possibility of Canada's entering the OAS ran at least four to one against joining.[12] In addition, the original government decision to seek permanent observer status was not prompted by public demand and remained of limited interest. The OAS was not mentioned in recent reports of the federal government on international relations. It is noticeably absent in the Hockin-Simard report of 1982. The overall conclusion, of course, was that the lack of public concern suggested little reason for federal politicians to encourage Canada's OAS entry. There were few votes to be gained from such an action and policymakers' attention could be focused more profitably elsewhere.

Traditionally, there were those who argued that by joining the OAS, Canada could make a greater contribution to regional integration and could provide technical development assistance. It could advocate greater human rights protection and help to reshape the structure of the organization. Nevertheless, one must be critical of these arguments. The United States continues to dominate the OAS. The OAS remains unable to ensure regional peace and security and suffers terrible administrative and financial problems. Furthermore, there appears to be no clear regional commitment to many of the central goals of the organization. The power to give it political muscle is not there in any meaningful way.

This is not to say that Latin American officials did not want Canada to join the OAS, however. Indeed, the opposite might have been the case at times. For example, Canada is known as a nation that pays its dues to international organizations on time and in full. This makes Canada nearly unique, as most OAS members are in arrears. In 1989, Canada, Guyana, and Belize were the only non-communist nations in the hemisphere that were not yet members, and the latter two joined in 1990. This would have left Canada as the only non-Marxist absentee--a rather conspicuous position. This might have exerted some external pressure on Canada to join the fold. Since most Canadians are only vaguely aware of any common interests with Latin America, however, this was not likely to be a sufficient argument for promoting Canadian membership.

As mentioned, some observers suggested that Canada might play a vital role in restructuring the OAS. Others maintained that Canada might help to diminish the dominant role of the United States and act as a conduit for Latin American interests.[13] Some stressed that Canada could be seen as a more legitimate contributor to the Esquipulas II peace process if it joined. Particularly annoying to Canadian officials was the contention heard occasionally that Canada's non-membership was a sign that it was willing to let the United States dominate the organization. In this way, Canada was seen as weak and deferential to its southern neighbor. Indeed, some insisted that by not joining, Canada contributed to the OAS's weaknesses whereas its participation would have contributed to the organization's legitimacy and effectiveness. These are decidedly minority opinions, however, for most Latin American officials were indifferent to, or ignorant of, the Canadian position and regional policy choices. As a result, there were no serious attempts by Latin American leaders to encourage Canada to join the OAS. Their interests, like Canada's, are directed to the United States, since that is where the predominant regional influence truly lies.

In sum, there have been many reasons expressed to explain Canada's decision not to join the OAS. Those that remain persuasive at this time include:

1.   Canada's ambivalent power relationship with the United States;
2.   the possible moral, if not legal, obligation to join the Rio Pact;
3.   the limited prospects for economic advantage;
4.   the uncertainty concerning future development aid obligations;

5.   the inefficiency of the OAS bureaucracy and the presence of more effective institutions elsewhere;
6.   widespread Canadian public indifference to Canada's entry into the organization; and
7.   limited Latin American interest in Canadian participation.

To many observers, Canada would not join the OAS until it was convinced that it could play a meaningful, and not just a symbolic, role. By downgrading its status, in December 1986, it appeared to be demonstrating that it had less faith in the organization's ability to make a difference than at any time in the previous twenty years. This view seemed reasonable, particularly since the OAS appeared to be in a miserable financial state on the eve of its centennial year.[14] Indeed, since so many OAS members have yet to fulfill their financial obligations to the organization, it is clear that they have limited faith in its viability as well.[15]

Further, some suggested that the OAS had become marginalized in the priorities of its member states. It was of decreasing value in dealing with the most pressing regional issues including Central American peace, the Latin American crisis, the developing needs of the region, and its own desperate financial situation.

The foreign minister of Barbados, in a speech to the extraordinary session of the General Assembly of the OAS in 1985, analyzed the problems of the organization on the basis of two propositions, which he acknowledged would sound to most of the members like "rank heresy." He stated:

The first is that the OAS is not an institution designed primarily for hemispheric cooperation as is fondly imagined, but is an institution whose main purpose was to mediate relations between Latin America and the United States . . . and as such has its underlying assumptions and its hitherto operational consensus firmly rooted in the fascinating history of these relations. The second proposition is that these historical assumptions and the consensus no longer hold true, and this fact, therefore, condemns the OAS to increasing anachronism, is precisely the cause of its present paralysis, and makes it unsuitable as an instrument of hemispheric cooperation.

In the face of this situation, Canada's best choice might well have been to continue its wait-and-see position. The circumstances that would lend themselves to Canada's joining the OAS as a full member were not evident, nor were they likely to be in the near future. Instead, Canada might have attempted to work for an organization that could promote regional integration and development far more efficiently. There is a possibility that it could accomplish these goals within the framework of the Esquipulas II Plan or as part of the United Nations. Why should it join an organization that is regarded as cumbersome, ineffective, and U.S.-dominated? Surely Canada's influence and resources could be put to better use in other forums.

Nevertheless, the Mulroney government decided to make a policy change. Had circumstances in Latin America changed dramatically? There is no real evidence of this. Could Canada's entry into the OAS demonstrate a substantial improvement over the status quo? It's hard to see how the Mulroney government would be enhancing its domestic prestige by joining. There is little direct proof of this, but perhaps the prime minister hoped that by joining he could deflect attention away from his economic problems and low popularity in public opinion polls. (This might be true even though most Canadians had limited interest in Canada's OAS position.) At the time of Canada's entry into the OAS, Mulroney's popularity was at 28 percent, his federal sales tax bill was nearly universally opposed, and a close friend and senator was being investigated for corruption. There are other factors that might have prompted the government's change of heart as well. Mexico and the English-speaking nations had recently called upon Canada to join, so as to partially offset the enormous U.S. influence on the organization. In addition, Canadian foreign policy officials were less wary of becoming associated with Latin American regimes, since most of their dictators had disappeared in recent years. Many of the nations of the hemisphere were now democracies, albeit fragile ones. In addition, joining the OAS would not be expensive and would be perceived as a positive development. Also, Canada might help to promote administrative efficiency and effectiveness. It could promote health and environmental issues.

Furthermore, the argument could be made that by joining, Canada could promote better coordination between the activities of the OAS and the United Nations. Another motivation for Canada's decision to join the OAS might have been the new initiatives that the organization had embarked on. Early in 1989, a three-man OAS delegation was sent to Panama in an effort to persuade General Manuel Noriega to step down and call free elections. Although that mission failed, Canadian diplomats considered it to be a signal that the OAS was prepared to play a more active role in the region. Of course, one might suggest the opposite perspective, that is, that the failure of the mission reflected the impotence of the OAS in resolving conflicts.

Other reasons for joining might be related to trade and investment. Joining promised increased trading opportunities, although this is purely a long-term prospect. So long as the international debt problem remains severe, Latin America is not likely to realize anything like its full potential as a market for Canadian exports. However, by joining the OAS, Canada could help solve the massive debt problem. Latin American countries can't buy Canadian goods if they must pay interest on their debt to North American banks. It is not clear, however, why Canada could not continue to work through such OAS-associated organizations as the Inter-American Development Bank to accomplish the same goal. It has also been suggested that Canada joined the OAS so as to build closer ties to Mexico. This might become necessary, it is argued, because Canada may have to import Mexican labor by the middle of the 1990s and because the Mulroney government is interested in pursuing a free trade agreement with Mexico. By joining the OAS, Canada could facilitate these goals. Perhaps so, but current unemployment is high enough in Canada to cause most observers to remain skeptical about the first explanation at least.

The argument is also made by Canadian officials that by joining, Canada can better understand, and help to resolve, the drug and crime problems, environmental pollution, and poverty. This may be true, but the OAS has been largely ineffective in ameliorating these problems so far.

Most important, the argument is made that if Canada wants a more stable political environment it can join the OAS and be an example of democratic stability, and an alternative model to the United States, for Latin Americans. This is possible, but Canada's geographic distance and cultural differences from Latin America will undoubtedly pose obstacles to this noble goal.[16]

It should also be noted that to the extent that Canada supports U.S. initiatives, it might well be regarded as an American lackey by Latin Americans. After Canada declared its support of the U.S. invasion of Panama, several Latin American diplomats in the OAS openly voiced their displeasure. Canada was not seen as an independent actor, and questions were raised about its ability to help mediate conflicts in Central America. Canadian officials appeared to have squandered much of the goodwill that had accompanied their entry into the OAS.

One Latin American diplomat in Ottawa was quoted as stating, "The problem for Canada is that this was the first action it took since it joined the OAS and everyone was watching. I can tell you that most of Latin America was disappointed."[17]

The last thing that Canadian officials wanted was to have Canada's credibility as an independent political actor hampered. Membership in the

OAS forced Canadian officials to face their country's foreign policy limitations head-on.

The arguments against joining remain persuasive even now. The OAS is still debt-ridden and poorly administered. It has limited clout, as evidenced by its inability to help resolve the debt crisis or stop the Falklands war. It has failed to resolve several long-standing border disputes and has taken little notice of human rights abuses in such member countries as Argentina and Chile.

By joining the OAS, Canada is more likely to find itself engaged in disputes with Washington over issues of secondary importance to its national interest. Little deliberation seems to have preceded the Mulroney decision. The prime minister did not refer the issue to a parliamentary committee for examination. No public hearings were held. Few voices were heard. Allowing more input might not have dissuaded the government, but it might have alerted Canadians to the potential risks involved. Proponents of the new Canadian policy suggest that by joining the OAS, Canada is demonstrating that it is more serious about its relations with Latin America. But Latin Americans themselves don't look to the OAS to help them resolve their disputes.

Critics charge that Canada can accomplish far more through its existing agencies than through the OAS. They point out that Canada will not increase substantially its diplomatic representation in the region, thereby partially undermining Canada's stated interests in Latin America. Interestingly, the government's decision reverses the September 1988 position of Ambassador Gorham, which argued that Canada should not join because of other financial priorities, Rio Pact concerns, and the risk of Canada's foreign policy independence. The evidence reveals that these concerns, and others, remain. The Mulroney government appears to have taken an unnecessary risk.

Nevertheless, Canada has joined the largest organization in the hemisphere. Most observers seem willing to give the government's decision the benefit of the doubt, or their attentions are focused on more pertinent issues like the implications of a free trade agreement with Mexico as well as the United States.

NOTES

1. For a fuller discussion of this point, see George Bell, "Canada and the OAS: Going around the Buoy Again?" in Brian MacDonald (ed.), *Canada, the Caribbean and Central America* (Toronto: Canadian Institute of Strategic Studies, 1986), pp. 87-108.

2. See, for example, "Memorandum from the Under-Secretary of State for External Affairs to the Prime Minister" *External Affairs Documents 1909-1946*, vol. 5 (December 11, 1941), p. 896.

3. Bell, "Canada and the OAS," p. 102. Interestingly, the OAS was called the Organization of American States precisely so non-republics in the hemisphere, and particularly Canada, might be encouraged to join. For evidence of this see "The Report of the Secretary-General of the OAS." *Annals of the Bogota Conference*, 1:1. For further discussion, see Marcel Roussin, "Canada: The Case of the Empty Chair," *World Affairs* (Spring 1953), pp. 15-16.

4. The expressed purposes of the OAS are, first, to maintain peace, and, second, to promote human welfare. Its stated principles are:

a. that international law is the standard of conduct of states,
b. that good faith shall govern the relations between states,
c. that military victory does not give rights,
d. that an attack against an American state is an attack against all American states, and
e. that controversies shall be settled by peaceful means.

5. It is interesting to note that Kennedy's advisers told him that two topics were not to be discussed during his parliamentary address. The first concerned the possible installation of U.S. missiles in Quebec. The second concerned Canada's possible entry into the OAS. For reasons of personal ego or his own perception of the national interest, Kennedy spoke on both issues. Prime Minister Diefenbaker advised the president to concern himself with his own country's affairs. This story was related to the author by Marcel Roussin, a professor and public servant who for many years was the leading external affairs department analyst assigned to study Canada's possible OAS role. The interview with Roussin took place on July 21, 1988, in Washington, D.C. Currently Roussin is a special adviser to the Department of External Affairs. In addition, for an interesting discussion of the points of departure between President Kennedy and Prime Minister Diefenbaker over Latin American issues, see Knowlton Nash, *Kennedy and Diefenbaker: Fear and Loathing Across the Undefended Border* (Toronto: McClelland and Stewart, 1990), pp. 114-116.

6. For an early discussion of this point, see F. H. Soward and A. M. MaCauley, *Canada and the Pan-American System* (Ryerson, 1948), p. 22 or Ian Lumsden, "The Free World of Canada and Latin America" in Stephen Clarkson (ed.), *An Independent Foreign Policy for Canada?* (Toronto: McClelland and Stewart, 1968), pp. 198-211.

7. One of the most notable discussions of this point is found in David Dewitt and John Kirton, *Canada as a Principal Power* (Toronto: Wiley, 1983).

8. See, for example, Professor Harvey Levenstein's article in the *Toronto Star* (January 14, 1974).

9. This was a view expressed by several officials in Ottawa but most clearly by Marcel Roussin and Dick Gorham in interviews in July 1988 in Washington, D.C. In this regard, see also Marcel Roussin's testimony to the Special Joint Committee of the Senate and the House of Commons, entitled "Canada's International Relations," vol. 37 (January 29, 1986), pp. 60-61.

10. Interview with Ambassador Richard Gorham (Washington, D.C., July 27, 1988).

11. For a comprehensive discussion of these points, see Benjamin Rogers, "The Extent, Focus and Changes of Canadian Public Interest in Latin America: 1967-1976," a report prepared for the Historical Division of the Department of External Affairs (Ottawa, March 1977).

12. Ibid., p. 75.

13. Certain of these views were expressed in an interview with Sergio Danese, counselor in the Brazilian embassy to the United States (Washington, D.C., April 19, 1988).

14. For a detailed discussion, see Lewis Diuguid, "Venerable OAS Threatened by Budget Axe," *Washington Post* (June 28, 1988), p. A-13, or John Goshko, "OAS: A troubled forum on Panama," *Washington Post* (May 16, 1989), p. A-16.

15. As of March 31, 1988, only eight countries had paid any part of their 1988 quota, with these total payments representing only about 16 percent of the total 1988 quota. In addition, twenty-two countries have such outstanding balances from previous years that the total unpaid balances represent 136 percent of the annual 1988 quota. One-third of the OAS's permanent employees (300) were laid off that year. By October of 1989, the United States was in arrears of $27 million, and Argentina, Brazil, Mexico, and Venezuela had paid none of their dues. Almost 700 employees were laid off. Canada is joining an organization that is in financial disarray.

16. Some of the advantages of Canada's membership in the OAS are summarized in Roger Paul Gilbert, "Le Canada et l'Organization des États Américains," *bout de papier*, 7:4 (1990), pp. 6-7

17. As quoted in Joan Godfrey, "The Invasion of Panama Bush League," *Financial Post* (December 25, 1989), p. 5.

3 Canadian Investment and Trading Ties with Central America

To the extent that scholars and journalists have examined the relations between Canada and Central America, their interest has focused almost exclusively on the prospects for peace, Canada's possible OAS involvement, developmental aid, and refugee patterns. Another topic of interest, however, concerns the extent to which there is a Canadian financial interest in the region. Although Canadian firms historically have had a limited number of investments in Central America, certain nickel and gold mining interests have had substantial holdings there.[1] All five of Canada's major banks have maintained Central American branches at various times, and Canada's resource, energy, and transportation sectors have also been represented. Official Canadian missions were sent throughout the 1960s, 1970s, and 1980s to investigate possible trade opportunities. In short, certain Canadian industrial, commercial, and financial concerns have realized that there is at least a modest profit to be made in Central America.

In general, Canadian economic ties to the region reflect areas of Canadian strength. That is, the Canadian emphasis has traditionally been placed on the development of an economic infrastructure and toward staple production. Canadian exports include newsprint, asbestos, aluminum, automotive parts, lumber, paperboard, fertilizer, fish, milk products, wheat, medical supplies, telecommunications equipment, and electrical products. Imports are concentrated in primary commodities including bananas, coffee, and metal products.

Canadian financial ties to Central America first became apparent at the turn of the century, when William van Horne, an engineer and entrepreneur who was integral to the building of the Canadian Pacific Railway, entered into a partnership with the United Fruit Company and

American military officers to build Guatemala's first railway.[2] The idea was to ship bananas from Guatemala's hinterland to North America. This was a most successful venture, as were the Canadian-owned tobacco and fruit plantations in Nicaragua.

Canadian financial institutions were also active. By the 1930s, all five of Canada's major banks and several insurance companies and utilities had branches in the region. In addition, Canadian institutions financed and owned the Salvadorean electrical system, which subsequently was nationalized in 1977.[3] These meager holdings were dwarfed by American interests there, of course, but they demonstrated that Canadian financiers were not completely indifferent to the commercial potential of Central America.

Canadian financial ambitions in Central America had to be tempered by consideration of U.S. motives there. There was a general understanding that the region was dominated by the United States due to a special relationship built on long-term trade and security arrangements. A sizable number of Canadian firms were subsidiaries of U.S. companies and were not permitted to export to Central America and compete with their U.S. parent companies. The 1970 government publication *Foreign Policy for Canadians* included a discussion of possible Canadian export markets in South America, but paid virtually no attention to Central America. At that time, Canada was intent on pursuing a "bilateral road" in its relations with Latin America.[4] This meant that Canada would devote its efforts to those countries that promised the most opportunity for trade and investment. The countries most frequently cited in this regard were Brazil, Mexico, and Venezuela. Few believed that any of the nations of Central America could provide similar commercial returns for Canada. As a result, the trading relationship remained limited until the 1970s.

Now, however, Canadian firms are more willing to pursue ambitious economic strategies in the area, even if occasionally they are at odds with U.S. government policy. For example, in Chapter 1 it was noted that Canada regarded the U.S. embargo of Nicaragua as an opportunity to do business there. The Canadian government had actively pursued a trading relationship with Nicaragua, although the Sandinista government's economic resources and capabilities remained limited, and its expansionist motives remained suspect. In addition, Canada has long retained an active trading relationship with Cuba, another U.S. nemesis.

Canada's trade promotion programs in Central America are dominated by federal and provincial government agencies, which in turn support private sector efforts at increasing trade. The federal government agencies include the Export Development Corporation (EDC), the trade offices of the Department of External Affairs and the Industrial Cooperation Division of the Canadian International Development Agency (CIDA). Ontario and Quebec also have notable trade promotion offices.[5]

Canadian trade with Central America increased dramatically between 1974 and 1984. Its exports of merchandise rose from $64 million to $149 million, while imports from the region went from $53 million to $215 million in that time.

During the same period, exports of engineering construction materials and various services also increased. It should be noted, however, that trade with Central America today accounts for less than 2 percent of Canada's worldwide trade, as can be seen in Tables 3.1 and 3.2. Canadian investment in the region is also limited--accounting for less than 1 percent of all foreign direct investment, worldwide (see Table 3.3).

Canadian trade with Central America declined between 1984 and 1989, primarily due to problems associated with political instability, foreign debt, and low prices for Central American produce. It remains considerably less than Canada's corresponding trade with Mexico, Colombia, and Venezuela. Furthermore, Canada runs balance-of-trade deficits with all Central American countries except Panama. As a result, both the Canadian government and a now-defunct lobby group, the Canadian Association for Latin America and the Caribbean (CALAC) have attempted

Table 3.1

Canadian Imports from Central America (thousands, $CDN)

	1985	1986	1987	Rounded to Nearest Thousand 1988	1989
Costa Rica	41,322	56,557	63,223	50,000	57,000
El Salvador	35,587	64,188	43,151	41,000	28,000
Guatemala	26,155	40,262	33,008	38,000	41,000
Honduras	20,894	20,678	16,945	27,000	25,000
Nicaragua	25,621	34,111	28,661	64,000	74,000
Belize	4,958	1,211	5,849	13,000	8,000
Panama	22,482	27,965	30,749	30,000	18,000
Total Canadian imports from Central America	177,019	244,972	221,586	263,000	251,000
Total Canadian imports from all countries of the world	104,355,196	112,511,445	116,238,614	No total available	No total available

Source: Statistics Canada, Annual Summary of Canadian Imports/Merchandise Trade, Catalogue 65-203 (1989).

Table 3.2

Canadian Exports to Central America (thousands, $CDN)

	1985	1986	1987	Rounded to Nearest Thousand 1988	1989
Costa Rica	21,379	28,099	35,862	29,000	23,000
El Salvador	15,173	11,294	15,669	20,000	11,000
Guatemala	17,779	15,274	20,282	18,000	21,000
Honduras	14,110	14,018	14,128	19,000	14,000
Nicaragua	18,873	23,163	10,293	23,000	23,000
Belize	4,409	4,026	6,180	7,000	5,000
Panama	54,961	45,572	37,458	37,000	19,000
Total Canadian exports from Central America	146,684	141,446	139,872	153,000	116,000
Total Canadian exports from all countries of the world	119,474,511	120,669,931	125,086,701	No total available	No total available

Source: Statistics Canada, Annual Summary of Canadian Imports/Merchandise Trade, Catalogue 65-203 (1989).

Table 3.3

Canadian Direct Investment in Central America (millions, $CDN)

	1978	1979	1980	1981	1982	1983	1984
Central America	159	225	235	239	230	----	255*

Source: Statistics Canada, Summary of Canadian Direct Investment Abroad, 1978-1984, Catalog No. 67202.

  *1984 figure does not include Nicaragua.

to expand Canadian trade with the Central American region. For example, in 1985, in an effort to stimulate trade contacts, the Department of Regional Economic Expansion (DREE) and CALAC jointly sponsored a tour for Central American businessmen in Canada. Periodically, Canadian businesses have indicated that they would like to pursue a higher level of trade with Central America, but complain that federal government support is too thin for Canadian firms operating in Latin America, and Central America in particular.[6] Government officials agree, but argue that the strife in Central America poses enormous obstacles to Canadian trade and investment there. Still, Canadian exports to the region, except for Nicaragua, have increased slightly since 1986. More than two hundred Canadian companies have discovered new markets there.

CANADIAN BANKING INVESTMENTS IN CENTRAL AMERICA

Since the 1970s, Canadian bank loans and investments in Central America have increased only marginally. A central obstacle to continued substantial Canadian bank involvement and credit extension is the perception that because of Central America's political instability and indebtedness, there is a major risk of overexposure. Banks feel vulnerable and look to South America for its apparently safer investment climate. Given the banks' concerns, it should not be surprising that they are liable to change their policies dramatically. For example, Canada's largest bank, the Royal Bank, had branches in Costa Rica and Panama, pulled them out, then installed them again, where they remain today. The Royal Bank currently has outstanding loans to all Central American countries. The other major Canadian banks also have loans outstanding to the region. All of the banks have placed their most problematic loans on the secondary market and built up reserves against losses.

Since 1987 Canadian bank loans have diminished substantially, following a trend set by banks in the United States and Western Europe. As a result, the largest current sources of financial facilities for Canadian trade and capital projects in Central America, and indeed in Latin America as a whole, are government aid programs (which are addressed in Chapter 4) and the government's export finance agency, the EDC.

The EDC offers short- to medium-term (one to five years) fixed rate export financing. Its loans are fixed at concessionary rates, and it is now the largest provider of export credits in Canada. For example, in 1978 the EDC offered Panama a (CDN) $1.12 billion financial package to support the development of the Cerro Colorado Copper Deposit. Approximately $742 million was slated to come from the EDC itself to cover the purchase of Canadian goods and services, while a consortium of banks would supply the rest. The Panamanian government ended the project in 1982, however.[7] A more successful EDC project was a $7.5 million loan to Guatemala, in July 1981, to purchase locomotives from Bombardier, Inc. of Montreal. Unfortunately, the EDC is refusing to insure private ventures in Central America until the political violence subsides there.

CANADIAN TRADE AND INVESTMENT PATTERNS IN NICARAGUA, GUATEMALA, EL SALVADOR, AND COSTA RICA

Canada's economic relations with Nicaragua have never been extensive, but a few investments have been of some consequence. Most notable perhaps was the Noranda Mine Ltd. subsidiary Empressa Minera El Sententrion. This project was initiated during President Somoza's regime and became the largest gold and silver mine in Nicaragua. It was nationalized by the Sandinista Government in November 1987.

Nicaragua maintains an embassy in Ottawa, but Canada has chosen not to reciprocate, stressing instead that its embassy in Costa Rica can serve Nicaragua adequately. In 1986 Nicaragua moved its trade office (Deltonic Trade) to Toronto, having been forced to vacate its Miami office following imposition of the trade embargo by the Reagan administration. The departure of the United States from the Nicaraguan trade picture during the Sandinista era left a vacuum which Canadian companies had attempted to fill, at least to a point. The situation was reminiscent of Canada's trading relationship with Cuba, another country faced with a U.S. trade embargo. In Nicaragua's case, however, its weak economy, shortage of foreign currency, and lack of export credits placed severe obstacles in the path of a vigorous trading link with Canada.[8] Interestingly, Spain, France, Denmark, and Sweden had been more generous with export credits and financing to Nicaragua than has Canada.

There are other obstacles to trade as well, for the U.S. embargo on Nicaraguan economic ties had negatively affected Canadian ties with that country. Soon after the U.S. embargo was announced, the Canadian Department of External Affairs told Canadian companies that they could no longer buy goods in the United States and ship them directly to Nicaragua. The fear was that Canada would be "circumventing" the embargo. While companies had to suspend direct shipments of goods-- mostly used parts for farm and industrial machinery--they were allowed to eliminate stockpiles. At the same time, they could continue selling goods made in the United States as long as they were bought in Canada.

This policy was not enforced until March 1989, when companies were told to suspend all shipments to Nicaragua of goods made in the United States. Soon after, however, the directive was rescinded, and the government called it a mistake.

Critics charged that Canadian officials' first instincts had been to kowtow to United States interests. Indeed, Daniel Ortega accused Canada of cutting off shipments because of the free trade agreement.[9] As always, Canadian officials worried about their first priority: bilateral relations with the United States. When the risks to the relationship were not perceived as overly damaging, Ottawa officials decided to resume trade with Nicaragua.

Canada imposed stiff quotas that halved Nicaraguan beef exports to Canada in 1986. There have been other trade restrictions imposed by the Canadian government as well. The reasons for these restrictions include the continued contra insurgency and Canada's interest in not diverging too sharply from U.S. policy. In addition, Nicaragua is nearly bankrupt and $90 million in debt to Canadian banks. Particularly ominous for Nicaragua is the fact that it is rated "off cover" by the Canadian Export Development Bank, which means the bank will not insure loans to fund Nicaraguan purchases from Canada.

Nevertheless, Nicaragua continues to seek increased trading ties with Canada and argues that Canada could do more to promote this trade. Its ambassador to Canada, Sergio Lacayo, has spoken repeatedly in the Canadian press about his government's desire for closer economic ties. "The two economies complement each other," he has stated. Lacayo has put particular emphasis on the prospects for Canadian tourism in Nicaragua. Although a relatively small number of Canadians have visited Nicaragua as tourists (most who go are development aid workers), Nicaragua does export seafood, beef, molasses, and metals to Canada, and it buys Canadian wheat, fertilizers, machinery, rapeseed oil, tallow, tobacco, milk powder, and medicine.

The federal government has suggested that Canada's investments in Guatemala would be limited, due to that nation's persecution of its Indian minority and its low level of economic development. However, Guatemala imports more goods from Canada than any country in the region, except for Costa Rica and Panama. Many Canadian financiers believe the Guatemalan economy has substantial potential for growth, and they are poised to take advantage of the situation. For example, and as earlier noted, with the help of a $7.5 million loan from the EDC in 1981, Bombardier, Inc. of Montreal was able to sell $13 million worth of locomotives to Guatemala in 1982. Canadian commercial interests have been particularly active in the Guatemalan transportation, communication, and energy sectors--most notably Inco's $250 million Exmibal nickel mine, which had been Central America's largest foreign investment of the 1970s. However, nickel deposits are very sensitive to world energy prices, and as prices plummeted, tax and financial problems ensued; the investment became unprofitable, and the mine was closed in 1981.

Canadian trade with El Salvador, although never substantial, grew during the 1970s, and then leveled off sharply in the 1980s, as evidence of human rights abuses there increased. Canadian exports to El Salvador include asbestos, aluminum, electronic equipment, food products, paper, and pharmaceuticals. The most important Salvadorean export to Canada by far is coffee. El Salvador is a desperately poor, war-ravaged country, however, and it would be unrealistic to expect trade or investment between the two nations to increase substantially in the near term.

Canada has more of a financial interest in Costa Rica, the only nation in the region to enjoy both long-term political stability and democratic practice. Traditionally Canadians have made up part of the country's large expatriate land-owning society. Twelve thousand Canadian tourists visited Costa Rica in 1987, up 31 percent from the previous year. One thousand Canadians live in Costa Rica. However, trade has declined since 1986 because the Canadian government will not extend credit until the debt issue is resolved. Canadian banks hold about 10 percent of Costa Rica's foreign debt ($130 million), and they are slowly negotiating repayment terms with the Arias government. Furthermore, in April 1989 Prime Minister Mulroney offered to ask Canadian banks to take a loss of up to (U.S.) $150 million on their commercial loans to Costa Rica. Under the proposed debt-relief plan, Canadian banks would receive $30 million. No final decision has been made by the banks at this writing, however. Canada continues to export newsprint and farm produce and import agricultural products from Costa Rica. In addition, Coldspring Resources and Rayrock Yellowknife Resources, both of Canada, have fairly substantial gold mines in Costa Rica.

CANADIAN SALES OF MILITARY EQUIPMENT TO CENTRAL AMERICA

One of the most controversial aspects of Canada's economic ties to Central America is its sale there of munitions and military hardware. According to the Stockholm International Peace Research Institute, between 1983 and 1988 Canadian military exports to Latin America averaged $13 million a year. The federal government has assisted more than 150 Canadian companies in providing arms. Ottawa channels its aid to the industry through the International Defence Programs Branch, an agency of the Department of External Affairs charged with promoting the sale of Canadian-made defense products abroad. Some of the most prominent instances of Canadian arms or military hardware finding their way to Central America include the following examples.

Since 1983, Canadian-made ammunition has been discovered in contra camps in northern Nicaragua and Honduras. According to Canadian law, no export permits are granted for arms shipments to countries engaged in conflict, under threat of conflict, or posing a strategic threat to Canada. As a result, Canadian arms are not to be sold to Central America, but the possibility exists for transfer of arms to third parties, such as the United States or a South American country.[10] Undoubtedly this is what occurred. Similarly, small amounts of Canadian guns and ammunition were shipped indirectly to El Salvador in 1979 and 1980. Canadian aircraft engines, sold during the 1970s to Brazil and India, ended up in planes flown by the Salvadorean air force.[11] In addition, as noted earlier, in 1983 the de Havilland Aircraft Company of Toronto sold helicopters with possible military applications to the Guatemalan air force. The Task Force on Churches and Corporate Responsibility (TCCR), a powerful coalition of Canadian churches opposed to any military involvement in Central America, decried the sale and suggested that the Guatemalan government might use the aircraft to strafe Indian villages, rather than for the stated purpose of promoting development. Nevertheless, the Department of External Affairs approved the deal. Ironically, at the same time that the Canadian embassy officials were negotiating the de Havilland sale, Ottawa was cosponsoring a United Nations resolution condemning human rights violations by the Guatemalan military regime. In the mid-1980s Canada also approached Honduras, from time to time, with offers to sell military hardware, despite church and labor opposition in Canada.

Furthermore, in February 1987 it was revealed that a Montreal-based arms dealer, Emmanuel Weigensberg, had been implicated in a plot to divert arms from Guatemala to the contra rebels in Nicaragua. The Guatemalan army was to have received up to one million rifle cartridges, 3,000 mortar grenades, and 50,000 unspecified other cartridges. The ammunition was never delivered to Guatemala, however, and contra leaders confirmed receiving the cargo. It was subsequently disclosed that the contras had paid (U.S.) $432,500 into an account at the Royal Bank in Montreal in return for the arms and weapons. These materials had been purchased by Weigensberg after he had been contacted by Richard Secord, a retired U.S. Air Force major general who had been implicated in the contra arms scandal. In addition, it was revealed that Propair, a Quebec regional air carrier, sold two Caribou transport planes to the CIA for the contra war. In these small ways Canada has played a part in the affair, although little information about Canada's indirect role in the scandal has been forthcoming.[12]

CONCLUSION

It would be stretching the truth to suggest that Canada's trading ties or military sales to Central America are a vital aspect of Canada's relationship with the region. Nevertheless, Canadian government officials and certain private firms have realized that there is a profit to be made there. One worrisome feature of this development, however, is the evidence that Canadian arms are being used by warring parties. To circumvent this problem the Department of External Affairs must demonstrate a measure of social responsibility when advising Canadian firms negotiating to sell weapons. Canada does not want to be drawn into the conflicts in Central America for ethical or strategic reasons. In this regard, Canadian government officials might also continue to insist that EDC export credits and insurance be withheld from countries that are notorious for human rights violations. Canadian actions will not, in and of themselves, end abuses, but they can be an important contributing factor to achieving that goal.

It should also be noted that there are a few uncertainties in the Canadian-Central American trading relationship, the resolution of which will have broad implications for economic relations. One concerns the role of foreign aid in Canadian external policy interests and questions what sort of links will exist between Canada's trade and its aid programs. What proportion of Canada's bilateral assistance will be tied to procurement of Canadian goods and services? At present it is 80 percent. Second, is Canada prepared to allocate a significant percentage of its export earnings to service Central America's debt? At this point the prospect appears doubtful. Will it support calls for the reform of traditional International Monetary Fund austerity measures? There has been some movement in this regard.

Undoubtedly, Canadian firms will continue to pursue an economic return in Central America. How successful they are will depend largely on the extent of government support, its policies regarding the regions' external debt, and the creativity and entrepreneurial spirit of the firms themselves. The federal government's greatest influence in Central America will come from its aid policies and peace-observing prowess, but its commercial ties can also be a contributing factor to the region's economic recovery and, ultimately, its long-term political stability.

NOTES

1.   For a good discussion of Canadian business ties to Central America in the early part of the twentieth century, see Peter MacFarlane, *Northern Shadows: Canadians and Central America* (Toronto: Between the Lines, 1989).

2.   For a comprehensive discussion of van Horne's business activities, see Tom Naylor, *The History of Canadian Business 1867-1914*, vol. 2 (Toronto: Lorimer, 1975). See also Peter MacFarlane, *Northern Shadows,* chap. 2.

3.   For a discussion of Canadian holdings in the region, see Tim Draimin, *Canada and Central America: An Overview of Business and Governmental Relations* (Toronto: CAPA, 1982).

4.   For a discussion of this point, see D. R. Murray, "The Bilateral Road: Canada and Latin America in the 1980s," *International Journal*, 37 (Winter 1981-82), pp. 108-131.

5.   For an excellent, if dated, discussion of Canada's trade promotion programs in the region, and particularly in Nicaragua, see a pamphlet written by Bob Thomson, *Canadian Aid and Trade Relations with Nicaragua* (Toronto: CAPA, November 1984).

6.   Many of these concerns are expressed in detail in a briefing written by Wilson Ruiz, published by the North-South Institute, entitled "A View From the South, Canadian/Latin American Links" (Ottawa, March 1988).

7.   This example is taken from Tim Draimin *Canada's Policy Toward Central America.*

8.   See Thomson, *Canadian Aid and Trade Relations with Nicaragua,* for a discussion of this point.

9.   See Andrew Cohen, "Nicaraguan Trade Rules Show Us Our Place," *Financial Post* (August 11-15, 1989).

10.   This point is discussed in detail in a pamphlet written by Julie Leonard and Tim Draimin, *Canadian Links to the Militarization of the Caribbean and Central America* (Toronto: CAPA, May 1985).

11.   As reported by the Latin American Working Group in "Taking Sides: Canadian Aid to El Salvador," *LAWG Letter*, 10:1 (August 1987), p. 7.

12.   For a summary of what information does exist, see John Picton, "Canada's Contra Connection," *Toronto Star* (April 29, 1990).

4 Canadian Government Developmental Aid to Central America

Undoubtedly, one of the most important contributions that Canada makes to Central America is developmental aid, also referred to as official development assistance (ODA). A significant amount of assistance comes from Canadian nongovernmental organizations, which will be discussed in Chapter 7. The federal government plays an important role as well, in providing this most obvious and tangible of contributions, and that is our present concern.

As noted earlier, the Canadian government makes aid available through the Canadian International Development Agency (CIDA). CIDA concentrates its aid to Central America in such sectors as rural development, forestry, flood control, communications, and transport. Wherever possible it tries to make its aid programs complement its commercial objectives in the region.

Three general considerations determine what kind of aid will be provided by CIDA, and how much it may be. These include:

Developing countries--their need, development performance, human rights record, and capacity to absorb aid.

Canadian interests--the political importance of the bilateral relationship, the country's regional role, historical ties, and commercial considerations.

Special crisis factors--natural calamities or major political or economic disturbances.

The Canadian government offers aid to Central America in a variety of forms:[1]

Bilateral aid includes loans or grants for development projects or for the supply of Canadian commodities such as fertilizer or food. Eighty percent of bilateral aid funds must be allocated for the purchase of

Canadian goods and services. This restrictive practice is called "tying" or "tied aid."

Multilateral aid includes loans, grants, and capital subscriptions to international banks and humanitarian agencies. These include the World Bank, the International Monetary Fund, the United Nations Development Program, and the Inter-American Development Bank.

Aid to nongovernmental organizations (NGOs) goes to Canadian private, voluntary organizations with projects in Central America, usually in the form of matching funds.

Food aid includes grains, for the most part, and is dispersed through bilateral, multilateral, and NGO channels.

Canada has also given generously to the Central American programs of such international organizations as the United Nations High Commission on Refugees (UNHCR) and the International Committee of the Red Cross. In 1972, Canada joined the Inter-American Bank, and by 1980 its contribution had reached over $1 billion. In addition, in July 1981 Canada helped to found the Nassau Group, a multilateral body that included Mexico, Venezuela, and the United States, and which was interested in promoting stability through a coordinated aid program for Central America. Its successor, the Caribbean Basin Initiative, includes more countries and seeks to accomplish essentially the same goals.

Nevertheless, CIDA, which was founded in 1968, is the primary Canadian agency that dispenses foreign aid. For example, in 1985-86 it disbursed nearly 75 percent of all of Canada's development assistance funds. The remaining 25 percent was and is managed by other ministries including Finance and External Affairs, as well as the International Development Research Center (IDRC) and the Petro-Canada International Assistance Corporation. Certain provinces work with nongovernmental organizations to distribute funds as well.

As with most Canadian interest in Central America, the effort to provide developmental assistance gained impetus only in the 1970s. Indeed, in 1971 Latin America became the last region of the world toward which Canada launched a bilateral assistance program. One factor inhibiting Canadian aid concerned the role played by outside armed powers in the region. Successive Canadian governments judged that their efforts would be largely ineffective unless their Central American aid recipients rejected outside military involvement. As former Secretary of State for External Affairs Allan MacEachen noted, "A common [Central American] effort of this sort could help to restore the political stability and confidence without which programs for development cannot succeed."[2]

Similarly, Canadian officials worried that any development strategies they might promote would come to nothing if the region was torn by intense internal conflicts. An ongoing dilemma was whether Canadian aid should be sent to authoritarian regimes that lacked the commitment to bring about the difficult structural reforms necessary to produce broad-based socioeconomic growth.

Another concern was CIDA itself. One study questioned whether its administrative resources were adequate to fulfill its mandate. It criticized the absence of high-quality personnel, the weakness of evaluative mechanisms, its inability to set priorities, and the pressure to disburse large sums in a limited period of time.[3] These concerns are still valid.

CIDA has also been adversely affected by intermittent budget cuts and reduced administrative growth, most recently in May 1989. When it has been interested in promoting small-scale community development projects, it has found itself increasingly reliant on the help of NGOs. Indeed, CIDA disbursements for NGO projects in Nicaragua and Honduras have equaled or surpassed ordinary bilateral disbursements in some recent fiscal years.

Notwithstanding these concerns, Canada's aid program to Central America grew somewhat during the 1970s. Indeed, by the end of the decade, Central America was receiving 54 percent of all Canadian bilateral aid to Latin America (excluding the Commonwealth Caribbean), even though that region contained only 6 percent of the Latin American population.[4] This is a bit misleading, however, for an inordinate amount of aid was designated for Honduras alone. In addition, there was a widespread consensus within the Canadian government that its level of Latin American aid was embarrassingly low.

In the early 1980s, circumstances changed dramatically. The United States launched a trade embargo against Nicaragua that offered Canadian officials a way of exploiting commercial ties while simultaneously asserting foreign policy independence and opposition to U.S. policy. A parliamentary subcommittee studying Canada's relationships with Latin America recommended aid increases to Nicaragua and Costa Rica. Church-based interest groups and NGOs reinforced this view. Government officials, including External Affairs Minister MacEachen, visited the region and promised increases.

Central American governments were either fully democratic (Costa Rica) or appeared to be adopting democratic practices. Regional peace was being suggested seriously. Simultaneously, Prime Minister Trudeau was facing domestic pressure to tie Canada's aid to sales of Canadian goods and services. Trudeau saw Canada's interests in Central America as being entirely consistent with his North-South development program. He was deeply conscious of the economic inequities between the power of the industrialized North and the weakness of the developing South. To advertise his concerns, the prime minister embarked on diplomatic missions around the world, seeking support for his aid programs.[5]

As a result of these factors, in October of 1981 the Trudeau government announced a five-year plan to triple the amount of aid to the region to $201.5 million. In addition, $18.3 million would be contributed to Canadian and international refugee relief programs in the area. Again, the priority aid recipient would be Honduras. Neither Guatemala nor El Salvador would receive assistance until their uncertain political climate was stabilized, their human rights record was improved, and any risks to potential Canadian assistance staff were eliminated. This being said, it is also the case that between 1982 and 1985, despite the aid suspension, more than $5 million in Canadian bilateral aid was delivered to Guatemala. This aid was justified by officials because it had been approved prior to the cut-off and was already in the pipeline. (See Table 4.1 for Canadian bilateral aid to Central America, 1970-1985.)*

The most prominent aid packages included a $32.3 million gift in January 1983, designated for the El Cajon Hydroelectric Project in Honduras. By 1985, the Canadian government had also provided Honduras with a line of credit allocated for sawmills and for heavy equipment purchases.

Honduras is the only "core" recipient of Canadian development aid in Central America.[6] It is characterized as such because of its abject poverty, its relative lack of political repression, and its apparent capacity to absorb Canadian aid. A core status implies that Canada's interest there is to systematically develop and implement projects and programs on a sustained basis. The remaining Central American countries are "non-core" and, in general, are recipients of much less assistance consideration. This does not imply that Honduras would always receive the most aid, however. In 1983-84, for example, Nicaragua and Costa Rica both received substantially more assistance than did Honduras (see Table 4.1). Nevertheless, Honduras does not have to pass as many bureaucratic hurdles to receive Canadian development aid. Other examples of Canadian aid during this time included a $15 million loan made to Costa Rica to finance the purchase of potassium and urea. In addition, $3 million was targeted to Central America for a scholarship program in Canada. The construction of rural housing in the region was also subsidized.

Of particular interest was a Canadian government-approved $13.4 million line of credit to Nicaragua, in January 1984, for agricultural supplies, livestock, and equipment. In addition, $7.5 million was designated for the construction of a potable water project, and $11.8 million for a geothermal power station called Momotombo II.[7]

*Tables 4.1 through 4.9 appear at the end of this chapter.

It should be noted that Canadian government representatives to the World Bank and the Inter-American Development Bank expressed disapproval of Washington's campaign to block development loans to Nicaragua, arguing that aid projects should be evaluated solely on their economic and technical merits. Ottawa had supported loans to El Salvador and Guatemala for the same reasons, and as a result faced criticism from domestic human rights groups.

Ultimately, Canada's decision to provide assistance to Nicaragua reflected Canada's serious misgivings about the U.S. embargo. Furthermore, it set Canadian policy apart from such European nations as West Germany and the Netherlands, which phased out aid to Nicaragua in the mid-1980s.

By December of 1984, the suspension of aid to El Salvador was lifted and Canada donated fertilizers and chemicals.[8] It appeared that the new Mulroney government was acknowledging the apparent human rights improvements under President Duarte. Ironically, that same month Canada joined other countries in the United Nations to condemn El Salvador's human rights abuses, thereby demonstrating again that consistency is not always a hallmark of Canadian policy.

As noted earlier, aid to Guatemala had been cut off in 1981, but economic relations continued. New credits were offered by Canada's Export Development Corporation on a commercial, rather than an aid, basis. Canadian representatives to multilateral institutions continued to support loans to Guatemala. The status of the Canadian embassy in Guatemala City was upgraded, through the appointment of a resident ambassador. Clearly the Canadian government was sending mixed signals to that country as well.

Canada's aid plan also incorporated many of the recommendations of the July 1982 parliamentary subcommittee on Canada's relations with Latin America, which called on international financial institutions to support aid projects based on developmental, and not ideological, criteria. The subcommittee also suggested the opening of one more embassy in Central America, presumably in Managua, and the use of aid, but not trade sanctions, as a lever to promote human rights. However, it was also maintained that "Canadian developmental assistance [should be] substantially reduced, terminated or not commenced in cases where gross and systematic violations of human rights make it impossible to promote the central objective of helping the poor."[9] This view was reinforced in the public hearings, in 1985 and 1986, of the Special Joint Committee of Parliament on Canada's International Relations, and became a theme of its final report *Independence and Internationalism*, published in June 1986.

This volume outlined suggestions for Canada's new foreign policy initiatives and priorities. Included in its recommendations was the renewed suggestion that development aid be terminated where human rights violations impede helping the poor. Instead, Canada would try to provide assistance through international organizations. In countries with a poor human rights record, but where cessation of aid is unjustified, the private sector and NGOs in particular would play a major role in providing development assistance. In countries where greater respect for human rights was apparent, higher aid allocations would be made available.[10]

Independence and Internationalism noted that because Canadian trade with the developing world was just a small part of Canada's total trade, development aid would become the major element of the government's North-South policy. This view was reinforced by polls throughout the 1980s which revealed that Canadians consistently believed that their country should be a generous donor.[11]

If one looks at the record, one finds that in fiscal year 1986-87, total bilateral disbursements to Central America were $21 million. David Haglund cites a Canadian aid official who maintained, "It's still peanuts by a lot of countries' standards, but by ours it's fairly significant."[12] Canadian support for the authoritarian Central American nations continued to be controversial in Canada, however. By March of 1987, a number of groups were again calling for the suspension of Canadian bilateral aid to those countries guilty of human rights abuses. Among the most prominent were the researchers at Canada-Caribbean-Central America Policy Alternatives (CAPA) in Toronto, who recommended that government-to-government assistance be suspended to Honduras until it committed itself to the peace process. In addition, CAPA suggested that El Salvador and Guatemala be entitled only to humanitarian aid until their civil strife ended. Earlier in 1985 CAPA and other groups suggested that because of repeated abuses, corruption, and an inability to absorb all of its designated aid, Honduras should lose its core status.[13] It is not clear whether Canadian government officials ever seriously considered this suggestion, but when Honduras held apparently democratic elections in November 1985, the criticism dissipated.

By contrast, Costa Rica and especially Nicaragua should be priorities for bilateral assistance--according to CAPA and other groups--because of their commitment and ability to provide economic aid to their citizens.[14] CAPA is but one of many Canadian NGOs or interest groups that emphasize their distaste for U.S. actions in Central America. These groups tirelessly pressured the Department of External Affairs to distinguish Canadian policy from U.S. policy and to support the Sandinista government's efforts to develop its economy, reduce social inequalities, and ward off the contra threat. Few Canadian interest groups have expressed support for the U.S. position in the region. Notwithstanding the normative question of whether the anti-U.S. government position is justified in their actions or not, the debate about Canada's future policy directions is distinctly one-sided.

Critics of Canadian government policy are also alert to the question of whether Canadian aid meets basic needs, in accordance with the United Nations Covenant on Economic, Social, and Cultural Rights, to which Canada is a signatory. This is particularly salient because commercial considerations can play a role in the Canadian decision to provide development assistance. Eighty percent of Canadian bilateral assistance is tied to the provision of Canadian goods and services, making Canada's aid program the second most tightly controlled of Organization for Economic Cooperation and Development (OECD).[15] Since Canadian costs are high, "tied aid" reduces the value of Canadian assistance. Also, because the procurement procedures associated with "tied aid" are complicated, administrative costs are high and the rate of disbursements is retarded. Development strategies are distorted toward projects for which Canada can furnish the required goods and services. Emphasis is placed on what Canada can best supply: potash fertilizer, machinery, communications support, and other products that might not be what grass-roots organizations in Central America most need. As a result, the emphasis is on outside priorities rather than local concerns. The rural poor suffer because their needs are met for the most part by the limited quantity of "untied" funds. Thus, "tied aid" for Canadian commercial advantage has stymied many of the most deserving development projects. This is despite Canada's ostensible commitment to concentrate resources on food production and other basic needs.

One result of this emphasis on the use of aid for trade promotion had been the establishment of a fund, under the auspices of CIDA, which was designed to absorb half of any ODA increase until 1990. Projects approved through the aid-trade fund had to satisfy both commercial and developmental criteria and include communication systems, transportation facilities, and the installation of electrical power outlets. This form of aid had also been repeatedly criticized for its stress on industrialization and its frequent inability to remedy the worst cases of dire poverty.[16] Critics charged that Canadian aid policy had too often been targeted for the construction of large projects like power stations, refineries, and telecommunications facilities, which served to generate more wealth for the already wealthy. Instead, aid might have been more frequently allocated to programs supporting primary health care, education, and expanding food production.

As a result, a number of pressure groups argued that Canada should reduce the percentage of "tied" goods and services required for the provision of bilateral aid.

Indeed, CAPA suggested that the Canadian government might channel some of its development assistance through CADESCA, the economic corporation arm of the Contadora peace process.[17] The European Economic Community had provided aid this way, and it had been argued that Canada could signify its support for the peace process by working with this organization. Canada would then be less reliant on CIDA, and could provide "untied aid" without losing face. At this writing, however, this idea has been a nonstarter.

It is worth noting that by February 1986 it had become clear that Canada would not be repaid for its outstanding Central American loans, at least in the short run. As a result, External Affairs Minister Joe Clark announced that CIDA loans to the region would be converted to outright grants. Furthermore, aid would be increased to all countries of the region, including El Salvador and Guatemala. Several Canadian human rights groups again voiced opposition to such aid, stressing that it would be taken as a signal that Canada endorsed the violent tactics of those regimes.[18]

Much of the Salvadorean aid was to be used to buy Canadian fertilizer, which was to be shipped to El Salvador and sold there at local market prices. The receipts from these sales would be placed in a fund, to be dispensed to Salvadorean NGOs by a private Canadian contractor.

This process, referred to as "counterpart funding," is similar to "tied aid," and is particularly vulnerable to corruption. In this case, the fertilizer would only prove affordable to wealthy landowners and farmers. A number of Canadian NGOs charged that this did nothing to reduce El Salvador's economic inequality, as it only strengthened the status quo.[19]

By 1986, the opposition that remained to providing aid to El Salvador was partially discredited by the Department of External Affairs. In a notable letter from Joe Clark to Professor Meyer Brownstone of the University of Toronto, Clark wrote:

The Salvadorean NGO projects which we have supported to date under the bilateral project include a shelter for homeless children in Santa Tecla, a health clinic in La Libertad, and a community nutrition center in San Salvador. These projects are not political and I find it difficult to understand opposition to humanitarian activities of this kind.[20]

Opposition to the resumption of Canadian aid to El Salvador was further diminished when an earthquake hit the country on October 11,

1986. Thousands of people were killed and 150,000 were left homeless. Canadian help was immediate. Financial aid was sent, and public health teams were mobilized to help clean up and arrange for the restoration of safe water supplies and acceptable housing.

Throughout 1986-87 the Canadian government continued to assert its opposition to human rights violators in Central America, while still providing humanitarian aid and other support. Its parliamentary committees continued to produce reports prescribing various noble goals. The cabinet continued to voice support for such efforts, while actually taking only very limited action to support these lofty ambitions. For example, on May 28, 1987, the House of Commons External Affairs and International Trade Committee issued a study entitled *For Whose Benefit,* which recommended that those governments around the world with the worst records of human rights abuses be denied direct Canadian government financial aid. Where possible, however, desperately poor segments of their populations would still receive assistance. No specific countries were cited, and Joe Clark insisted that it was often difficult to define human rights standards. Nevertheless, the chairman of the commons committee that issued the report, William Wineguard, stated that CIDA's decision-making process "boggles the mind" and that Canada's foreign aid programs were "beset with confusion of purpose."[21]

The Wineguard Committee recommended that CIDA be decentralized, so that fewer decisions would have to be made at its Hull, Quebec, headquarters. Such a reorganization, it was argued, would speed up CIDA's work, bring aid recipients into the decision-making process, and give on-site aid officials more flexibility to meet changing circumstances. Previously, CIDA had been one of Canada's most centralized agencies.

The committee report also mentioned that aid-giving had frequently reflected the economic interests and convenience of the donor, and had taken too little account of recipients. It recommended instead that Canada's aid policy should help the poorest countries and people. It proposed emphasizing human development--educating, training, and working with people--and decreasing emphasis on building physical structures. Finally, the Wineguard Committee report suggested an acceleration in Canada's timetable to increase its aid, and a decrease in the proportion of "tied aid" from 80 percent of Canadian government total government-to-government assistance to 50 percent.

In general, the recommendations of the Wineguard report mirrored the Canadian aid strategy of 1975-80 (such as it was) which had deemphasized the "commercialization" of Canada's aid programs. The policy of disposing of surplus food in the form of aid, or of subsidizing sales of uncompetitive Canadian goods to developing countries, was explicitly rejected in the Wineguard report.[22] The government's initial response to the report was resoundingly positive. All recommendations were accepted in principle, except for the following: those pertaining to the reduction of food aid's share of total aid, the creation of a banking institution to help Canadians invest in developing countries, and the creation of an advisory board on aid. Indeed, in November 1987, in response to the Wineguard report, the Canadian government announced plans to decentralize CIDA over the ensuing years and to open local support offices facilitating its aid programs in Honduras, Nicaragua, and El Salvador. These offices would be staffed by local technical and administrative experts who would, in turn, be supervised by Canadian aid program officers. This effort reflected the government's desire to respond to calls for greater aid involvement from Canadian interest groups and a mass media focused on the problems of the region. As is frequently the case, however, economic considerations outweighed charitable ones. In May 1989 the Mulroney government announced large-scale budget cutbacks. The aid program was slashed dramatically, and few of the recommendations calling for increased expenditures would be realized in the foreseeable future. This point will be discussed subsequently.

Interestingly, the federal government repeated its earlier statements that CIDA would weigh human rights considerations in its aid decisions. Its emphasis on this point worried some members of the Canadian business community, who feared repercussions for general trade if a country's aid was suddenly cut off. It should be reiterated that Canadian business has long been a prime beneficiary of the foreign aid program. About sixty-five cents out of every dollar spent on aid stays in Canada, or returns through aid-related purchases: goods and services, food, equipment, and the hiring of Canadian personnel. The Canadian government pledged to find new ways to encourage Canadian businesses and NGOs to provide more assistance, however. This program, too, has been put on hold.

Furthermore, the government pledged to spend more on health care, education, and training programs to help aid recipients to manage their own affairs. The level of "tied aid" was to be reduced from 80 percent to 66 2/3 percent. The expectation was that the developing country would use the "untied" dollars for local procurement, thus enhancing domestic industry. The criteria under which Ottawa would decide which governments would receive funds would be kept confidential, with a parliamentary committee briefed each year on the matter. At this writing, however, no actions have been taken to implement these goals.

During External Affairs Minister Clark's visit to Central America in November 1987, President Daniel Ortega of Nicaragua acknowledged that Canada had an active and positive policy toward Nicaragua, through its aid programs and its quiet refusal to take part in the U.S. economic block-ade.[23]   Of course, it is only Canada's aid contributions that have been acknowledged by the Central American political actors. Its other interests in the region generally go unrecognized.

Ortega called for increased levels of Canadian aid, and stated that rich countries including Canada "can have a greater impact in our country" by helping Nicaragua repair the economic damage done during seven years of civil war.[24] It is also the case that Nicaragua impressed Canadian officials by delivering its aid effectively. However, Clark insisted that his government's aid budget could not be increased. Canadian directors of NGOs criticized this decision, emphasizing that Canada's professed support for the peace plan should be backed with concrete action. These concerns went unheeded.

While Clark was in Costa Rica, President Oscar Arias suggested that he consider using aid to encourage countries to comply with the peace plan. Clark did not support this view, however, stressing that Canada did not wish to link aid to overtly political considerations.[25] Conditionality would not be a part of Canada's aid program.

The director of Canadian University Service Overseas (CUSO) referred to Clark's modest intentions in the region as "spineless" and "intellectually inept."[26] Clark was lambasted for failing to criticize U.S. support for the contra rebels. But what became abundantly clear during the minister's visit was that Canada simply did not possess a great deal of political clout in the region. Nor was a large infusion of Canadian assistance likely to make a substantial difference.

It should also be noted that the Canadian government's assertion that it provides aid where it is most needed--even if the recipient's political leaders are inefficient or corrupt--does not stand up to examination. For example, Canada gives more aid to Costa Rica than to its neighbors, even though it has Central America's highest per capita income. Also, Canada has cut off aid to Guatemala and El Salvador because of their govern-ments' human rights abuses. One could reasonably argue that delivering aid is a political, as well as a moral, decision.[27]

If it is the case that foreign aid is political, then it might be possible to encourage democracy and peace through aid, while respecting a society's right to self-determination. CAPA and other groups suggest that Canadian foreign aid delivery be contingent on its use for peaceful purposes, while encouraging popular participation in decision making. It must be delivered in a corruption-free environment (as far as possible) and must encourage the development or transfer of appropriate technol-ogy. This is admittedly a tall order in the Central American context, but the argument is frequently advanced that efforts should be made to promote these noble goals. As noted, successive Canadian governments have voiced these sentiments from time to time; but rarely have they supported these views with concrete action.

On the other hand, a reasonable, and perhaps a more persuasive, argument could be made against Canada's use of aid to exercise political influence. For example, Canadian aid is dispersed to more than 100 recipient nations, thus making it difficult to target any one nation for influence. Furthermore, the volume of assistance is not so great as to carry much political weight in Central America. Instead, the rationale for Canada's continued commitment to providing aid may be better justified by the international and domestic prestige that it enjoys as a result of such action. Secondary factors affecting Canada's desire to provide aid might include true altruistic motives (i.e., a desire to do "what's right"), and pressure from domestic interest groups.[28]

By August 1987 the most important Canadian government aid projects in Central America included the following:[*29]

For *Costa Rica*, there was a three-year (1985-87) commitment to provide a line of credit to assist the agricultural sector. In addition, a four-year (1986-1990) grant of $3 million was provided to create a scholarship program providing technical and college-level training in agriculture. Assistance was also provided to aid in the construction of houses and to provide drilling equipment.

For *El Salvador*, $8,140,000 worth of Canadian fertilizer was provided to support that country's balance of payments and to assist the displaced and the poor.

For *Honduras*, assistance was provided to support many projects including the upgrading of its national hydroelectric network, the improved management of its tropical forests, and the production of a master plan for the integrated rural development of the Guayape valley. Funding was also provided to build 260 potable water systems for two different projects, to support the Honduran cooperative movement, to support ten community health clinics, and to construct housing for 1,200 low-income Honduran families.

For *Nicaragua*, lines of credit were provided to improve the supply of potable water, to assist its food production capacity, and to produce electricity from its Momotombo II geothermal project. In March 1988, $1 million in food aid (i.e., kidney beans--a staple of the Nicaraguan diet) was donated during a severe drought.

*See Tables 4.1-4.9 for a breakdown of aid disbursements.

In November 1987 bilateral aid was restored to Guatemala. The Canadian government wanted to demonstrate its support for the Cerezo government's efforts to withstand pressures from its military to impose order by persecuting dissidents. The aid was also a reflection of Canada's interest in President Cerezo's efforts to promote economic development and democracy. Finally, it was a recognition that Cerezo had been an invaluable actor in the effort to devise the Esquipulas II peace plan. Most human rights groups charged that Canada was making a mistake, however, since there remained ongoing evidence of serious human rights abuses by government officials in Guatemala.

It should be mentioned that in its 1987 report on Guatemala, Amnesty International pointed out that when President Cerezo disbanded Guatemala's notorious secret police, its members were simply retrained and integrated into regular police units. Politically motivated killings and disappearances continued, and a brutal military organization continued to run large portions of the country. Renewed Canadian aid could thus be interpreted as a vote of confidence for that situation. Indeed, External Affairs Minister Clark was told by Nineth de Garcia, a leading human rights activist in Guatemala, that Canada should channel aid through private agencies and not the government, since the army had appropriated some of the assistance. Furthermore, she maintained that political violence had actually been increasing.[30] One might also suggest, although not substantiate, a thesis that suggests that Canada resumed aid under pressure from the United States (not a viable possibility, since the United States has almost always tolerated a relatively independent Canadian foreign policy stance) or because it wanted to appease Guatemala, which was angry that Canada had reduced its diplomatic presence there. The latter is the more likely scenario. Whatever the motivation for the Canadian resumption of aid, by early 1990 it was proceeding without hindrance. A formal "memorandum of understanding" was signed between the governments of Canada and Guatemala, whereby a new four-year $8.8 million bilateral aid project would be initiated. As noted earlier, some critics charge that Canada's largess toward Honduras is also unwarranted. Canada donates, on average, $10 million per year to that country, but President Azcona is lukewarm, at best, about the Central American peace plan. Also, it is undoubtedly the case that some of Canada's aid falls into corrupt hands. Furthermore, Canada has helped to build the Honduran hydroelectric industry, but much of the lighting produced by the El Cajon dam is exported to the rest of Central America. It is not providing sufficient electrical power to the Honduran countryside and to the people for whom it was destined. Government officials insist that Honduras remains a "core" country, however, and as such will continue to receive substantial support from Canada.

In fiscal year 1987-88, Canada's development assistance funds to the Central American nations included CDN $21,555,500 for Costa Rica, $8,111,400 for El Salvador, $3,677,600 for Guatemala, $7,690,700 for Honduras, $15,037,600 for Nicaragua, and $981,900 for Panama. Costa Rica, Nicaragua, and Honduras received large increases from the previous year--the first two a recognition of the effort to promote the peace process by Presidents Arias and Ortega, and the last an acknowledgment of the "core" country status of Honduras.

In March 1988 CIDA released a set of new goals and principles for its worldwide aid program, in a report entitled "Sharing Our Future." No increase in development aid was announced, but a renewed emphasis was to be placed on human rights considerations, "untied" aid, and decentralized management of aid programs. Sixty-five percent of Canadian assistance would go to Commonwealth and francophone developing countries, whereas little aid (16 percent) would be targeted for Latin America, although an aid office would be opened in San Jose, Costa Rica. The report was vague on how human rights would be assessed, and defined human rights abuse as "gross and persistent abuse without further qualification."

A major part of the report was devoted to discussion of the biggest innovation of Canadian development strategy: "the partnership program." This program would use fully 50 percent of aid dollars to finance NGOs, universities, multilateral organizations, and businesses to do development work. This was a risky proposition, however, for development money was scarce, and well-intentioned but ultimately futile projects could be financed. Therefore money would have to be allocated carefully, although the shared responsibility advocated by the federal government would allow for a pooling of expert views, and would be an incentive for private and public institutions to become involved in the aid program. Here again the government's stated goals were noble and ambitious.

In July 1988 an all-party parliamentary committee on the Central American peace process issued a report entitled "Supporting the Five."[31] With regard to development aid the report urged the government to raise an international fund for reconstruction (totaling $100 million over five years, and entitled the Esquipulas II fund), encouraged the United States to end its economic embargo against Nicaragua and maintain its cut-off of military aid to the contras, and prompted the Soviet Union and its allies to participate in multilateral efforts to support recovery and development in the region. The reconstruction fund would likely be administered by the United Nations and would reduce Central American dependence on bilateral aid and the consequent influence of countries like the United States.

In September, Joe Clark announced that the government would spend $100 million for reconstruction and development assistance in Central America between 1988 and 1994. This would double the bilateral aid given over the previous five years, and was clearly a positive response to the parliamentary group recommendations. There was no discussion of how the $100 million would be apportioned, however. Clark also pledged to work within the United Nations and the World Bank to promote more effective coordination and prioritization of development assistance to the region. Clark failed to acknowledge the suggestions of "Supporting the Five," however, and made no reference to discouraging U.S. contra support or encouraging Soviet aid involvement.[32]

In October 1988 Nicaragua was devastated by a hurricane on its Atlantic coast, and Canada contributed $250,000 of emergency aid. Relief agencies criticized what they saw as Canada's stinginess, particularly since it extended $6.6 million in immediate and long-term aid to Jamaica after it was similarly devastated by a hurricane. Indeed, Nicaragua suffered many more fatalities. Perhaps the difference was related to the fact that many more Jamaicans than Nicaraguans live in Canada, and thus Jamaicans were better equipped to lobby for assistance from federal authorities. Of course Jamaica is also part of the Commonwealth.[33]

Pressure increased on government authorities to be more generous, and $2.3 million in additional funds were targeted for Nicaragua. In addition, various NGOs raised $900,000 for the relief effort. By contrast, the United States blocked all humanitarian aid shipments to Nicaragua as part of its overall embargo.

Interestingly, Canadian aid to El Salvador also increased at this time, amid accusations that it was being used to support a repressive regime and was not being directed to those who most needed it. Although CIDA denied the charge made by Salvadorean labor leaders, convincing evidence was presented to show that Canadian aid was being controlled by the Salvadorean military and corrupt government officials.[34] Critics of the Canadian government reiterated this position in December 1988, when a Canadian aid worker in El Salvador was severely injured by a hand grenade, probably thrown by military forces at a refugee settlement.

Providing aid for all of Central America, even where human rights violations were rampant, continued to be justified by Canadian government officials on the grounds that according to the Esquipulas II Agreement, peace and development were inseparable. The economic health of all Central American countries was intertwined. Canada would be promoting regional rivalry and civil unrest if it were to make the case for aid to one country at the expense of another.[35] This is not to say that human rights considerations would always be ignored, but they would not be an immediate priority.[36]

Furthermore, Canadian government officials maintained that by providing aid to all of the countries of the region, they enjoyed some credibility with each country. On the other hand, Canada's aid donations were not substantial enough to have a meaningful influence. As long as making a vital difference in the region is not a priority, and External Affairs officials insist this is the case, then limited assistance is not a problem. Some Canadian observers claim that by stressing Canada's limited clout in the area, the federal government is simultaneously providing itself with an excuse for not making more of a difference.[37] This is a complaint made frequently by left-wing critics of Canadian External Affairs policy. They, and others, use Sweden as the model of a nation that targets its aid to one country, in this case Nicaragua, and not to all of the countries of the region. In this way, it is argued, Sweden becomes a country with influential policies.[38]

As if to excuse the situation, government officials have always stressed that if Canada is not exerting a vital influence, neither are Canada's aid projects assisting the armed forces or corrupt officials of any of the recipient countries. (If this statement is more than just rhetoric, the government may want to reevaluate its aid program in El Salvador in light of the election of the Arena party.) Future aid decisions--indeed decisions of all sorts regarding Central America--would depend upon budget allocations, the ability to target aid where it is needed most, and the absorption capacity of the recipient nation.

Unfortunately, the May 1989 announcement that foreign aid allocations would be dramatically reduced foreshadows an ominous future for CIDA and its beneficiaries. Canadian proponents of aid, whether for reasons of national prestige or altruism, have been stifled by the budget cutters who saw an institution that was vulnerable to massive cuts. Although the Canadian economy grew steadily in 1988, its deficit grew precipitously. The result for foreign aid planners was a large-scale budget slashing and a reevaluation of priorities. Aid will be cut by $1.8 billion from 1989-1994, with a cut of $335 million from the 1989 budget alone--a reduction of 12.2 percent. Canada's official development assistance will plummet to 0.43 percent of GNP in 1989-90, from a target of 0.7, a lower percentage than when the Mulroney government took office in 1984. Canada will support the U.S. "Brady Plan" on debt, and slash contributions to both the Inter-American Development Bank and Caribbean Development Bank by 40 and 80 percent, respectively. The immediate future of Canada's aid program looks precarious. In April 1989 Prime

Minister Mulroney promised Costa Rican President Arias that: "We know the impact of poverty and violence in Central America. For this reason, Canadian economic assistance has more than tripled in the past decade and will increase significantly during the next."[39] With the announced cuts in the government foreign aid budget, the prime minister has had to reverse his position. He realizes that there is no strong constituency for foreign aid, and that cutting assistance programs is easier than slashing domestic programs. The aid cuts were immediately condemned by those who believed that Canada was abandoning the developing world, but to no avail.

Not only is the aid program troubled by budget cutbacks, but it has been crippled by a lack of consistent purpose. The government has released several policy papers and reports calling for renewed aid, an emphasis on human rights considerations, and strategies for using development assistance to promote peace in Central America. It has rarely followed its pronouncements with concrete action. (One notable recent exception was the August 1989 visit by a Canadian elections delegation to Nicaragua to assess options for Canadian assistance. The delegation returned with a favorable evaluation of the legal/technical election framework, and confirmed the need for international assistance. In September, Canada announced a $700,000 program to support the electoral process, including provision of materials for ballot boxes, voter-privacy screens, manuals for local election officials, and technical and financial aid to Nicaragua's supreme electoral council.) Overall, however, the government's policies are consistent with those of its Liberal government predecessors. "Tied aid" remains an important tool to promote commercial interests, notwithstanding the problems associated with it, and the government's repeated pledge to reduce its impact. Indeed, Cranford Pratt argues that the pursuit of economic interests has become the predominant concern of those who shape Canadian policies on North-South issues.[40] In addition, government officials are, at times, inconsistent in their statements about the extent to which human rights considerations enter aid decisions. One is forced to conclude that Canada's promotion of human rights is made on a case-by-case, rather than on a systematic, basis. CIDA remains disorganized and problematic, and it would be unreasonable to expect a major reform of the agency in the near future.

Canada might be able to make a concrete and positive difference in Central America by targeting its aid where it can do the most good. But other priorities have taken hold, and it is hard to be optimistic about the "helpful fixer" making a distinctive contribution to the diminution of the region's poverty and underdevelopment.

Table 4.1
Canadian Bilateral Aid to Central America, 1970-1985
(bilateral aid disbursements, millions $CDN)

Country	1970-71	1971-72	1972-73	1973-74	1974-75	1975-76
Costa Rica	-	-	-	.05	.15	.14
El Salvador	.11	.19	.07	.11	1.42	2.07
Guatemala	-	.01	.13	.05	.02	3.32*
Honduras	-	.16	.53	.31	2.19	1.44
Nicaragua	-	.01	.01	1.41	1.02	.13

	1976-77	1977-78	1978-79	1979-80	1980-81
Costa Rica	.04	.20	.16	.17	.14
El Salvador	.90	.49	.63	1.37	2.66
Guatemala	1.48	1.88	4.61	2.94	1.33
Honduras	.43	1.79	9.88	4.62	3.68
Nicaragua	.57	.40	-	.20	.20

	1981-82	1982-83	1983-84	1984-85
Costa Rica	.35	3.23	6.34	6.64
El Salvador	6.21	.54	.53	.51
Guatemala	1.17	2.57	.86	.82
Honduras	3.25	3.57	1.97	19.36
Nicaragua	4.65	.59	7.15	6.61

Source: Canadian International Development Agency *Annual Reports* and *Annual Reviews*, various years, Ministry of Supply and Services, Ottawa.
*The sudden sharp increase in aid to Guatemala in 1975-6 is accounted for by relief aid following the 1976 earthquake.

Aid Disbursements to Central America (1982/83 - 1986/87)*

Acronyms for various kinds of development assistance listed in Tables 4.2-4.9.

ICOD	International Centre for Ocean Development
INC	Industrial cooperation
MAF	Mission-administered funds
NGI	Nongovernmental institution
NGO	Nongovernmental organization
PCIAC	Petro-Canada International Assistance Corporation
IDRC	International Development Research Centre

Source: Federal government publication entitled *Summary of Aid to Central America* (August 1987)

*Summary of Canadian Aid to Central America, August 1987.

Table 4.2
Total Aid to Central America, 1982/83 to 1986/87 (in $CDN)

	Costa Rica	El Salvador	Guatemala	Honduras	Nicaragua	Panama	Activities	Total
Bilateral*	26,246.8	7,150.9	3,339.6	30,490.3	22,153.5	-	3,773.8	93,154.9
MAF	1,667.8	1,780.5	1,747.5	1,646.3	1,672.4	680.4	-	9,194.9
NGO	1,036.0	4,577.0	4,315.0	7,897.5	9,542.7	1,122.9	-	28,491.1
NGO (Food Aid)	18.6	2,748.0	756.0	1,058.7	1,334.4	40.0	-	5,955.7
NGI	1,882.0	44.5	508.9	1,252.0	2,521.0	1,239.1	-	7,447.5
INC	762.9	0.5	571.9	255.1	259.3	41.7	-	1,891.4
Food Aid (Govt. to Govt.)	-	-	-	-	2,816.0	-	-	2,816.0
IDRC	5,164.0	408.0	1,372.0	1,076.0	556.0	1,258.0	-	9,834.0
PCIAC	7,560.0	-	-	-	-	-	-	7,560.0
ICOD	-	-	-	-	-	-	-	-
Humanitarian Aid**	-	570.0	590.0	-	80.0	-	-	1,240.0
Total Direct	44,338.1	17,279.4	13,200.9	43,675.9	40,935.3	4,382.1	3,773.8	167,585.5

*Includes country focus projects.

**Except for FY 85/86 and 86/87, direct disbursements are included in other categories. Amounts exclude assistance provided through the multilateral channel.

Table 4.3
Aid Disbursements to Costa Rica, 1982/83 to 1986/87 (in $CDN)

	82/83	83/84	84/85	85/86	86/87	TOTAL 82/83-86/87
Direct						
Bilateral*	2,878.1	5,993.6	6,315.8	6,604.9	4,454.4	26,246.8
MAF	352.7	348.6	321.0	282.8	362.7	1,667.8
NGO	168.0	248.0	320.0	60.0	240.0	1,036.0
NGO (Food Aid)	-	-	-	18.6	-	18.6
NGI	128.0	286.0	298.0	140.0	1,030.0	1,882.0
INC	285.0	185.0	169.0	3.9	120.0	762.9
Food Aid (Govt. to Govt.)	-	-	-	-	-	-
IDRC	715.0	660.0	649.0	1,530.0	1,610.0	5,164.0
PCIAC	-	-	-	60.0	7,500.0	7,560.0
ICOD	-	-	-	-	-	-
Humanitarian Aid**	-	-	-	-	-	-
Total Direct	4,526.8	7,721.2	8,072.8	8,700.2	15,317.1	44,338.1

*Includes country focus projects.

**Except for FY 85/86 and 86/87, direct disbursements are included in other categories. Excludes assistance provided through the multilateral channel.

Table 4.4
Aid Disbursements to El Salvador, 1982/83 to 1986/87 (in $CDN)

	82/83	83/84	84/85	85/86	86/87	TOTAL 82/83-86/87
Direct						
Bilateral*	4,335.5	347.4	332.8	71.0	5,964.2	7,150.9
MAF	275.8	351.6	350.8	303.0	499.3	1,780.5
NGO	542.0	1,613.0	912.0	240.0	1,270.0	4,577.0
NGO (Food Aid)	170.0	1,008.0	260.0	1,250.0	60.0	2,748.0
NGI	-	4.5	-	-	40.0	44.5
INC	-	-	0.5	-	-	0.5
Food Aid (Govt. to Govt.)	-	-	-	-	-	-
IDRC	101.0	122.0	95.0	20.0	70.0	408.0
PCIAC	-	-	-	-	-	-
ICOD	-	-	-	-	-	-
Humanitarian Aid**	-	-	-	30.0	540.0	570.0
Total Direct	1,524.3	3,446.5	1,951.1	1,914.0	8,443.5	17,279.4

*Includes country focus projects.

**Except for FY 85/86 and 86/87, direct disbursements are included in other categories. Excludes assistance provided through the multilateral channel.

Table 4.5
Aid Disbursements to Guatemala, 1982/83 to 1986/87 (in $CDN)

	82/83	83/84	84/85	85/86	86/87	TOTAL 82/83- 86/87
Direct						
Bilateral*	2,187.1	511.3	483.5	90.0	60.0	3,339.6
MAF	350.0	350.0	350.0	347.5	350.0	1,747.5
NGO	636.0	848.0	1,121.0	730.0	980.0	4,315.0
NGO (Food Aid)	296.0	-	70.0	240.0	150.0	756.0
NGI	73.0	55.9	154.0	6.0	220.0	508.9
INC	206.0	105.9	-	40.0	220.0	571.9
Food Aid (Govt. to Govt.)	-	-	-	-	-	-
IDRC	65.0	4.0	303.0	380.0	620.0	1,372.0
PCIAC	-	-	-	-	-	-
ICOD	-	-	-	-	-	-
Humanitarian Aid**	-	-	-	150.0	440.0	590.0
Total Direct	3,813.1	1,875.1	2,481.5	1,983.5	3,047.7	13,200.9

*Includes country focus projects.

**Except for FY 85/86 and 86/87, direct disbursements are included in other categories. Excludes assistance provided through the multilateral channel.

Table 4.6
Aid Disbursements to Honduras, 1982/83 to 1986/87 (in $CDN)

	82/83	83/84	84/85	85/86	86/87	TOTAL 82/83-86/87
Direct						
Bilateral*	4,579.5	2,879.5	19,005.8	2,590.6	1,434.9	30,490.3
MAF	249.3	350.0	349.9	347.9	349.2	1,646.3
NGO	2,844.8	1,986.7	726.0	720.0	1,620.0	7,897.5
NGO (Food Aid)	388.0	232.0	70.0	138.7	230.0	1,058.7
NGI	55.0	11.2	63.8	122.0	1,000.0	1,252.0
INC	52.1	94.0	98.0	11.0	-	255.1
Food Aid (Govt. to Govt.)	-	-	-	-	-	-
IDRC	114.0	137.0	215.0	380.0	230.0	1,076.0
PCIAC	-	-	-	-	-	-
ICOD	-	-	-	-	-	-
Humanitarian Aid**	-	-	-	-	-	-
Total Direct	8,282.7	5,690.4	20,528.5	4,310.2	4,864.1	43,675.9

*Includes country focus projects.

**Except for FY 85/86 and 86/87, direct disbursements are included in other categories. Excludes assistance provided through the multilateral channel.

Table 4.7
Aid Disbursements to Nicaragua, 1982/83 to 1986/87 (in $CDN)

	82/83	83/84	84/85	85/86	86/87	TOTAL 82/83- 86/87
Direct						
Bilateral*	785.2	5,752.7	6,261.8	5,807.0	3,546.8	22,153.5
MAF	353.2	349.5	350.3	269.6	349.8	1,672.4
NGO	1,772.0	2,396.7	1,867.0	877.0	2,630.0	9,542.7
NGO (Food Aid)	60.0	56.0	310.0	798.4	110.0	1,334.4
NGI	419.0	197.0	235.0	270.0	1,400.0	2,521.0
INC	117.0	135.0	7.3	-	-	259.3
Food Aid (Govt. to Govt.)	-	2,816.0	-	-	-	2,816.0
IDRC	203.0	183.0	-60.0	40.0	190.0	556.0
PCIAC	-	-	-	-	-	-
ICOD	-	-	-	-	-	-
Humanitarian Aid**	-	-	-	80.0	-	80.0
Total Direct	3,709.4	11,885.9	8,971.4	8,142.0	8,226.6	40,935.3

*Includes country focus projects.

**Except for FY 85/86 and 86/87, direct disbursements are included in other categories. Excludes assistance provided through the multilateral channel.

Table 4.8
Aid Disbursements to Panama, 1982/83 to 1986/87 (in $CDN)

	82/83	83/84	84/85	85/86	86/87	TOTAL 82/83- 86/87
Direct						
Bilateral*	-	-	-	-	-	-
MAF	151.1	150.6	149.2	79.6	149.9	680.4
NGO	154.0	205.9	473.0	80.0	210.0	1,122.9
NGO (Food Aid)	-	-	20.0	20.0	-	40.0
NGI	306.0	72.9	20.2	-	840.0	1,239.1
INC	20.0	11.7	-	-	10.0	41.7
Food Aid (Govt. to Govt.)	-	-	-	-	-	-
IDRC	102.0	316.0	190.0	380.0	270.0	1,258.0
PCIAC	-	-	-	-	-	-
ICOD	-	-	-	-	-	-
Humanitarian Aid**	-	-	-	-	-	-
Total Direct	733.1	757.1	852.4	559.6	1,479.9	4,382.1

*Includes country focus projects.

**Except for FY 85/86 and 86/87, direct disbursements are included in other categories. Excludes assistance provided through the multilateral channel.

Table 4.9
Regional Aid Disbursements to Central America,
1982/83 to 1986/87 (in $CDN)

	82/83	83/84	84/85	85/86	86/87	TOTAL 82/83-86/87
Direct						
Bilateral*	855.3	323.0	862.0	1,259.6	473.9	3,773.8
MAF	-	-	-	-	-	-
NGO	-	-	-	-	-	-
NGO (Food Aid)	-	-	-	-	-	-
NGI	-	-	-	-	-	-
INC	-	-	-	-	-	-
Food Aid (Govt. to Govt.)	-	-	-	-	-	-
IDRC	-	-	-	-	-	-
PCIAC	-	-	-	-	-	-
ICOD	-	-	-	-	-	-
Humanitarian Aid**	-	-	-	-	-	-
Total Direct	855.3	323.0	862.0	1,259.6	473.9	3,773.9

*Includes country focus projects.

**Except for FY 85/86 and 86/87, direct disbursements are included in other categories. Excludes assistance provided through the multilateral channel.

NOTES

1. This breakdown of aid programs is adapted from the Latin American Working Group's "LAWG Letter" entitled "Overview of Canadian Aid to Central America: 1980-85," 9:3 (February 1988).

2. See the statement of Secretary of State for External Affairs Allan MacEachen, "Address to the 38th session of the United Nations General Assembly" (New York, September 27, 1983).

3. Thomas C. Bruneau, Jan J. Torgensen, and J. O. Ramsay, *CIDA: The Organization of Canadian Overseas Assistance,* 24, Centre for Developing Area Studies, McGill University (Montreal, October 1978).

4. Tim Draimin, "Canadian Foreign Policy in El Salvador," in Liisa North (ed.), *Bitter Grounds* (Toronto: Between the Lines, 1981), pp. 99-100.

5. For a discussion of Canada's aid programs in the 1970s, and problems associated with their allocations, see *In the Canadian Interests: Third World Development in the 1980s* (Ottawa: North-South Institute, 1980), pp. 5-18.

6. For an overview of Canadian aid to Honduras, see "Paved with Good Intentions: Canadian Aid to Honduras," published by the Latin American Working Group *LAWG Letter*, 44 (February 1989).

7. For an excellent overview of Canadian aid to Nicaragua until 1984, see Bob Thompson, "Canadian Aid and Trade Relations with Nicaragua," a pamphlet published by Canada-Caribbean-Central America Policy Alternatives (Toronto: CAPA, November 1984).

8. For an overview of aid to El Salvador, see "Taking sides: Canadian Aid to El Salvador," published by the Latin American Working Group, *LAWG Letter* 10:1 (August 1987).

9. See the report of the Parliamentary Subcommittee on Canada's Relations with Latin America and the Caribbean (Queen's Printer, 1982).

10. See the Canadian government's volume *Canada's International Relations* (December 1986), pp. 73-74, for the federal government's positive response to *Independence and Internationalism.*

11. See for example, *Report to CIDA: Public Attitudes Toward International Development Assistance* (Hull: Canadian International Development Agency, 1988).

12. David Haglund, "Missing Link: Canada's Security Interests and the Central American Crisis," *International Journal* 43:4 (Autumn 1987), pp. 789-820.

13. See, for example, Michael Czerny and Tim Draimin, "A Secret Foreign Policy: Canada and Central America," a pamphlet published by CAPA (Toronto, Winter 1985).

14. See the statement published by CAPA, and entitled "Pro-Active Peace Proposals for Canada," (Toronto, March 5, 1987).

15. For a discussion of the problems associated with "tied aid," see Terence A. Keenleyside, "Foreign Aid and Human Rights," *International Perspectives* (March/April 1987), pp. 15-18.

16. This point is discussed in detail in the Latin American Working Group's *LAWG Letter*, pp. 3-4.

17. For example, see the discussion in Liisa North, "Measures for Peace in Central America" (Ottawa: CIIPS, May 8-9, 1987), p. 55.

18. For example, see the "Statement by the Victoria International Development Education Association (VIDEA)," *House of Commons Minutes of Proceedings and Evidence of the Standing Committee on External Affairs and International Trade* (November 4, 1986) 7, pp. 57-60.

19. This point is discussed in more detail by Stephen Dale, "Abetting Uncivil Warfare," *Now* (September 25-October 1, 1986).

20. For a reference to this point, see a public letter from the secretary of state for external affairs to Professor Meyer Brownstone (Ottawa, February 9, 1987).

21. Ottawa Citizen (May 29, 1987).

22. For a good critique of the Wineguard report, see John Tackaberry, "Getting Development Right," *International Perspectives* (July/August 1987), pp. 12-14.

23. The Montreal Gazette (November 25, 1987), p. A-13.

24. "Ortega Says More Aid Vital If Peace Plan Is to Succeed," *Globe and Mail* (November 25, 1987), p. A-14.

25. As reported in *Globe and Mail* (November 30, 1987).

26. "Clark's Troubled Tour," *Maclean's* (December 7, 1987), p. 26.

27. For an extended discussion of this point, see "Aid for Poorest, Poor Way to Go?" *Globe and Mail* (December 15, 1987), p. A-8.

28. For a critical discussion of the motives underlying Canada's aid policies, see Kim Richard Nossal, "Mixed Motives Revisited: Canada's Interest in Development Assistance," *Canadian Journal of Political Science* 21:1 (March 1988), pp. 35-56.

29. For a comprehensive overview of Canadian government aid projects as of August 1987, see a booklet published by the federal government, *Summary of Canadian Aid to Central America* (August 1987). See also Tables 1-9 in the appendix.

30. "Guatemala Death Squads Active as Canada Ready to Resume Aid," *Toronto Star* (November 25, 1987).

31. Supporting the Five: Canada and the Central American Peace Process (Ottawa: Queen's Printer, July 5, 1988).

32. The complete text of Clark's response to the Bosley all-party report can be found in a public letter sent by Joe Clark's office to John Bosley, and released by the Department of External Affairs on September 23, 1988.

33. For a thorough discussion see Charlotte Montgomery, "Nicaragua Aid Called Inadequate," *Globe and Mail* (November 12, 1988), p. A-9.

34. For a discussion of the controversy, see Charlotte Montgomery, "Salvadoreans Echo Canadian Concerns over Bilateral Aid," *Globe and Mail* (December 3, 1988), p. A-23.

35. For example, see a paper written by Ambassador Richard Gorham, Canada's roving ambassador to Central America, *Peace and Development in Central America*, released by the Department of External Affairs (not dated).

36. See, for example, the statement by International Development Minister Monique Landry, who was quoted by Charlotte Montgomery in "Human Rights Records Ignored in Aid Decisions, Minister Says," *Globe and Mail* (June 9, 1989), p. A-4.

37. For example, see the statement by Tim Draimin of CAPA in "What Should Canada Do?" *Hamilton Spectator* (March 14, 1989).

38. See, for example, Gerald Caplan, "Our Foreign Policy is Amoral, Illogical and Subservient to U.S. Interests," *Toronto Star* (April 16, 1989).

39. As quoted in "A Broken Promise," *Toronto Star* (May 4, 1989).

40. Cranford Pratt, "Canada: An Eroding and Limited Internationalism," in Cranford Pratt (ed.) *Internationalism Under Strain: The North-South Policies of Canada, the Netherlands, Norway and Sweden* (Toronto: University of Toronto Press, 1989), pp. 24-69.

5 Finding Peace in Central America: The Promise and the Reality

A solution to the bitter strife in Central America continues to prove elusive.[1] Recent attempts to resolve the serious problems there, most notably through the Contadora initiative and the Esquipulas plan (also referred to as the Arias or Guatemala plan), have been stymied. The points of dispute in the region include civil war in El Salvador, insurgency in Guatemala, abject poverty in all five of the republics, social dislocation in the region, and the interventions of outside powers pursuing their own interests--often to the detriment of the Central American nations them-selves. Clearly, it should be no surprise that peace remains a rare commodity.

This chapter departs from the discussion of Canadian policy in Central America. Instead, it offers a background to the peace process as a whole. Central America has been torn apart by internal conflicts since the early part of the nineteenth century, but the regional strife took on a new and dangerous element after the successful victory of the Sandinista National Liberation Front in Nicaragua in 1979, and the escalation of the civil war in El Salvador since 1980.[2] These events not only intensified and internationalized the tensions within Central America between radical movements of the left and conservative oligarchies on the right, but they also heightened the involvement of both the United States and the Soviet Union in the region. In this way, regional conflicts became aggravated by superpower strategic interests.

In January 1983, in an effort to achieve regional peace and to limit the growing involvement of the superpowers in Central America, four Latin American neighbors--Mexico, Panama, Colombia, and Venezuela--agreed to serve as mediators between the various parties involved in regional conflicts. These nations, which became known as the

Contadora states (after the Isla de Contadora, off the coast of Panama, where they met) struggled to find regional solutions to regional problems.

In a declaration issued on May 13, 1983, they stated that the purpose of the group was to fulfill for Central America "a diplomatic function aimed at seeking, through a political route, the solution of the conflicts and counting, in order to accomplish this, on the collaboration of the involved parties."

The Contadora countries were soon joined by the "Latin Support Group," composed of Brazil, Argentina, Peru, and Uruguay. However, obstacles to peace were enormous. The U.S. government was never enthusiastic about Contadora. Equally disadvantageous was the lack of those economic, political, and social advantages that would be necessary for reducing the region's tensions. Violence, which was common in most of Central America, sprang from poverty, the unequal distribution of wealth, rigid social structures, and the absence of effective vehicles for popular participation in politics.

Nevertheless, it was hoped that a Latin American solution to the difficulties might help reduce tensions, promote the peaceful settlement of ongoing disputes, and discourage direct or indirect external intervention.

The goals of the Contadora nations were quite clear-cut--at least at first glance. First, they sought to demonstrate that the problems of Central America originated there and could best be settled by regional actors. By contrast, the 1984 report of the Kissinger commission (officially referred to as the National Bipartisan Commission on Central America) implied that the problems emanated from the strategic interests of the Soviet Union and its allies. The Contadora states insisted that the region's strife had emerged from long-standing social, economic, and political problems that had then been aggravated by superpower involvement. The Contadora nations hoped that a regional approach to conflict resolution, rather than an emphasis solely on the internal situations of the states, might provide the impetus necessary to separate the turmoil in Central America from superpower competition.

To facilitate this process a census would be introduced in each country (as well as a calendar of reduction) to help eliminate all foreign military advisers, and others, from participation in military or security activities. In addition, efforts would be made to identify and end all forms of financial and other support for irregular forces involved in the destabilization of any Central American governments. Any forces engaged in undermining any government in the region would be removed (for excerpts from the Contadora Treaty, see Appendix A). Contadora deliberately excluded U.S. involvement. The assumption was that each of the Central American countries would be acting in its own national interest.

Another goal of Contadora was to provide a neutral forum for the articulation of grievances, the resolution of conflict, and the promotion of national reconciliation. It was hoped that within a Contadora treaty, strategies could be devised to provide long-term approaches to conflict management in Central America. These strategies would be based on the universally desirable goals of justice, freedom, and democracy. A complete set of diplomatic and legal proceedings and rules of involvement were to be created. Human rights protection and electoral guarantees ensuring effective and popular political participation were to be instituted.

Another goal, vital, but secondary at the time, centered on the notion of "economic Contadora"--the economic revival of the area. It was generally agreed that the provision of regional peace and security could not be guaranteed until progress had been made in overcoming Central America's low level of economic development. To that end, a variety of economic development strategies were to be suggested for eventual implementation. Also, refugee aid programs were to be introduced, and existing ones augmented. International and humanitarian organizations would be sought out to help facilitate voluntary repatriation of refugees, with the cooperation of the Central American governments involved.

Clearly the goals of Contadora were quite ambitious, and it should come as no surprise that the effort to implement its provisions has been fraught with difficulties. One initial problem focused on Contadora's primary mandate. The intent of the Contadora participants had been to find a consensus among the five Central American countries and to create a mechanism for reconciliation. However, some observers of the process declared that Contadora should be solely concerned with solving the root causes of instability in the region: social, economic, and political injustice. To them, national reconciliation was secondary. Conflicting motives would hamper the peace process.

Other obstacles included the presence of externally supported guerrilla campaigns in El Salvador, Nicaragua, and Guatemala, and growing East-West interests in the region. Barriers to peace included the ever-present threat of military coup d'etat in all of the countries but Costa Rica, and competing national interests and priorities. Nicaragua and the four other countries mistrusted one another, and, in general, the requisite degree of political will necessary to overcome the region's problems was not apparent. For example, during his inaugural address in August 1983, then-Guatemalan President Mejia Victories declared: "The Contadora Group has nothing to do with Central America. . . . the Nicaraguan Government represents a threat not only to Guatemala, but to the entire continent."[3] Clearly, convincing the leaders of Central America that the goals of Contadora were both viable and in all of their national interests would be an uphill battle.

To summarize, the goals of Contadora in 1983 included:

1. The removal of foreign military advisers from Central America. The Contadora ministers shared a distaste for unilateral U.S. interventions in the region (e.g., Guatemala in 1954, Cuba in 1961, the Dominican Republic in 1965). They also shared a desire to moderate and contain the Sandinista regime in Nicaragua and the FMLN revolutionaries in El Salvador, and to avoid the expansion of a Soviet bloc presence in Nicaragua. The Contadora ministers feared any repetition of these activities, and they wanted to avoid the conversion of the region into an epicenter of East-West tensions.
2. An end to arms imports and arms smuggling.
3. An end to international military maneuvers.
4. The closing of all foreign military bases.
5. An end of support for guerrilla movements.
6. Comprehensive control and verification procedures.
7. The eventual institution of democratic, pluralistic governments, with major socioeconomic reconstruction.[4]

From the outset the Contadora negotiators recognized that the United States had legitimate security concerns in the region, and they worked to reduce Soviet and Cuban influence there. However, they disagreed fundamentally with the Reagan administration about the underlying cause of the turmoil in Central America. If the United States saw the problems as being caused by Soviet-Cuban expansionism, the Contadora countries saw the basic causes of civil strife to be internal (i.e., poverty and social justice). Moreover, they blamed the United States for having tolerated repressive right-wing regimes for decades, thereby contributing to instability.

The solution of the Contadora ministers was to seek a regional solution to their problems, thereby challenging U.S. hegemony in the region. In addition, they felt that negotiation and dialogue would have to become standard devices in restoring political stability and social peace to Central America. There was also a consensus that negotiations with Cuba to limit Soviet/Cuban influences in the region were mandatory. Above all, the threat of regional wars had to be ended.

At first the United States ignored the Contadora group. Later it publicly professed support, while continuously undermining the peace process. For example, in July 1983, just as the Contadora countries were producing their first comprehensive proposals, President Reagan dispatched naval vessels to the Pacific and Caribbean coasts of Nicaragua and announced that the largest U.S. military exercise to date, Big Pine II, would take place in Honduras during the fall.

In September of 1983, the Contadora support group of Mexico, Colombia, Panama, and Venezuela presented a 21 point proposal, with political, economic, and security measures designed to eliminate or reduce any foreign military presence in the region. Although the Reagan administration supported the document in principle, it simultaneously attempted to revive CONDECA (the Central American Defense Council), a body for regional military cooperation, which had ceased to function after the downfall of President Somoza in Nicaragua. The plan failed when the Guatemalan army balked at the idea.

In spite of the U.S. efforts to sabotage the Contadora effort, the 21 points were put into treaty form. More than 100 regional advisers and diplomats were involved. Finally on September 7, 1984, after several revisions, the four Contadora countries agreed on a compromise version entitled "Act for Peace and Cooperation in Central America" and submitted it to the Central American governments.

If implemented, the proposed treaty would have reversed the thrust toward militarization by such measures as suspension of limits on personnel, and the removal of foreign military bases. Further external support for insurgents fighting against El Salvador or Nicaragua would be ended. The holding of free elections in the region's nations was also promised.

Nicaragua agreed to the draft version on September 21. Although it had frequently voiced its verbal support, the Reagan administration was caught off guard. It had expected the draft to be rejected by the Sandinistas out of hand. Administration spokespersons now called the treaty proposals unfair, citing, for example, the fact that foreign military advisers engaged in training and operations (such as U.S. personnel in El Salvador) would have to leave, while those involved in maintenance (such as the Cubans and Soviets in Nicaragua) would not. They stated further that it was one-sided to end U.S. military exercises and close U.S. military bases without exacting anything from Nicaragua. The United States argued as well that the proposed procedures for monitoring and verifying of the Contadora Treaty were vague and unenforceable. Finally, the Reagan administration was troubled by the Contadora provision freezing military aid to El Salvador and Honduras, thus permitting Nicaragua to maintain a considerable military advantage over the two nations considered most susceptible to Nicaraguan interference.

By October 19, 1984, there began a series of counterproposals[5] formulated by U.S. allies Costa Rica, El Salvador, and Honduras, and culminating in the Act of Tegucigalpa. These three were members of the Central American Democratic Community--a euphemism for nations heavily influenced by the United States.

The Act of Tegucigalpa had provisions that limited the powers of the Nicaraguan military, permitted foreign military maneuvers under certain conditions, allowed for certain categories of military advisers, and generally permitted more favorable treatment of the members of the Central American Democratic Community than had prior proposed treaties.

A leaked U.S. National Security Council document, discussed in press reports on November 6, 1984, indicated that the Reagan administration felt that the Act of Tegucigalpa had "effectively blocked" the adoption of the draft Contadora treaty.[6] Nicaragua issued a statement revealing that it found the provisions of the Act of Tegucigalpa unacceptable.

The Contadora Treaty became the subject of lengthy negotiations which failed to reach a satisfactory resolution. A summit on the treaty proposed by the Contadora countries, scheduled for February 1985, had to be canceled because El Salvador and Costa Rica insisted on preconditions for their attendance. By late February, Deputy Foreign Minister Victor Tinoco of Nicaragua stated that his government considered the Contadora peace process "dead."[7]

While Contadora was being undercut, the United States initiated a more aggressive policy against Nicaragua. On January 17, 1985, the United States ended the bilateral talks with Nicaragua that it had initiated in mid-1984 at the urging of the Contadora nations. On the next day the United States suspended for two years its recognition of the International Court of Justice's jurisdiction on matters relating to Central America. This followed the court's calling on the United States to desist from mining Nicaraguan harbors or engaging in threatening military activities directed at that country.

On February 21, 1985, President Reagan stated that the United States wanted to "remove the present structure" of the Nicaraguan government. He added that the Sandinistas would be acceptable only if "they'd say uncle."

On May 1, 1985, the United States announced the imposition of a trade embargo against Nicaragua. Soon after, relations were further strained when Nicaraguan president Daniel Ortega visited the Soviet Union, and the U.S. Congress subsequently approved "humanitarian assistance" to the contras.

Amidst this climate of exacerbated tension and conflict, the Contadora countries initiated efforts to iron out a second draft treaty. Border clashes on the Costa Rican-Nicaraguan frontier became more frequent.

In December 1985 the Contadora group announced the suspension of its activities until May 1986. A Contadora foreign minister noted that the suspension was caused by the "deep confrontation" between the United States and Nicaragua. The decision to postpone further negotiations reflected a serious impasse in the Contadora process, but it also provided a breathing space before the elections and changes in government in Costa Rica, Guatemala, and Honduras, in late 1985 and early 1986.

The Contadora group met with the so-called Lima group of countries (Argentina, Brazil, Peru, and Uruguay) on January 11-12, 1986, and produced the Caraballeda message, which reaffirmed the original Contadora principles as a basis for peace in Central America and outlined a plan for immediate action. Subsequently, the Guatemala Declaration, signed on January 17 by the Contadora and Lima groups as well as the five Central American countries, reaffirmed the Caraballeda message. A month later, on February 10, the foreign ministers of the Contadora and Lima groups held their first combined talks in Washington with U.S. Secretary of State George Shultz. They asked Shultz to cooperate with their efforts at negotiation by halting aid to the contras. He denied their request.

It appeared that after four years of talks and multiple draft treaties, the negotiations were deadlocked. Behind the stalemate, the key issues were regional arms limitations, democratization in Nicaragua, and U.S. support for the contras. Each of these issues, in turn, touched directly upon the principles of nonintervention, self-determination, and respect for national sovereignty upon which the Contadora group's basic consensus rested. The United States and its closest Central American allies--Costa Rica, Honduras, and El Salvador--demanded that the Sandinistas reduce the size of their armed forces and install a "democratic" political system before they would halt support for the contras. The Sandinistas, in turn, refused to "disarm" or to negotiate with their political opposition until the United States and the neighboring Central American governments halted aid to the contras. On May 24-25, 1986, the five Central American presidents met again to try to reach a consensus on the Contadora peace treaty. Their meeting collapsed without substantial agreement, although the creation of a Central American parliament was proposed and discussed.

On June 25, 1986, the U.S. House of Representatives reversed its two-year ban on military assistance to the contras and approved the Reagan administration's request for a $100 million U.S. aid package in military and "humanitarian" assistance to the rebel forces. In August, President Reagan publicly acknowledged for the first time that it might ultimately be necessary for the contras to overthrow the Sandinista government militarily.

The Contadora process remained a reality, although it was clearly moribund. If the United States did not intervene directly, then the contras alone would not be able to defeat the Sandinistas. The Nicaraguan government would continue to rely on Soviet and Cuban aid, thus permitting an external presence in that country as well. The Sandinistas would not be able to completely defeat the contras as long as the latter could continue to retreat to sanctuaries in Honduras and El Salvador. The prospects, then, were for protracted war in Nicaragua, accompanied by inevitable spillover effects in Costa Rica, Honduras, and El Salvador.

Nevertheless, the effort to find a peaceful solution to the region's problems continued and, in August 1986, an apparent breakthrough, Esquipulas II, was reached. Before discussing this point, however, the interests and motives of the main political actors in Central America until 1986 will be discussed in more detail.

NICARAGUA AND THE CONTADORA PEACE PROCESS

Nicaragua's priority had been to consolidate its revolution and protect its borders. To that end, any attempt to broaden peaceful ties with its neighbors was welcomed, at least on the surface. As a result, Nicaragua appeared to look quite favorably upon the Contadora process as a possible vehicle for arriving at peace in the region. Until recently, however, Nicaragua claimed that it could not be a signatory to the agreement until all parties were subject to its provisions. By this it meant that the United States would have to cease its support of the contras, end the CIA mining of Nicaraguan harbors, and terminate its attempts to destabilize the Sandinista regime.

Furthermore, Nicaragua insisted that it would sign the Contadora Act, reduce its military buildups, and withdraw Soviet and Cuban advisers only if the United States simultaneously ceased hostilities directed at the Sandinista regime and signed a protocol committing itself to respect the provisions of the Contadora agreement. As far as Nicaragua was concerned, this would effectively prohibit support for the contra forces.[8]

When the Contadora process was first discussed, Nicaragua favored bilateral nonaggression pacts with its Central American neighbors and joint border patrols with Honduras and Costa Rica.[9] When the talks appeared to be ready to collapse soon after, Nicaragua agreed to accept a multilateral negotiating framework.

In October 1983 Nicaragua resumed its attempt to negotiate bilateral treaties with the United States and Honduras. The United States immediately rejected this approach, stressing instead that a peace accord could be achieved only through the Contadora process. In the ensuing three years, Nicaragua resisted pressure by the United States and the other Central American countries to reduce its military forces, and continued to maintain that its large standing army and heavy military expenditures were necessary to resist the American threat and to maintain its sovereignty and political independence. In addition, it stressed that its military preparedness would remain at a high level until the United States signed the Contadora Treaty and thereby stopped supporting the contra insurgents. It rejected the view that its forces and arms should be commensurate with the other four Central American countries, arguing instead that it required a high force level in order to deter the contras and a potential U.S. invasion. The United States, in turn, accused the Sandinista government of resisting the peace initiatives and, in fact, of ostensibly supporting Contadora only in an effort to maximize its public relations potential. At about this time, the Reagan administration was flushed with its success in Grenada and was taking a particularly aggressive stance against what it labeled the Marxist-Leninist regime of Nicaragua. Indeed, there were suspicions in many circles that, with the defeat of the Marxist regime in the Caribbean, Nicaragua would be a prime target for U.S. military intervention.

In September of 1984, a circulation draft of the Contadora peace treaty was signed by Nicaragua. The document banned international military maneuvers, restricted the buildup of military forces, and outlawed support for insurgent forces against other nations in Central America. As mentioned, the United States was caught off guard by this Nicaraguan action.

The United States immediately denounced Nicaragua's support for Contadora and called it a publicity stunt. In fact the United States was put in an uncomfortable position, for it could not now legitimately accuse the Sandinista regime of taking every opportunity to create unrest in the region. In addition, Washington was stifled in its efforts to isolate Nicaragua internationally. Finally, the United States could not easily justify its hostility as long as Nicaragua appeared to be making a peaceful gesture.

The United States then pressured Honduras, El Salvador, and Costa Rica to reverse their acceptance of the Contadora draft, and to insist upon revisions. In addition, the United States accused Nicaragua of agreeing to the draft in its early stages only if no further changes occurred. In other words, the Reagan administration attempted to portray Nicaragua as inflexible. Soon after, the United States successfully encouraged its Central American allies to block acceptance of the treaty.

In the next two years no unanimous agreement was reached on the Contadora Treaty. Nicaragua continued to insist that although it supported the peace process in principle, it could not reduce its military establishment until its borders were secure and the U.S.-contra threat was ended. The United States also claimed to support Contadora in principle, yet could not sign the treaty until Nicaragua reduced its military commitment. U.S. officials began to call for a new regime in Nicaragua. Of course, underneath all of this was the U.S. desire to avoid anything that would serve to "legitimize" the Sandinistas.

By November of 1985, the negotiating process had produced few concrete solutions, and further discussions were postponed until April 1986. At that time the talks resumed, but the parties would soon be deadlocked again.

EL SALVADOR AND CONTADORA

El Salvador is a country that has been torn apart by civil war, poverty, and social injustice. The Duarte government had expressed support for the Contadora peace process, but it was absolutely dependent upon U.S. economic aid and military assistance in its attempt to develop economically and provide political stability. These goals were especially difficult to reach given the high costs of the struggle against the FMLN guerrillas. President Duarte was therefore forced to adopt positions within the Contadora negotiations that were consistent with the U.S. position. El Salvador was not alone in this regard. Costa Rica and Honduras had also found it advantageous to support the U.S. position when required. As a result, it was conventional wisdom that Washington's close relations with the governments of El Salvador, Honduras, and Costa Rica gave the Reagan administration veto power over any agreement drafted by the Contadora nations, since no agreement could take effect unless all five of the Central American nations signed.

HONDURAS AND CONTADORA

Like El Salvador's, Honduran interests are closely tied to the United States. This precluded any strong support for the Contadora peace process unless the American position on Nicaragua was tempered. Honduras's foreign policy initiatives were further circumscribed because of its position as the poorest of the Central American republics and one of the poorest countries in the hemisphere.

In 1982, following a decade of military government, Honduras returned to civilian rule and formal democratic political institutions. The United States continued to support the government militarily and provided development aid in exchange for U.S. military use of Honduran territory and unofficial sanctuary for the contras.

Honduras was concerned about the Nicaraguan military buildups on its border and the possibility of Nicaraguan reprisals for contra attacks launched from Honduras. As a result, it was reluctant to alienate its American ally and demonstrate greater enthusiasm for the peace process than it already had. Indeed, Honduras regularly took the lead in promoting the U.S. position at Contadora-related meetings and repeatedly accused Nicaragua of obstructing the peace process. Honduras worked to increase the Sandinistas' diplomatic isolation. Furthermore, when the United States felt that the peace negotiations had proceeded too rapidly, Honduras predictably slowed down the negotiations by raising technical objections for presenting new proposals.[10]

GUATEMALA AND CONTADORA

Guatemala is the largest and most industrialized Central American country. In the 1970s and 1980s its military rulers had a grim record of human rights violations, which prompted the United States (and other western countries) to scale back donations of economic or military aid. Ironically, Guatemala's leaders were fervently anticommunist, but the country received little support from the bastion of anticommunism--the United States. This is particularly interesting given the constant threat of armed insurgency within Guatemala and the terrible economic problems it faces in the form of a burgeoning debt and a severe recession.

Because of its strained relations with the United States, its lesser degree of economic dependence on American aid, and the apparent capacity of the Guatemalan military to contain domestic insurgents, Guatemala has maintained foreign policy positions more independent of the United States than has any other Central American nation except Nicaragua. The Christian Democratic government of President Vinicio Cerezo (inaugurated in January 1986) had been particularly interested in promoting the Contadora process. Guatemala feared a direct confrontation with Nicaragua and sought to distance itself from its anti-Sandinista neighbors and the United States.

This point must be qualified, however, for Guatemala continued to face an economic crisis; its military was still a potent force, and always a threat to overthrowing the government; and U.S. aid had increased in

1986. How long Guatemala could continue its policy of "active neutrality" was anyone's guess, and remains so today.[11]

COSTA RICA AND CONTADORA

Costa Rica is the only Central American country, and one of the few in Latin America, to have retained a civilian government and democratic institutions for most of its history. It is also unique in that it retains no standing army. Like many of its neighbors, Costa Rica has modeled its constitution on that of the United States, but it is almost alone in its ability to practice the principles that its constitution embodies.

Costa Rica, like Honduras and El Salvador, is reluctant to diverge too sharply from the U.S. on foreign policy issues. Accordingly, Costa Rica's position on the Contadora peace process has been hesitant. Although it was in its interest to support Contadora as a means of preserving its democratic stability, Costa Rica would not go so far as to undermine American interests. It shared President Reagan's concerns about the Sandinista threat and has depended heavily on U.S. markets and economic assistance to sustain its fragile economy.

Nevertheless, the Costa Rican government officially opposed using its territory as a base for contra operations or U.S. military maneuvers. It was reluctant to provoke open conflict with Nicaragua. In practice, however, the contras did operate out of Costa Rican territory. Along with Honduras and El Salvador, Costa Rica remained a member of the Central American Democratic Community and continued to support the isolation of the Sandinista regime in Nicaragua. Costa Rica's tie to the United States is a primary concern, and it would support the United States even if that country continued to demonstrate its doubts about the peace initiatives.[12]

THE UNITED STATES AND CONTADORA

The United States is a major political actor in Central America.[13] It has a myriad of strategic, political, and investment interests in the region, and as a result, all efforts to find a peaceful solution to the strife in Central America must take U.S. concerns into account. Indeed, one motivation for the formation of the Contadora peace talks was to demonstrate that the countries of Latin America could reach peaceful agreements without the intervention of external powers like the United States. Intervention is one thing, however, and interests quite another, for U.S. interests are always a factor in the Central American peace process. The United States and the Soviet Union are the most prominent external powers, and their involvement in Central American affairs has had enormous repercussions for the region. The United States, in particular, has been able to mobilize vast political, economic, and military resources; reward cooperative nations in the region; sanction any attempt to challenge its hegemony; and intervene when it considers such action necessary.

The United States supported the removal of the Sandinista regime from power, the reinforcement of democratic interests in El Salvador, and the containment of radical or revolutionary movements in the rest of Central America. The U.S. administration managed to convince most members of Congress, and much of the public, that the Sandinista regime constituted a threat to its neighbors and to the United States. In February 1985 President Reagan stated that his objective in Central America was "to remove [the Nicaraguan government] in the sense of its present structure." Reagan regarded Cuba and Nicaragua as Soviet proxies in the Americas and insisted that U.S. policy direction was essentially defensive. This strategy has been described as the "four pillars" of American policy toward, or goals for, Nicaragua. These pillars include democracy, an end to foreign subversion, reduction in arms and the size of military forces, and an end to outside military support.

However, President Reagan could not generate a national consensus in support of the overthrow of the Nicaraguan government, or for the use of overt military force against Nicaragua. As a result, Washington was not in a position to apply the full range of U.S. power resources in Central America and had to rely on "second-best" strategies, such as covert support for the contras.[14]

This support was suspended, however, as the House and Senate opposed the President's contra policy by approving a special resolution to withhold $40 million of military aid still due the contras. The revelation that U.S. officials secretly diverted Iranian arms payments to the contras alienated Congress across ideological lines and jeopardized further support for contra aid.

With regard to the peace process, the United States was in an awkward position. The U.S. government supported a peaceful solution to the problems of the region. President Reagan declared that the Contadora process was the best tool available to resolve the difficulties there. However, many analysts argued that the President was only paying lip service to Contadora and that his real goals were military: to undermine the Sandinista government, to support the Duarte regime (since defeated), and to safeguard U.S. strategic interests. Accordingly, the United States discouraged Nicaraguan participation in Contadora, supported the contra forces, and encouraged El Salvador, Costa Rica, and Honduras to protect U.S. interests.

Some American observers stress that had a successful Contadora agreement been reached, it could have been a useful vehicle for the survival and consolidation of the Nicaraguan revolution.[15] This might well have been another reason for President Reagan's less than whole-hearted support for the Contadora process. Indeed, Undersecretary of State Elliott Abrams declared that the U.S. government would prefer no treaty at all to a "bad" agreement, by which he meant that the United States would prefer no agreement to one that would permit the retention of the Sandinista regime. Furthermore, on May 20, 1986, the U.S. Defense Department released its study of the Contadora peace plan, in which the peace effort was severely criticized as giving Nicaragua "a shield from behind which they could continue their use of subversive aggression." This would require sending 100,000 U.S. troops to Central America within several years.[16]

Although this was a Defense Department view, and not necessarily a State Department one, it is clear that there was a great deal of U.S. government concern over the possible repercussions of Contadora. As far as the United States was concerned, Contadora's efforts to negotiate a verifiable treaty that neutralized Nicaragua as a security threat via agreements on the withdrawal of foreign bases and advisers, limited the size of military establishments, and controlled arms build-ups and mutual nonaggression pacts, were inadequate because communists simply could not be trusted.[17]

As a result, it was decided that the best American strategy for the region was to promote the contra forces, rather than the Contadora process. The United States, then, would demand that the Contadora draft include two provisions that the Nicaraguans could not live with. These included the continuation of U.S. military maneuvers in Honduras, which Nicaragua wanted to eliminate, and a provision to set limits on the size of each Central American country's military, which would require Nicaragua to make sharp reductions in troop levels, scrap some of its arsenal, and repatriate its Cuban advisers (if any existed). Also, strict compliance with the provisions of the Contadora Treaty would have required an end to Nicaraguan press censorship and harassment of the Catholic church and political parties. The provision for internal reconciliation would have required negotiation with the U.S.-backed contras. Finally, the ban on cross-border subversion would have ruled out Sandinista aid to the Salvadorean rebels.

The main explanation which President Ortega offered for his resistance to the treaty was that his government needed all the arms it could obtain in order to keep the U.S. imperialists at bay. One might argue, however, that this was a curious rationale, since the terms of Contadora provided his best opportunity to evict U.S. military power from the region.

Costa Rica and Honduras, the two Central American states that have harbored the contras, would have been bound by the treaty, to deny such sanctuary. Honduras and El Salvador would have had to restrict the presence of U.S. military advisers on their soil. Contadora, then, had the potential to dismantle most of the anticommunist infrastructure that the United States had so elaborately built up in Central America in recent years.

On the other hand, one could make the credible argument that by supporting Contadora, the Reagan administration would have gained a solid base of support in both domestic and international public opinion for a tough policy toward Nicaragua, had the Sandinistas violated the treaty. Richard Bloomfield, for example, argued that Contadora could have put the United States on the side of principle and put the onus of violating principle on Nicaragua.[18] In signing the agreement, the United States would have gained the Contadora governments--Colombia, Mexico, Panama, and Venezuela--as allies. These countries represent three of the major democracies of the region (Panama excepted, at that time) and a significant percentage of Latin America's population. Further, one might argue that by joining these allies in supporting Contadora, the United States would have been in a stronger position to demand that allies abroad join it in sanctions against a Nicaragua that was breaking its commitments.

This was always an unlikely scenario, however, as subsequent events have made clear. The United States suffered foreign policy defeats in Panama and Haiti, and an enormous climate of mistrust existed between Washington and Managua. Neither country could demonstrate strong support for Contadora under the circumstances.

ESQUIPULAS II AND THE PROSPECTS FOR PEACE

On August 7, 1987, in Esquipulas, Guatemala, an accord was signed by the five Central American presidents. It was entitled Procedure for the Establishment of a Strong and Lasting Peace in Central America, and was also referred to as Esquipulas II, the Guatemala plan, or the Arias plan. This agreement was the result of the combination of a tenacious four-and-a-half-year negotiation process led by the Contadora countries, diplomatic backing provided by the Contadora support nations, and a ten-point peace plan offered by Oscar Arias Sanchez, president of Costa Rica.*

The Arias plan reflected an assertion of Central American autonomy, and was based on the proposition that it was less costly to live with the Sandinistas than to overthrow them. The proposals originated in Central America accepted the current composition of the Nicaraguan government, and did not depend on direct negotiations between the Sandinistas and the contras. There was recognition that U.S. support for the contras was unpopular in the region and that any solution to Central America's strife must be indigenous in origin. Nicaragua responded favorably to the announcement of the Guatemala accord, and the United States Senate voted almost unanimously to support it. The Reagan administration was lukewarm at best, however.

Special provisions regarding security concerns included a call for renewed regional arms control negotiations, the termination of all foreign aid to rebel groups, and the understanding that a Central American nation's territory could not be used to support attacks on another country in the region. Political provisions of the agreement included the following: a dialogue between Central American governments and their unarmed opponents, the requirement that prisoners held by insurgent groups be released in advance of planned Central American parliamentary elections, the restoration of a free press, an end to states of emergency, and, in general, a return to democracy throughout the region. Finally, the agreement's participants discussed new sources of economic and refugee aid.

Taken together, the main elements of the plan were congruent with the earlier Contadora drafts. In response to the agreement, Nicaragua, as a sign of good faith, withdrew its case against Costa Rica in the International Court of Justice for allegedly tolerating contra bases on its territory. It was clear that all five of the signatories to the agreement assumed a vital stake in the accord's success--or at least in appearing to comply with it--and demonstrated a growing sense of regional independence from the United States.

Arias's brilliance was most apparent in his plan for the implementation of the accord. Essentially, he emphasized three main strategies for implementation. The first was his notion of "simultaneity," that is; a cease-fire, amnesty for prisoners, cessation of foreign involvement, and no use of the territory of one Central American country (by troops or

*For a text of Esquipulas II, see Appendix B.

equipment) to wage war against another country--all had to take place simultaneously. This could not be a step-by-step process if it was to work.

Second, Arias advocated the use of concrete timetables for implementing the different phases of the accord. Unlike the Contadora plans, which possessed no rigid timetables, the Arias plan set a maximum of 90 days for its provisions to be implemented, and then 120 days for a review.

Third, Arias advocated the opening up of the peace process to permit outside verification by an international organization such as the United Nations or the Organization of American States.

Arias was instrumental in solving many of the problems that might have emerged among the Central American presidents. He did so by traveling to each Central American capital to consult with its president and his most important advisers. Out of this process the Arias plan emerged. "Good deeds will not go unpunished," as the saying goes, however. President Cerezo of Guatemala, and perhaps a few of his colleagues, argued that all five presidents should have received the Nobel Peace Prize. Arias's efforts were unique and exemplary, however, and he deserved the acclaim that he received.

Although the U.S. Congress expressed support for the plan, President Reagan demonstrated little enthusiasm. Undaunted, Arias worked with Speaker of the House Jim Wright, who subsequently worked closely with the Reagan administration to develop his own plan for peace in Central America, which was modeled partly on the Arias plan. Wright believed that his plan could serve as a fallback if the Arias plan encountered serious problems.

On August 4, 1987, three days before the Esquipulas II agreement, and contrary to Wright's expectations, the U.S. government publicly announced the Reagan/Wright plan. Its main provisions called for a negotiated cease-fire, democratization in Nicaragua, cessation of Soviet military bases or aid in Nicaragua, and no support for any insurgents elsewhere in the region. The United States agreed to halt contra aid, reduce the number of military advisers, and cease combat maneuvers by U.S. troops in Honduras.

Crucial to the implementation of the plan was the notion that the United States would agree to abide by its provisions only if Soviet military aid to the Sandinistas was ended simultaneously. The Reagan administration hoped to ensure the survival of the contras if negotiations broke down. Also, Reagan hoped to rebuild American credibility after the Iran-contra affair. Instead, one could argue that the Reagan/Wright plan was just an attempt by the United States to dominate the peace process, and so it was rejected in favor of the Arias plan.

This being said, Esquipulas II was not without serious drawbacks. One problem related to the provision that declared all five countries to have equal status and, by implication, equal situations. Honduras balked at this idea, however. Unlike the other countries, it faced U.S. pressure to continue providing a haven for the contra fighters. Further, all five countries--but particularly Honduras, Nicaragua, and Guatemala--had dramatically different strategic situations. Honduras, El Salvador, and (to a lesser degree) Costa Rica were closely tied to the United States. Guatemala was relatively neutral, and Nicaragua's ties were to the socialist bloc. Treating all five equally, and having them reach unanimous agreement on divisive issues, would prove terribly difficult in the months to come.

In addition, the provision for democratization of the region was subject to interpretation. The United States equated democratization with complete freedom of the press, free and monitored elections, and viable opposition parties. In Nicaragua however, and to a lesser degree in Guatemala, democratization was thought to be a long-term process, with a viable opposition being tolerated only at an unspecified future date.

Furthermore, there was no clear evidence that any of the five countries was willing to make difficult sacrifices for the sake of the peace process. All professed support and a willingness to work together, but convergence is not the same as a willingness to make concessions.

It should also be noted that since only the Central American governments participated directly in the Esquipulas II accord, there was a bias toward maintaining the political status quo in their nations. The accord reinforced the dominance of the existing governments by stipulating that opposition groups could participate only after giving up their struggles and their arms. Although one could understand the accord's preoccupation with such measures, it tipped the scale drastically in favor of the existing regimes in power.

In addition, each of the presidents faced immediate and enormous economic and social problems that deflected attention from the long-range goals of the peace process, to the exclusion of his nation's high inflation and burdensome economic debt. Nonetheless, most Costa Ricans remained strongly supportive of Arias.

In Guatemala, the peace process had gotten bogged down, with no progress toward a cease-fire with the guerrillas. In El Salvador, there remained the threat of violence from forces on both the left and the right. Concerns in Nicaragua about a U.S. threat were dwarfed by the multitude of economic problems that the country continued to face. The Sandinista government cracked down on internal dissent, frequently closed the main opposition newspaper, and expelled U.S. diplomats accused of abetting unrest. Border fighting continued, with both the government forces and the contra rebels claiming a willingness to negotiate--but not to lay down arms first.

Honduras failed to comply with sections of the Arias accord that called for an end to rebel bases on foreign soil. The contras were almost totally based and supplied in Honduras, and were supported by the United States.

Some diplomats suspected that the peace plan was dead, although the Central American presidents continued to discuss renewed negotiations and strategies for regional compliance with Esquipulas II. President Arias, however, appeared less optimistic, stating, "I honestly believe we have ourselves to blame. We always found an excuse not to comply."

Nevertheless, hopes remained for peace in the region. Nicaragua was concerned about the possibility of securing a commitment from the United States to end support for the contra rebels in neighboring countries, thereby permitting it to rebuild its economy and consolidate its revolution. It was far easier for Nicaragua to accept reforms imposed and supervised by its neighbors than it was to have them instituted by the North American "imperialists." Nicaragua had permitted at least the appearance of some internal liberalization in order to end internal conflict, foreign intervention, and economic sanctions.

In December 1987 the Sandinista government opened indirect talks with the contra insurgents for the first time, under the auspices of Cardinal Obando. The purpose of the meeting was to discuss prospects for a cease-fire and to demonstrate an attempt to comply with the Esquipulas II agreement. The talks broke down and fighting resumed, but efforts to bring the two sides to the bargaining table continued. Indeed, representatives of the Sandinistas and the contras met in Sapoa, Nicaragua, on March 24, 1988, and agreed on a 60-day cease-fire. Other provisions included a gradual amnesty for Nicaragua's estimated 3,300 political prisoners, the return of exiles, and the movement of the contras to "truce zones" within Nicaragua borders. The talks broke off, however, and since then U.S. military aid to the contras has ceased. The impetus for negotiation had diminished, although a cease-fire held for four months in 1988. Nicaragua and the United States expelled each other's ambassadors. Most of the contras retreated to base camps in Honduras, and Sandinista troops reinforced their positions along contra infiltration routes.

In July 1988 the Nicaraguan government reimposed restrictions on its opposition. It violently broke up an opposition rally, and kept six leaders in jail during long trials. Some suggested that Nicaragua's economic problems might have forced it to make concessions to the United States in the form of internal liberalization, but there was little evidence of this. For advocates of peace in the region, Nicaragua's noncompliance was particularly distressing.

In Guatemala, President Cerezo's government survived a military coup on May 11, 1988, and, although ostensibly a democracy, had been employing increasingly repressive tactics on insurgents. Little or no constructive dialogue had occurred between the government and the armed opposition. Economic poverty remains endemic, as it does throughout the region.

In El Salvador, the government was threatened by extremists on both the right and the left. President Duarte's power base diminished following the announcement of his terminal illness; right-wing gains in municipal elections; the growth of the left-wing guerrilla movement FMLN; and a split in the governing Christian Democratic party. In the hope of dampening growing polarization, the Catholic church became actively involved in organizing a national debate involving all sectors of society. However, this noble attempt at national reconciliation produced few concrete positive results. In subsequent national elections, the candidate of the right-wing Arena party, Alfredo Christiani, was elected president. Marxist FMLN guerrillas vowed to continue fighting, and a number of terrorist incidents were reported. Christiani pledged to promote the democratic process in his country, but few were optimistic as long as the nation's economy remained in dire straits.

Honduras was also in a precarious economic position and faced a substantial degree of pressure from the United States to support its interests. Honduras depends on the United States for economic and military aid, and harbored approximately 10,000 contras and at least 15,000 Nicaraguan refugees within its borders. Government repression had risen since the announcement of the Esquipulas II accord, and the Azcona Administration remained clearly suspicious of Nicaragua's intentions.

Costa Rica, the only long-standing democracy in the region, retained close ties with the United States and stressed the need for greater economic and technological collaboration with the superpower. President Arias emphasized the importance of debt rescheduling as a vehicle for his nation's economic development. However, Costa Rica was overwhelmingly supportive of the peace process and had established a national reconciliation commission.

An Esquipulas III meeting of the five presidents, held in San Jose, Costa Rica, on January 15-16, 1988, broke up without an agreement on the criteria necessary to implement the Arias plan. The details proved overwhelmingly complex; the Nicaraguan and Honduran presidents disagreed repeatedly; and the United States pressured the presidents of

Honduras, El Salvador, and Costa Rica to try to persuade Daniel Ortega to implement fully the democratic provisions of the accord. If Ortega was unwilling, the presidents were urged by the United States to abandon the existing peace process. The United States warned that it might "lose interest" in Central America, leaving the three countries without military or economic aid. At first, only Arias stood firmly behind the peace plan, while Duarte and Azcona remained lukewarm. Ultimately, only presidents Arias and Cerezo appeared to remain fully committed to the peace process, with Nicaraguan president Ortega supportive only if outside aid to the contras was terminated.

On November 30, 1988, the five Central American foreign ministers met in Mexico and agreed to ask the secretary-general of the United Nations to approach Canada, West Germany, Spain, a Latin American country, and the OAS to design a verification mechanism for the Esquipulas II accord. Although this was clearly a positive step, no agreement was reached as to exactly what was to be verified. Renewed talks, scheduled for January 15-16, 1989, were postponed until March in San Salvador, El Salvador, so that the five presidents could have a chance to evaluate President Bush's Central American policies.

At the time, observers maintained that if the Bush administration dispensed with much of the knee-jerk anticommunism prevalent in the rhetoric and policies of the Reagan administration and adopted more pragmatic policies in the region, then the prospects for a peace process directed by Latin Americans would dramatically improve. Secretary of State James Baker was certainly no ideologue. During his confirmation hearings before the U.S. Senate, Baker warned that Central America may be ripe for crisis: "I don't see an issue coming at us any quicker than this one, I think it is going to be right on our doorstep when we take office. These problems are not going to go away, they're going to multiply."

Baker's statement indicated a pragmatic attitude that was perceived as advantageous to the peace process.

There were other promising signs as well. In February 1989 Vice President Dan Quayle attended the presidential inauguration of Carlos Andres Perez of Venezuela. While there, Quayle avoided meeting with Nicaraguan president Daniel Ortega and sharply criticized the Sandinista government. Nevertheless, Ortega praised Quayle: "I thought he showed an ability to understand the political reality of Latin America." Quayle also stressed U.S. support for the Arias peace plan--a reversal from President Reagan's position--and added that there were no immediate plans to resume military aid to the contras. Quayle's position was most encouraging to the advocates of Esquipulas and provided a clear sign that the United States would provide no obstacles to the next planned Central

American presidents' discussions scheduled for February 13-14, 1989, in San Salvador. It was clear, however, that the United States would not help the process either. The Bush administration remained suspicious that the Sandinista government might try to manipulate a peacekeeping or peace-observing force, so that the contra forces would be kept at bay, while government troops could move more freely. The United States retained many vital interests in Central America and would be hard-pressed not to intervene if it perceived its interests to be threatened. The intervention into Panama was only the most recent example.

This was also demonstrated during the February 1989 meeting of the Central American presidents, when U.S. officials reiterated their lack of faith in the goodwill of the Nicaraguan leadership. The presidents agreed that the contras would be disarmed simultaneous to the Sandinistas ceasing their support of the FMLN guerrillas in El Salvador, releasing Nicaraguan political prisoners, moving up elections, and allowing rigorous verification by international observers of human rights and democratic reforms. As part of the agreement, Honduras would insist that the 11,000 contras and their dependents be disarmed and "repatriated" to Nicaragua or another country. Removal of the rebels would be subject to verification by a United Nations-sponsored peacekeeping force. As an overture to the United States, the Sandinistas proposed to invite the United States to participate in a multinational effort to combat drug trafficking in Central America. The plan immediately stalled on the question of how to monitor Nicaragua's progress toward democracy. Most analysts agreed that the clear winners in this agreement were the Sandinistas, whose contra adversaries would be disbanded within 90 days of the presidents' agreement. The United States was not consulted during this process, but this was due, in part, to the policy vacuum existent during the first months of the Bush administration. Also, it was consistent with the Central American presidents' desire for outside nonintervention.

President Bush announced that he wanted to analyze the agreement in detail, before commenting on it. Vice President Quayle expressed skepticism over whether the Nicaraguan promises of early elections and democratization would be fulfilled. By contrast, Canadian External Affairs Minister Joe Clark said the presidents' communique gave grounds for renewed optimism that the political will to attack the roots of their regional problems still existed.[19]

Contra leaders were not prepared to lay down their arms just yet, however. Excluded from the Central American presidents' meeting, they agreed to disband only if the Sandinistas implemented their promised democratic reforms. But the summit agreement underlined the widely held view that the contras were a spent force, militarily and politically. Yet, one could also make the argument that Nicaragua had to reform, since it needed U.S. loans and an end to the trade embargo. Its economy was failing, with inflation approaching 20,000 percent per year. In his rhetoric, President Ortega compared his nation's goals to those of social democratic Sweden, not Marxist Cuba.

In March a United Nations spokesman announced that the United Nations had drafted plans for a 160-man Central American peacekeeping force to monitor a halt in foreign aid to the contra rebels and to ensure that none of the countries of the area harbored guerrillas fighting neighboring governments. Officials from the Central American nations subsequently approved the draft. This was the closest that the five countries had come to agreeing on concrete proposals for verifying the noninterference clauses of the Esquipulas II agreement.

Of course, the establishment of any peacekeeping force required the approval of the United Nations Security Council, where the United States has veto power. However, U.S. officials pledged not to veto such a plan, since a peacekeeping force would test Nicaragua's willingness to implement political reforms and hold free elections. This was by no means a unanimous position within the U.S. State Department, however. Many officials vigorously opposed the peacekeeping plan. They worried that the Sandinista government might eliminate the contras and thereby feel no pressure to institute democratic elections.

Furthermore, President Bush, although more cautious than his predecessor, had not indicated that he rejected the notion that military action would be the ultimate way to end communism in the region. The appointment of contra lobbyist Bernard Aronson as assistant secretary of state for international affairs was also a sign that the Bush administration might choose to pursue hard-line policies. This view was further reinforced on March 25, with the announcement that the president and Congress jointly agreed to extend nonmilitary aid to the contras through February 28, 1990, notwithstanding the agreement to demobilize the Nicaraguan rebels.

On August 7, 1989, however, a positive sign emerged. In Tela, Honduras, the presidents of the five Central American nations agreed on a plan to disband the contras by December 8, and left implementation of the plan up to an international commission made up of the secretaries-general of the United Nations, the Organization of American States, and their representatives. The contras would be demobilized and repatriated to Nicaragua. The plan also called for negotiations and a cease-fire between the Salvadorean government and the FMLN guerrillas.

The agreement was seen as a sharp rebuke to the Bush administration, and also posed potential problems for the United Nations. The

United Nations was charged with a major role in starting the demobilization process, and would require that the contras disarm, before a U.N. force would participate in that process. Furthermore, the United States could veto deployment of such a force if it came to a vote in the Security Council, although U.S. administration officials had implied that they probably would not take such action. In addition, although the contra forces appeared to be incapable of extracting any more meaningful support, they had not yet surrendered their arms. Their spokesmen stressed that they had no faith in Sandinista promises of no reprisals.

The Tela agreement was a clear sign that the Central American leaders were continuing to strive for peace in the region. Indeed, on November 7, 1989, the United Nations Security Council approved the creation of the United Nations Observer Mission in Central America (ONUCA). Its primary mandate was to monitor the Honduran-Nicaraguan border. Perhaps the most important boon to peace, however, was the surprising victory of the National Opposition Union party (UNO) in the March 1990 Nicaraguan elections. The Sandinistas relinquished power, most of the contras were disarmed, and the United States pledged economic support. Good fortune had fallen into President Bush's lap without the need for American military intervention. From a U.S. government perspective, the UNO victory had fulfilled the best possible scenario for U.S. interests. Nevertheless, the peace process remains fraught with difficulties. There remains a substantial amount of distrust between adversaries. Assassination attempts on President Cerezo have continued. The Arena government of El Salvador has been charged by some critics with committing human rights abuses. All of the countries of the region continue to experience economic setbacks.

CONCLUSION

At the present time, one must remain suspicious about the short-term prospects for a successful agreement on the peace process, notwithstanding the Tela agreement and the UNO victory in Nicaragua. El Salvador continues to be engulfed in a civil war, all of the countries are desperately poor and unstable, and the parties to the Esquipulas II agreement are not demonstrating the required degree of enthusiasm for cooperation toward peace.

One can take an opposite tack, of course, and stress that the peace plan has had a considerable significance for Central America. One can emphasize that Esquipulas was a major cooperative endeavor for Latin America, an indication of a new willingness to coordinate policies in the face of the region's problems, and a symbol of Latin America's greater independence from U.S. influence. Certainly the Chamorro victory will also reduce regional enmity.

This is putting the best face on a worrisome situation, however, for thus far the peace process has not attained its primary objectives. It has not been able to ensure peace and stability in the region. There has been no reconciliation between the Salvadorean government and the FMLN, or the Guatemalan government and its insurgents. Although it is true that Contadora and Esquipulas were the most significant displays of Central American unity since the long-expired Central American Federation of 1824-39, they have not yet accomplished their central purpose.

This is not to say that peace is not on the horizon. From time to time political analysts have proclaimed Contadora or Esquipulas dead, and then, like phoenixes emerging from ashes, they reappear. The effort continues, for not only does the possibility of peace remain, but with the peace plans the Latin American countries can continue to demonstrate that they have the means to solve their own problems, and are no longer reliant on outside powers. One should not underemphasize this powerful rationale for an accord.

NOTES

1.   An earlier version of this chapter appeared as "Contadora and the Central American Republics: A Slide Down a Slippery Slope," in Scott MacDonald et al. (eds.), *The Caribbean After Grenada: Revolution, Conflict and Democracy* (New York: Praeger, 1988), pp. 197-211.

2.   For a more comprehensive overview of the root causes of Central America's problems, see Howard J. Wiarda (ed.), *Rift and Revolution: The Central American Imbroglio* (Washington, D.C.: AEI, 1984); Morris Blachman, William Leo Grande, and Kenneth Sharpe (eds.), *Confronting Revolution: Security through Diplomacy in Central America* (New York: Pantheon, 1988); Robert S. Leiken and Barry Ruben (eds.), *The Central American Crises Reader* (New York: Summit Books, 1987); Harold Dana Sims and Vilma Petrash, "The Contadora Peace Process," in *Conflict Quarterly* 7:4 (Fall 1987), pp. 5-28.

3.   George Black, *Garrison Guatemala* (London: Zed Books, 1984), p. 6.

4.   For a comprehensive review of these points, see Bruce Michael Bagley, "Contadora: The Failure of Diplomacy," in Abraham Lowenthal (ed.), *Latin America and Caribbean Contemporary Record* (New York: Holmes and Meier, 1987).

5.   For a comprehensive discussion of these proposals, see Everett A. Bauman, "The Strengths and Weaknesses of Contadora as Regional Diplomacy in the Caribbean Basin" (unpublished working paper for the Latin American program, Woodrow Wilson International Center for Scholars, 1985).

6.   This last point is reported in Liisa North, *Negotiations for Peace in Central America: A Conference Report* (Ottawa: Canadian Institute for International Peace and Security, 1985), p. 1.

7.   As quoted in the *Ottawa Citizen* (February 26, 1985).

8.   For a detailed discussion of this point, see the "Press Communique from the Office of the Presidency," Republic of Nicaragua, Managua (April 12, 1986).

9.   See William LeoGrande, "Rollback or Containment? The United States, Nicaragua, and the Search for Peace in Central America," *International Security* (Fall 1986), 11:2, pp. 89-120.

10.   For a detailed discussion of this point, see Bruce Bagley (ed.), *Contadora and the Diplomacy of Peace in Central America* (Boulder: Westview, 1987).

11.   For a good discussion of Guatemala's foreign affairs interests, see Robert Trudeau and Lars Schoultz, "Guatemala," in Morris Blachman, William LeoGrande, and Kenneth Sharpe (eds.), *Confronting Revolution*, pp. 23-49.

12.   For an excellent discussion of Costa Rican policy initiatives, see Chalmers Brumbaugh, "Costa Rica: The Making of a Liveable Society" (unpublished Ph.D. diss., University of Wisconsin, 1985).

13.   For a comprehensive discussion of U.S. policy in Central America, see Edward Best, *U.S. Policy and Regional Security in Central America* (New York: St. Martin's Press, 1987); Richard Fagen, *Forging Peace: The Challenge of Central America* (New York: Basil Blackwell, 1987); Mark Falcoff and Robert Royal, *The Continuing Crisis: U.S. Policy in Central America and the Caribbean* (Lanham, MD: UPA, 1987); John E. Findling, *Close Neighbors, Distant Friends: United States Central American Relations* (Westport, CT: Westview, 1987); Peter Kornbluh, *The Price of Intervention: Reagan's Wars Against the Sandinistas* (Washington, D.C.: IPS, 1987); Abraham F. Lowenthal, *Partners in Conflict: The United States and Latin America* (Baltimore: Johns Hopkins University Press, 1987); Harold Molineu, *U.S. Policy toward Latin America: From Regionalism to Globalism* (Boulder, CO: Westview, 1986); Robert A. Pastor, *Condemned to Repetition: The United States and Nicaragua* (Princeton, NJ: Princeton University Press, 1987); Thomas W. Walker (ed.), *Reagan Versus the Sandinistas: The Undeclared War on Nicaragua* (Boulder, CO: Westview, 1987).

14.   For a good discussion of U.S. ties to the contra forces, see Morris J. Blachman et al., *Confronting Revolution*, pp. 295-386.

15.   For a good discussion of this point, see William M. LeoGrande, "Cuba," in Blachman et al., *Confronting Revolution*, pp. 229-55.

16.   This statement is quoted from "Latin America: Chronology 1986," *Foreign Affairs* (Winter 1987) 65:3, p. 687.

17.   For a comprehensive discussion of this point, see Bruce Michael Bagley and Juan Gabriel Tokatlian, "Contadora: The Limits of Negotiations" (unpublished paper for the Latin American Studies Program of the School of Advanced International Studies, Johns Hopkins University, 1986).

18.   Richard J. Bloomfield, "Using the Contadora Solution," in the *New York Times*, February 17, 1987, p. A23.

19.   On November 18, 1987, the United States congressional committees on the Iran-contra affair revealed the arms sale diversion from Iran to the contras and thereby undermined U.S. diplomatic credibility in much of Central America, at least for a time. With the charge leveled against the Reagan administration that it had willfully circumvented the law in its efforts to fund the contras, the gulf between the Sandinista government and Washington widened even further. The Nicaraguan government had little incentive to advance the peace process by engaging in talks with the contras as long as the United States was prepared to aid the insurgents. Since then, U.S. aid has drastically diminished, and sporadic talks, most notably on June 9, 1988, have occurred between the Nicaraguan adversaries, although almost all collapsed, with little evidence of progress. With the Chamorro victory, of course, this may all be moot.

6 Canada and the Peacekeeping Process in Central America

For over thirty years Canada has played an active role in the United Nations peacekeeping forces. It is currently participating in all seven of the existing U.N. missions in various troubled parts of the world. Of late, Canadian peacekeepers are performing a similar service in Central America. Furthermore, Canada has played a supportive and advisory role with regard to the various regional peace plans that have been considered. For example, Canada has offered suggestions to the signatories of the Contadora plan and its successor, the Esquipulas II plan concerning strategies for arriving at peaceful solutions to the region's problems.

Canadian government officials stress that their years of peacekeeping experience in countries as diverse as Vietnam, Cyprus, Lebanon, the Congo, and other countries will be put to good use in Central America. Canadian involvement entails the dispatch of Canadian troops under the umbrella of the United Nations, and the offering of advice. It should be acknowledged, however, that Prime Minister Mulroney, like his immediate predecessors, maintains that the Central American countries will have to resolve their problems on their own. There is a place for multilateral dialogue and cooperation, and external powers must encourage the peace process, but peace is an internal matter. Outside powers, particularly the United States and the Soviet Union, should stay out or they would almost certainly aggravate tensions. However, if superpower noninterference is coupled with both a viable agreement and the political will to make it work, then a long-standing peace might be realized in the region.

BACKGROUND TO CANADIAN INVOLVEMENT

Canada first pledged to support the peace process in March 1982, when External Affairs Minister Mark MacGuigan stated: "We have had general encouragement from both Cuba and Nicaragua to participate in . . . the resolution of problems in the region on the grounds of our high credibility".[1]   This was followed by a September 1983 statement by MacGuigan's successor Allan MacEachen, who announced that Canada would support the Contadora peace plan proposals "to stop the process of militarization and to verify and monitor the progressive withdrawal of all foreign military personnel from the region."

This view was reiterated soon after by Minister of International Trade Jean-Luc Pepin, who stated that Canada would be prepared to play a role in monitoring the border zones and controlling the movement of foreign arms if so requested by the Central American countries. Pepin insisted that any Canadian role would be modest, but his government would send jeeps and communications equipment to help implement the peacekeeping process if formally asked by the countries of the region.[2]

A further step was taken in February 1984, when MacEachen indicated that Canadian officials would be available to consult with the social, economic, and security commissions that had been set up by the parties to the Contadora plan. There was some thought that Canadian assistance might include a peacekeeping force, although this suggestion was rejected by Mexican president Miguel de la Madrid during a visit to Ottawa in May 1984. In any case, the offer was not taken up by the Contadora countries. In April of 1984, MacEachen visited Costa Rica, Nicaragua, Honduras, and Colombia to obtain first-hand knowledge of the problems arising from military intervention and the growing numbers of refugees. The extent of the problems he witnessed, and the frustration he felt about the inability of Central American officials to outline specific steps that Canada might take to help, caused MacEachen to note:

> In my discussions in every country the possibility was mentioned that Canada might help at a certain stage, particularly in the field of verification and arms control, if there developed an agreement on arms control or arms limitation. But nobody was able to tell us yet what we might be able to do and they don't know themselves yet how we may be able to help, so no request was made to us.[3]

Upon returning, MacEachen again pledged Canada's support for Contadora and made particular reference to Canada's possible role in the design of a Control and Verification Commission (CVC). Canada also called for the removal of foreign armies from Central America. In July 1984 the Contadora countries officially requested Canada's comments on the verification process, and on August 23, 1984, Canada presented its comments to those countries.

The comments were universal in scope, rather than specific to Central America. They related to the funding, composition, communications, and structure of the proposed verification commission. Further discussions concerning the CVC were then scheduled between Canada and the Contadora countries. On September 27, 1984, MacEachen told the U.N. General Assembly that Canada supported the Contadora proposals "to stop the process of militarization and to verify and monitor the progressive withdrawal of all foreign military personnel from the region."

In November 1984 the new external affairs minister, Joe Clark, provided a revised set of detailed comments[4] pertaining to the second draft of the Contadora act, as well as the Tegucigalpa amendments. These comments were presented in confidence and included suggestions that the United Nations coordinate and supervise the work of all commissions formed to implement the Contadora act. The mass media were to be granted detailed knowledge of the CVC and "irregular or insurgent forces would not be a party." Other points discussed included "time limits on the CVC mandate, the need for specific guarantees relating to freedom of movement, access by the Control and Verification Commission, their physical security, definition of size, logistic and communications support, and recommendations with respect to financial operations."[5]

The presentation of Canada's comments was coupled with the external affairs ministers' concerns about the viability of the Contadora plan. On November 13, 1984, Clark stated: "the Act that has been prepared by the Contadora group is not as good as it needs to be, and that any country charged with that [control and verification] responsibility would want to have the best instrument available." In subsequent years Clark's misgivings would increase.

From June 2-8, 1985, Clark visited Costa Rica, Nicaragua, and El Salvador to sign aid agreements and to reiterate Canada's commitment to the Contadora process. On August 23 Clark issued a statement of encouragement to the newly formed Lima Support Group, which included Argentina, Brazil, Peru, and Uruguay, and which supported the Contadora process. Then from September 12-13 the Contadora foreign ministers presented another draft of the Contadora Act, relating to verification and control mechanisms. Nicaragua rejected the plan on November 11, however, and cited its failure to prohibit U.S. military activity in the region as a reason. It was particularly concerned about American support for the anti-Sandinista forces.

Canada continued its effort to contribute to the reconciliation process, however, and sent an observer delegation to the Guatemalan presidential elections on November 3, 1985, and another observer team to the Honduran elections on November 24, 1985.

Canada's interest in the region received a measure of publicity on November 25 when its U.N. Ambassador, Stephen Lewis, spoke of Central American peace to the United Nations General Assembly. On December 8 another Canadian delegation was sent to Guatemala to monitor the second round of presidential elections there.

All this time Canada continued to offer detailed comments and suggest modifications to subsequent versions of the Contadora plan.[6] It remains unclear, however, how seriously Canada's suggestions have been taken. Favorable responses were initially offered by the Contadora group and the Central American governments, but this may have been simply a courtesy, or a desire not to offend. They may also have reflected a desire for increased developmental aid or financial investment in the region. As noted in Chapter 1, there is no strong evidence that Canada's efforts will make a decisive difference in the peace process. In this chapter it will be noted that Canada's suggestions have been incorporated in some of the subsequent drafts of the Esquipulas II Treaty,[7] but here again it is not clear how integral these suggestions have been.

It must also be recognized that although Canada's views carry weight and are respected in Central America, Canadians could never presume to exert a vital influence there. Canada does not have a global foreign policy. Indeed, what influence it has would probably deteriorate if it were to take sides or become too vocal in its criticism of the political actors in the region.

Nevertheless, Canada continues to seek solutions to the region's strife. External Affairs Minister Clark endorsed the Caraballeda Declaration, the statement of the Contadora nations, and the Contadora support group of January 1986, calling for an end to aid to the contras and the resumption of peace talks in Central America. Soon after, Clark voiced support for the Esquipulas II plan. He emphasized that "the need for a comprehensive agreement and for a workable and effective verification process remains urgent and essential."[8]

From May 24-25, 1986, the five Central American presidents convened under the auspices of Esquipulas I, named for the small town in Guatemala where they originally met, to discuss the creation of a Central American parliament. They failed to reach agreement on a new draft treaty, because Nicaragua insisted that it would not sign until the United States stopped aiding the Contras.

As noted in Chapter 5, on August 7, 1987, the five regional presidents did sign a peace plan proposed by President Oscar Arias of Costa Rica, the Esquipulas II accord (or Arias plan). The agreement was met with enthusiasm within Central America and in most of the rest of the world. Joe Clark immediately endorsed it.

At various times in 1987 and 1988 Clark again endorsed the Arias plan, the meetings between Central American political leaders, and the various efforts to bring democracy to all countries of the region. Canada reiterated that it was prepared to send advisers to the verification and control portions of the Contadora/Arias peace plans. Joe Clark continued to argue that Canada's long experience in peacekeeping efforts around the world might be invaluable in Central America. Furthermore, the vice president of Nicaragua, Sergio Ramirez, visited Canada on October 20, 1987, to ask for help in ensuring that the peace plan would hold. This reinforced the view, ostensibly held by Central American leaders and reinforced in the Canadian media, that Canada could play an important role in the region. Undoubtedly, the visit was also useful as a demonstration, or recognition, of the legitimacy of Nicaraguan concerns in Canadian eyes.

Canada was quick to applaud Nicaragua's apparent good faith regarding the Arias plan, but, as was to be expected, Clark would not address Nicaraguan fears about the perceived U.S. military threat. As usual, Canada would not diverge too sharply from the United States. Clark also refused requests by some opposition members of parliament to issue specific criticisms of continued U.S. military involvement in the region. Nor would Ottawa respond to informal and individual calls by some signatories to the Guatemala agreement--most notably President Oscar Arias--offering strong support that might include officials or troops to monitor the peace. Clark maintained that Canadian help of this kind could come only if a formal request from all five countries involved--Nicaragua, Costa Rica, Guatemala, El Salvador, and Honduras--was received. This was necessary to ensure that the Canadian government was perceived as being helpful.[9] Finally, Canada would not offer substantial increases in development aid to the region, although it had been reasonably generous historically. Currently, 1.2 percent of Canadian foreign aid goes to Central America.

Nevertheless, in an effort to lend support to the peace process, Joe Clark suggested in November 1987 that Canada might be prepared to admit Nicaraguan contras into Canada as part of a general peace settlement. Canadian government immigration officials insisted, however, that political refugees accepted into Canada would have to be noncombatants. Accepting contras, who advocated violence as a means to their political ends, would necessitate a change in immigration regulations. As a result, the question of what to do about the Nicaraguan insurgents was left open.

During a visit to Central America in November 1987 by Clark, Nicaraguan president Daniel Ortega voiced renewed support for Canada's peace initiatives. Ortega emphasized that Canadian peace observers might monitor Nicaragua's borders with Costa Rica and Honduras, and thereby discourage any incursions. Furthermore, he mentioned that if Canada was to support peace in the region, it might also take steps to support political and economic institutions that would broaden the prospects for democracy there. For example, Canada might devise strategies for rescheduling, forgiving, or working with, the debt problem.

At this point Clark expressed confidence that Canada could be a peacemaker in Central America. On the eve of his trip to the region, he stated: "I think that there's an opportunity for us to encourage the momentum of the peace process . . . whether in some kind of peacekeeping or observing role or in something else."[10] Joe Clark's primary aims were to show Canadian interest in, and support for, the peace plan and to let the regions governments know that Canada understood their predicament as they tried to escape domination by external powers. As Clark put it, "they need space to achieve their own peace in their own way."[11]

Unfortunately for the external affairs minister, his trip was characterized by a number of minor errors and misunderstandings. Indeed, at one point he complained that his officials did not give him current information about the suggested strategies for compliance with the Central American peace plan. Clark then promised to familiarize himself with the region so as to better promote policies directed toward attaining peace. He insisted that any peace plan would have to be unique to the region, and stated, "You can't take it off the shelf."[12] In a subsequent speech to parliament, Clark emphasized that he had spoken with each Central American president and that they all intended to participate in the effort to create peace.[13]

On January 22, 1988, it was announced that the five Central American presidents had accepted Canada's offer to send military experts and a peacekeeping force to the region to help set up a verification system. These forces, also referred to as an auxiliary technical group, would first design the inspection mechanism for the on-the-ground verification of the agreement.

Once the verification system was in place, Canadian soldiers (as well as West Germans, Spaniards, and others--all under United Nations auspices) would be sent as observers to the region. Canada also announced that it would be prepared to send the force even if its role was confined to a part of the region, such as the volatile Nicaraguan-Honduran border. No timetable was set for the dispatch of the troops, and Canada would not send forces to Central America until a formal request was made by all five presidents, with a specific time frame made clear.

The Canadian government wanted to stay informed about the changing situation in the region, however. It also wanted a measure of publicity for its peace efforts. With that in mind, a motion was introduced in the Canadian Parliament on January 29, 1988, to set up a bipartisan parliamentary committee to examine and report on the Central American peace process. The specific mandate of this group was to examine the extent of compliance and noncompliance with the Esquipulas II agreement, and to suggest additional ways that Canada might play a constructive role.

The committee visited the five Central American countries in mid-May of 1988, and received decidedly mixed signals. President Duarte of El Salvador questioned the wisdom of involving neutral countries like Canada in the peace process. Honduran officials could offer no details about how Canada could assist. But Nicaraguan president Daniel Ortega again praised Canada for its efforts.

In February of 1988 the leaders of Nicaragua's contra forces revealed that they wanted Canada to help police any cease-fires called in their seven-year guerrilla war with the Sandinista government. As far as they were concerned, several countries would be called upon to monitor the peace, but only Canada was unanimously accepted as a peace observer. At about this time, Liberal party leader John Turner announced that if elected prime minister (he was not), he would make Canada a pioneer in the development of technology to ensure that nations would live up to the terms of their peace treaties. To this end, he would have increased funding on the verification research program from its $1 million budget to an unspecified sum. This would have had a direct application to the peace process in Central America. Like Mulroney, Turner had a goal of maintaining Canada's reputation as a helpful fixer on the world stage.

In March 1988 Canada offered to help implement the Arias plan, and suggested that its role might now include putting observer teams in each Central American capital, hearing complaints about human rights violators, monitoring arms shipments through the region's ports, and installing sensors along borders where troop movements were common. Canada might even investigate the validity of the American claim that Cuban troops were in the area. However, no Central American response was immediately forthcoming.

But on March 24, 1988, an important development occurred. Sandinista and contra representatives agreed, in Sapoa, Nicaragua, to finalize discussions leading to a sixty-day cease-fire which would commence on April 1. Provisions included a gradual amnesty for

Nicaragua's political prisoners, the return of exiles, and the movement of the contras to so-called "truce zones" within Nicaraguan borders. In the following months, the U.S. Congress failed to pass contra aid legislation, thereby leaving the contras militarily impotent. With these developments and the excitement surrounding the Arias plan, Canada and other interested observers revealed a renewed optimism for the prospects for peace.

Amid all this discussion of Canada's involvement in the Central American peace process, it is worth discussing why involvement is in Canada's interest. First, Canadian security interests are enhanced by stability in its hemisphere. A resolution to the conflicts in Central America discourages major power involvement in the region. In turn, there is a reduced strategic threat to all the countries of the hemisphere, including Canada.

Second, Canada's involvement allows it to play a leading role on the world stage, a role for which it is ideally suited, given its long record of effective peacekeeping. By engaging in such an enterprise, Canada's prestige is enhanced; it is likely to be asked to participate in similar missions again; and it is better able to pursue its interests successfully within the United Nations and other international organizations. Canada's 1989 election to the U.N. Security Council may facilitate this process. Also, the Canadian military regards Canadian involvement favorably because of the experience and pride it brings to the armed forces.

Third, one might argue that Canada's effective peacekeeping and peace-observing missions enhance the governments's prestige domestically. Although Canadians rarely vote on the basis of foreign policy concerns, a successful mission and the goodwill that is usually generated as a result cannot but have some positive spillover effects for the governing party. Similarly, one might argue that a successful mission, by enhancing national pride and prestige, would in turn help to promote national unity. To reiterate, this would not be a necessary condition for unity, but it might well be a contributing factor.

Fourth, a peacekeeping mission in this area of great East-West interest demonstrates that Canada's foreign policy strategies differ at times from those of the United States. Their motives are similar, as both desire peace, but--at least in Central America--the strategies diverge somewhat. Also, as discussed in Chapter 1, Canadian participation would provide a counterweight to closer bilateral ties. Free trade is the most obvious example of this. Finally, it should go without saying that Canada gains if it can help to remedy human misery by promoting peace, development, and democracy.

To the extent that Canada's diplomatic initiatives might make a difference in Central America, then, what might such efforts include?

First, if Canada is seen as a friend of the region and of the United States, then it might influence all of the parties, particularly the United States and Nicaragua, to cease hostilities. Finding a strategy to reach this goal while allowing both countries to "save face" would require a statesmanlike effort. The Canadian government might be ready to take on such a role if all parties to the conflict were to agree, however.[14]

As part of such an effort, some suggest that Canada should help to create a "Northern friends of Contadora."[15] Presumably this might also include a "Northern friends of Esquipulas." Such a group of nations, which might include countries in Western Europe as well as multilateral institutions like the United Nations, could provide diplomatic support and financial assistance to the peace effort while remaining independent of it. A sufficient degree of political will would be crucial for creating an effective international role. In the absence of such a support group, nongovernmental organizations from outside countries might advise their governments and the public concerning developments in Central America. In this way, international awareness of the region's strife might grow, and new strategies might be suggested to counter the problems of the area. Nongovernmental organizations in Canada are already active in providing financial aid and technical advice, and encouraging public awareness.

In addition, Canada might continue a position first articulated in the Trudeau era--and reiterated by all subsequent governments--that is, to repeatedly emphasize that any lasting solution to Central America's difficulties can emerge only if all parties to the conflict seek a lasting peace and are willing to make the political sacrifices necessary to arrive at such a goal. As noted earlier, such a decision must be coupled with noninterference from the two superpowers. Other countries might provide aid and technical assistance, but not direct involvement that might aggravate existing tensions. If necessary, the United Nations might help to maintain the peace.

Canada might also speak out on Central American issues at international forums, as a spur to action. Also, some groups call for the establishment of a Canadian embassy in Nicaragua. They maintain that only in this way could Canada accurately monitor developments there and thereby make informed policy decisions. Such an action would further demonstrate Canada's foreign policy independence from the United States. For budget reasons, and other reasons related to bilateral sensitivities, Canada has chosen not to pursue that option. It has, however, appointed a roving ambassador to the region, Richard Gorham. His mandate includes collecting information, arranging meetings, offering peacekeeping and other advice to the Central American countries, and maintaining a clear signal that Canada is willing to help if asked.

Another suggestion, offered in 1988 by the bipartisan parliamentary committee focusing on the Central American peace process, was that a political office be assigned to each of the Esquipulas countries.[16] Their report also suggested that a chargé d'affaires be introduced in Nicaragua who would report to the Canadian ambassador in Costa Rica. Furthermore, Guatemala might be restored to full ambassador status, (it was in 1990) and the Canadian government would appoint chargé d'affaires in El Salvador and Honduras--both would report to the ambassador in Guatemala. The report suggested that all of these efforts could be realized at a relatively small cost. At this writing government leaders have spoken favorably about these recommendations, but, have not yet acted upon most of them.

Where else might Canada become involved diplomatically? The report of the International Commission for Verification and Follow-up (a commission outlined in the Esquipulas II plan) indicated that El Salvador, Guatemala, and Honduras were taking few steps to democratize, and that democratization had been monitored closely only in Nicaragua. The contras had received much attention, and finding confidence-building measures to improve relations between Nicaragua and its neighbors had been a priority. The sluggish progress made by the other nations of the region was a disappointment, however. If the commission's findings prove accurate, then Canada might choose to press for universal compliance with the peace accord.

In the meantime, Canada has been quietly promoting steps toward peace in Guatemala. In 1989 it co-sponsored a United Nations resolution to monitor Guatemala's increasing number of human rights violations. In August 1990, Canadian officials hosted a groundbreaking meeting in Ottawa which promoted contact between Guatemala's rebels and the countries' business and religious communities. In September 1990, Canada appointed a senior official, Brian Dickson, as ambassador to Guatemala. In addition, in October External Affairs Minister Joe Clark received the head of one of Guatemala's leading human-rights groups. All of these actions were carried out with virtually no fanfare so as not to raise false expectations.

As mentioned, part of Canada's involvement has also included sending peacekeeping or peace-observing troops to Central America. Over the last forty years Canada has sent more peacekeeping soldiers (80,000) to more troubled areas of the world than has any other country. Canadian forces are unique in that they have served in every one of the United Nations peacekeeping operations. Peacekeeping has become the proudest postwar tradition in the Canadian military. Although Canada's record has won accolades, they have paid a high price. Of the 733 U.N. troops killed in the field, 78 have been Canadian. At present Canada has sent 175 of the total U.N. contingent of 350 peacekeepers. They are based in Tegucigalpa, Honduras.

Central America is no stranger to peacekeeping forces. For instance, such a force served in the area following the El Salvador-Honduras war in 1969. Most often the peacekeepers have been U.S. troops acting to suppress conflict in the area and, most assuredly, to protect American interests in the region. The current peacekeeping force, however, is distinctive for its international character, devoid of superpower membership.

It should be stressed that peacekeepers have to be sensitive to the connotation that peacekeeping has in Latin America. American "peace-keeping" in the Dominican Republic was perceived as an invasion, for example. Therefore the number of international forces should not be excessive, and the terminology used in the peace effort should be neutral in order to avoid inflaming passions. Also, the central objective of a mission should not be to report every violation, but only the most flagrant ones threatening peace. It must be seen as impartial, however, to assure its credibility and effectiveness, particularly since it could not employ force. In April 1990 Canadian troops, serving under the United Nations rubric, were sent to the region.

The primary tasks of the U.N. peacekeepers include reacting swiftly to requests for investigation, verifying all verbal agreements between parties, and checking on movements of host countries' troops and insurgents (FMLN, the contras, etc.) and monitoring the presence of military advisers. Further, peacekeepers engage in overseeing the exchange of POWS and examining inventories to track small arms. They monitor activity in as visible fashion as possible. Their task is a difficult one, for they have to prevent one country from being used as a staging ground or weapons trans-shipment point in support of a military uprising in another nation. They must keep two belligerent factions apart. To that end, they need complete freedom of movement and access, and the confidence of all parties involved. As a result they operate under a clearly defined mandate from the United Nations.

Before Canada agreed to contribute to the Central American peace process, whether by contributing advice or peacekeepers, it insisted upon certain preconditions. Most important, any solution to the region's problems would have to be arrived at by the parties to the conflict, and not by outside forces. Outside powers, and particularly superpowers, often aggravate an already bad situation. An international organization like the United Nations can provide advice and peace-observing troops, but it cannot become directly involved in negotiations between the parties to the dispute. Nevertheless, Canada wanted the United Nations to oversee the peace process because of its peacekeeping expertise, its international legitimacy, and its ability to generate the required funds for the mission. Also, Canada favored U.N. involvement because its own soldiers could then be regarded as international actors. If there was to be trouble they would not be agents of a foreign government, but of a respected international body.

Canada also favored the entry of more nations' forces on the peacekeeping team. The participation of other nations would increase the legitimacy of the effort and bring different perspectives to the region's security concerns.

In addition, any Canadian involvement required a clear and well-defined mandate. Canada's strategies, goals, time limits, and other crucial factors were to be spelled out at the inception of any involvement. Freedom of movement for observers was assured. The peacekeepers would receive the latest information and have all necessary powers to supervise the mandate of the mission. Canadian officials would strive to avoid any repeat of the problems incurred during their missions in Vietnam, for example, when their uncertain status at times made it unclear if they were to be seen as U.S. allies, as purely international forces, or whatever.[17] Relations between Canada and another peacekeeping nation of the time, India, were damaged due to frequent misunderstandings. Also, the Canadian government would insist that decisions reached concerning regional strategies for peace could be arrived at by majority vote and not necessarily by unanimity. The effort to push for unanimous support for every measure failed miserably in Vietnam.

Furthermore, all of the Central American nations would have to help pay for the peacekeepers, which would cost about $2.5 million (CDN) a year to maintain. One could make the reasonable argument that their military spending is such that they could afford it if they chose to. In other peacekeeping efforts around the world however, funds have not always been easily forthcoming. Clearly, Canada's advice to the peace process might include not only how to promote the conflict resolution but how to avoid the myriad of pitfalls that could emerge along the way.

It should be clear that all parties to the disputes would agree that international peacekeepers would be performing a vital and desirable function and would not be subject to interference. All nations of the region would have to agree that seeking an equitable and workable peace agreement would be of the highest priority and in their national interests. At this time, however, there exists a disparity in the Central American governments' enthusiasm for the peace process. Nicaragua and Costa Rica are obviously excited. Guatemala is relatively indifferent, at best, since it faces no direct threat from its neighbors. For the process to succeed, however, all governments must lend more than just token support.

A number of military preconditions existed for Canadian involvement as well. These were detailed in a working paper distributed by the Canadian government on November 1, 1987, entitled "Central America Peacekeeping Observer Organization (CAPOO)". To paraphrase the military section of this paper, Canadian officials were to be concerned with such issues as the role of each contingent of troops. Would they be operational, specialist support, or a combination of these roles? (They were a combination.) Would troops just be expected to observe and report on violations of the peace accords, or would they be expected to help influence a return to normalcy? (Mostly the former.) Could Canadian troops carry weapons and be able to defend themselves? (No.) To what extent would the five Central American nations be responsible for ensuring the protection and security of the mission? Could a cease-fire be guaranteed in the areas where verification is requested? What facilities would be provided, and under what conditions? How would communications and transportation facilities be established between military forces and their governments? How would the peace observers' freedom of movement, which includes the right to stop any trucks or to look into any warehouse, be implemented? Granted, the free movement of peacekeeping troops might be perceived as a violation of a nation's sovereignty, but it is a necessary means of stopping arms traffic. Also, would peacekeeping forces be subject to their own criminal and disciplinary jurisdiction, and would they be immune to the civil laws of the host countries? Some of these questions remain to be answered at this writing.

A clear mandate was of great importance. Equally vital was a precise time limit for the participation of international forces. These and others are lessons that Canadian officials have learned from previous missions. But the application of these lessons was difficult in Central America, given the large number of irregular forces involved in the conflict. The contras and the FMLN demanded a significant role in the peacemaking process, and at times this introduced a major stumbling block to regional negotiations.

In sum, the most important preconditions for Canadian participation included the need for a sufficient degree of political will to make the process work, the presence of an independent advisory body to which peace observers could report, and adequate financing of the peace effort.

Other preconditions included suspension of the rule dictating that international forces must unanimously agree to all decisions. Canada learned from its Vietnam experience that unanimity is not always possible, and that such a rule can complicate relations. Also, there had to be freedom of action and movement. This is essential for any force respon-sible for supervising, observing, or monitoring a peace, cease-fire, or truce. In addition, Canada insisted that the force be a combination of military and civilian personnel. It had to be well organized with tasks clearly defined. They had to be seen as reliable and credible supporters of the peace process.

At first, there were reasons to be a bit pessimistic about the prospects for such a mission, however. Asked in February 1985, for his gut feeling about the chances for success of the Contadora effort, Clark replied: "I'm not really optimistic. . . . It's the best that's there, it's got lots of troubles . . . but it's the best vehicle there is."[18] In the months to follow, Clark's doubts would persist. On July 7, 1986, he said: "So much dedicated effort directed to creating an atmosphere and finding a formula for peaceful reconciliation in Central America has not yet achieved success."

Nevertheless, the minister pledged Canada's continued support. One of the most worrisome obstacles was the Central American region's terrain--especially near Nicaragua's borders--which is rugged and difficult to traverse. Border regions are 150 to 400 miles long, which presents communications and patrolling difficulties. One solution was to implement unmanned sensors as verification aides to simplify the process.[19] A Canadian peacekeeping expert, Lt. Col. Don Ethell, visited Central America with External Affairs Minister Clark in November of 1987, and suggested that 300 people, nearly as many vehicles, and eleven helicopters would be needed to patrol the border areas. Sophisticated radar capable of detecting supply planes traveling at night would have to be used as well. Some experts noted that the helicopters most likely to be used were also underpowered for the climate and unlikely to do the job effectively. Lt. Col. Ethell remarked that the Central American officials and military officers were somewhat complacent about setting up a peacekeeping operation and were unaware of the complexity of setting up an observer-group mission. They appeared more willing to discuss the philosophy of peace than to get bogged down in the technical details of how to preserve it.[20] Of course, this is all part of a learning process that would succeed only if regional officials were truly willing to work toward an equitable and lasting cessation of hostilities.

The peacekeeping mission patrols the cease-fire zones and borders across which guerrillas and supplies move. It investigates alleged violations by either side, and files regular reports. Careful planning is mandatory.

An additional concern relates to the requirement for time limits for the mission. Canadian forces arrived in Cyprus in 1964 for what was believed to be a temporary mission. They remain there to this day. Could Central America prove to be a similar quagmire? Since a number of the Central American governments were unenthusiastic about international troops inspecting their territories, (although they had all formally requested it), and since the tasks of any mission remain unspecified, it is hard to be enthusiastic about the short duration and clear success of an international mission.

Costa Rican president Oscar Arias and Nicaraguan president Daniel Ortega had publicly suggested that they might be willing to consider a Canadian role in enforcing peace. But as noted, the argument could be made that their interest lay not so much in gaining Canadian peacekeeping expertise, as in receiving increased development aid. There was another important Canadian consideration as well, and that had to do with the serious financial constraints that Canadian external affairs personnel are facing, globally. On December 16, 1986, the Government announced cutbacks to the mission in Guatemala, including the removal of the ambassador, leaving just three officers in charge of political, immigration, and aid affairs. The embassy in Costa Rica also felt the financial pinch, while simultaneously it was assigned more responsibilities. These cutbacks affected embassies and consulates worldwide, but they were particularly difficult in Central America where Canadian diplomats had been called upon to do so much. Indeed, many observers predicted that the Mulroney government's deficit-reduction policies would particularly hamper the efforts of diplomats in Central America.[21] The rapid gathering of accurate first-hand information by seasoned diplomats became much more difficult. Critics stressed that the promotion of trade and the regulation of immigration had become much more difficult. At present, only fifteen Canadian diplomats remain to cover the Central American countries in matters of politics, aid, trade, immigration, cultural affairs, and the needs of Canadians in the region. Undoubtedly, the cutbacks have diminished Canada's understanding of the area and reduced Ottawa's ability to initiate actions and respond to events there. Future cutbacks are expected in the next few years.

It should also be mentioned however, that Canada's peacekeepers have come under great domestic public scrutiny. In one survey, 80 percent of the Canadians polled stated that Canada should be concerned about Central America.[22] Thousands of Canadians have traveled, worked, or been missionaries in Latin America. Many Canadian church leaders had explicitly called for a Canadian peacekeeping role in the region.[23] Also, some critics of Canadian policy argued that Canada should let its commitment determine its policy, and its interests enhance its capabilities. For example, if Canada's commitment to NATO drives its capabilities, would a parallel commitment not apply to Central America? Of course, one could argue that Canada's role in NATO is clearly established and recognized as integral. Its interest in Central America is not so long-lasting or vital, nor is there evidence that Canada is willing to make the sacrifices necessary to be a major player in the peace process, as evidenced by its financial cutbacks and its more important international obligations elsewhere. Put simply, Canada is not yet sufficiently committed, nor are its interests sufficiently clear-cut to satisfy those who seek greater involvement in Central America.

Nevertheless, Canadian public interest is not likely to disappear, whether or not settlement is reached or a clear military victor emerges. Unlike the conflict in Vietnam, which prompted much Canadian interest and anti-American rhetoric for only a short time, Central America will remain a Canadian concern for at least two reasons. First, unlike Vietnam, the Central American region is geographically close to Canada. There is particular Canadian interest in refugees, development aid, and human rights abuses in its own hemisphere. Second, the United States will always have a major role to play in the region, and its policies will remain a target for Canadian criticism. More important, Canadian foreign policy planners, reacting to ongoing U.S. policies in Central America, will be forced to weigh the consequences of Canadian actions there.

On November 30, 1988, an agreement was reached to begin the process of forming an auxiliary technical group to act as part of a verification commission that would include Canada. This was just a beginning. In the absence of a comprehensive agreement ironing out the details of peacekeeping, Canadian officials considered an incremental approach to supporting a series of bilateral agreements--such as a joint Nicaragua/Costa Rica border commission. To quote one official: "We would go, even if the agreement is less than perfect. . . . We would consider doing just the Nicaraguan/Honduran border or something inside Nicaragua."[24] John Graham stressed that such a plan would focus on particular points of tension, addressed separately and in advance of a comprehensive settlement.[25] At the time Canadians dominated numerically the peacekeeping mission in Central America. At present, however, there are grounds for optimism. In April, 1990, Canadian peace observers under the United Nations flag were sent to repatriate contra fighters from their Honduran sanctuaries to Nicaragua. During operation "Home Run", as the U.N. forces dubbed it, more than 23,000 former rebels surrendered their weapons to U.N. soldiers. The weapons were destroyed and the demobilized rebels were relocated to United Nations protected "Security Zones" in Nicaragua. Ironically, this disarmament role had not been envisioned for the peace-observing force.

The job is not complete of course. El Salvador and Guatemala continue to be racked by internal violence and ONUCA continues to stop cross-border shipments of arms and troops to guerrilla forces in the region. They continue to patrol the entire area looking for violations of the ceasefire. Also, it is not clear how long the peace observing force will have to remain in Central America. Nevertheless, on balance the U.N. mission has been an unexpected success thus far. A lasting peace is not guaranteed, however.

To promote the peace process, it has also been suggested that Canada might provide advice leading to the formation of a Central American parliament. This idea has reemerged periodically over many years. In fact, as noted earlier, between 1824 and 1839 there existed a Central American federation, but external and internal pressures forced its dissolution.

Another way that Canada might encourage Central American peace could be by helping to conduct democratic elections or by offering to train indigenous election officials. A group of Canadian nongovernmental organizations worked to support the Nicaraguan elections through the Committee for Peace and Democracy in Nicaragua (CPDN). The CPDN organized observer teams to monitor all phases of the electoral process and provided the public with relevant information about the election. It is hoped that other nations will be motivated to follow Canada's example in promoting peace.

This last point is particularly salient; although Canada has consistently supported the peace efforts for the region, other influential countries including Great Britain, France, West Germany, and the Netherlands have wavered in their support. Joe Clark has stated that Canada would be prepared "to help devise a mechanism for peace and then participate in the mechanism."[26] Realistically, however, Canada would not pursue any of these actions unless it was assured that the United States would not stand in opposition to them. As well-meaning as Canada's motives might be, it will not endanger the interests that are truly important--the bilateral ones.

CONCLUSION

Prime Minister Mulroney acknowledges that the peace process has problems, but he also maintains that it has helped keep the lid on an increasingly explosive situation, has provided for frequent dialogue among the five Central American countries, and has become a possible framework for peace. As a result, the government is likely to pursue the following policies in the next few years with regard to the peace process:

1. Canada will continue to help in the design of essential security provisions of a peace treaty in response to requests from the nations of the area.
2. It will continue to argue that all parts of the agreement must be workable.
3. It will stress that there must be the political will on the part of all five countries that the agreement should work. Each Central American country must agree that a peace treaty serves its long-term self-interest.
4. It will attest that a settlement must be perceived by the major external powers as being in their interests.
5. Finally, Canada will emphasize that a solution must be regional and without outside interference. "Contadora is an indigenous Latin American crisis--albeit a crisis with serious international dimensions."[27]

The Canadian government remains cautiously optimistic that a workable peace plan can be implemented. Its efforts in Central America could help save lives, build financial and other ties to the region, and demonstrate foreign policy initiatives somewhat independent of those of the United States. So far, the peace observing mission has been a successful one. By making a contribution to the peace process, Canada enhances its prestige internationally and increases domestic pride and security. The arguments for a limited Canadian involvement in the Central American peace process are compelling, notwithstanding the attendant problems. Put simply, the benefits of such participation far outweigh the costs.

NOTES

1. As quoted in the *Winnipeg Free Press* (March 16, 1982), p. 34.
2. *Winnipeg Free Press* (October 6, 1983), p. 1.
3. Quote taken from "Prospects Look Poor for Peace," *Winnipeg Free Press* (April 23, 1984).
4. The "Comments" were comprehensive enough to be written directly into any final Central American peace treaty. For a discussion of this point, see *Maclean's* (February 11, 1985).

5.   John Graham, "Canada and Contadora," text of a speech delivered to the Canadian Institute of Strategic Studies (Toronto, Nov. 8, 1985), p. 7.

6.   For example, between July 1984 and September 1985, Canada provided a series of five written contributions at the request of the Contadora countries.

7.   The Esquipulas II plan calls for amnesty to insurgents, ends the state of emergency, halts outside aid to rebel forces, encourages refugees to go home, reaffirms basic freedoms, and establishes commissions to help the move toward free elections.

8.   Department of External Affairs press release "Contadora" (Ottawa, March 1986).

9.   See Ross Howard, "Nicaragua to Seek Canadian Peace Role," *Globe and Mail* (October 20, 1987), p. A-4.

10.   As quoted in the *Washington Post* (November 20, 1987), p. A-31.

11.   Gordon Barthos, "Joe Clark a Hit on Latin Trip," *Toronto Star* (November 29, 1987).

12.   Paul Knox, "Clark Wrestles With Fine Points of Central American Politics," *Globe and Mail* (November 30, 1987), p. A-12.

13.   Text of a statement in the House of Commons by the Right Honourable Joe Clark, Secretary of State for External Affairs, on his Central American Trip, November 21-29, 1987 (Ottawa, December 2, 1987).

14.   The United States was skeptical about the chances for a successful resolution to the conflicts in the region, but it had accepted Canada's role in peacekeeping or peace-observing, even though it might mean putting Canadian forces between Nicaraguan troops and the U.S.-supported contras.

15.   Liisa North (ed.), *Negotiations for Peace in Central America*, a conference report published by the Canadian Institute for International Peace and Security (Ottawa, September 27-28, 1985), p. 36.

16.   See the report of the House of Commons Special Committee on the Peace Process in Central America entitled "Supporting the Five" (Ottawa, July 5, 1988), pp. 34-35.

17.   For a good overview of Canada's peacekeeping experience in Vietnam, see Douglas A. Ross, *In the Interests of Peace: Canada and Vietnam 1954-1973* (Toronto: University of Toronto Press, 1984); Ramesh Thakur, *Peacekeeping in Vietnam: India, Poland and the International Commission* (Edmonton: University of Alberta Press, 1984; Victor Levant, *Quiet Complicity: Canadian Involvement in the Vietnam War* (Toronto: Between the Lines, 1986).

18.   "Clark to Seek Freer Information Flow," *Globe and Mail* (February 8, 1985), p. 1.

19.   This suggestion is made in Calvin Bricker (ed.), *Central America and Peacekeeping: A Workshop Report*, (Toronto: CISS, 1986).

20.   Ethell's report is discussed in Paul Knox, "Keeping the Peace Wouldn't be Easy," *Globe and Mail* (December 1, 1987).

21.   See, for example, Paul Knox, "Canada's Cutback Will be a Millstone," in the *Globe and Mail* (December 9, 1986), p. A-9.

22.   As quoted in John Graham, "The Caribbean Basin: Whose Calypso?" speech delivered to the Canadian Institute for International Affairs (Toronto, May 4, 1985).

23.   A few of the many organized groups in Canada interested in Central America include the Support Committee for the People of Guatemala; the Human Rights Commission of El Salvador; the Table de Concertation pour El Salvador; the Social Justice Committee of Montreal; and CAPA. A more complete list is presented in Chapter 7.

24.   As quoted in the *Globe and Mail* (Tuesday, May 17, 1988).

25.   John Graham, "Contadora--The Moving Target," text of a speech delivered at the Centre for International Studies (Toronto, Canada, May 23, 1986).

26.   As quoted on CBC Radio's "As It Happens" (November 30, 1987).

27.   John Graham, "Canada and Contadora."

7 Canadian Pressure Groups, Nongovernmental Organizations, and the Effort to Promote Human Rights in Central America

Until now this study has focused on the Canadian government's role in Central America. A reasonable argument could be made that without the activity of various pressure groups and nongovernmental organizations (NGOs), Canada would remain fairly indifferent to the region. Canadian NGOs have planned and administered aid programs. Canadian pressure groups have published newsletters, lobbied members of parliament and the bureaucracy, demanded an increase in refugee quotas, and attracted widespread attention to the region through the mass media. This is not to suggest that such groups are the decisive factors in a political decision, for a credible case can be made that government officials act entirely independently of them. Nevertheless, in this chapter we will explore the extent to which pressure groups and nongovernmental organizations can make meaningful differences.

Canadian interest groups, and particularly church-based groups, began to focus attention on Central America after two significant events. In 1979, the Sandinistas overthrew the Somoza regime in Nicaragua, and took power.[1] After an interval, the United States condemned what was perceived to be a Marxist threat to the hemisphere. Certain Canadian interest groups immediately called for Canada to recognize the new regime in Nicaragua and support it with development aid. Soon after, Archbishop Oscar Romero of San Salvador and four nuns were murdered in El Salvador. This inspired calls for Canadian government condemnation of the right-wing death squads that perpetrated these crimes.[2] In March 1982 representatives of several Canadian churches issued a public statement rebuking the government for its failure "to take creative and appropriate action," and suggesting strategies for opposing U.S. military aid to the region and supporting political negotiations between warring parties.[3]

Since the early 1980's several religious and nonreligious groups, including the Canadian Labour Congress, CAPA, the Louis Riel Brigade, Tools for Peace, and many others have demanded greater Canadian government attention to remedies for the terrible problems of the region.[4] Many aid workers have traveled to Nicaragua to offer support. The Canadian embassy has formally advised Canadian development workers "to take the utmost care and caution in their daily lives, and particularly to avoid areas of conflict whenever possible."

Tools for Peace was organized by nongovernmental organizations, community and solidarity groups, churches, and individuals across the country. In December 1985, it stocked a boat with (CDN) $1 million worth of goods and supplies to be sent from Vancouver to Nicaragua. Since that time this coalition has organized many deliveries of goods and has offered expert advice to Central America, particularly to Nicaragua.

Canadian interest groups kept up the pressure on the federal government throughout the early 1980s. Fifteen hundred prominent Canadians signed an open letter to Prime Minister Trudeau stating that

Global peace is threatened by the growing conflict in Central America. The United States, under President Ronald Reagan, is threatening to destroy Nicaragua. It is turning Central America into a war zone by arming privileged elites against the pressures for social change. Canada, by taking decisive public action, can reinforce the threatened prospects for peace. We urge Prime Minister Trudeau to:

- state publicly and clearly Canada's unequivocal opposition to U.S. military intervention in Central America;
- press publicly for immediate concrete initiations to demilitarize Central America, including an end to all foreign military aid, withdrawal of foreign military forces an end to the covert war against Nicaragua;
- urge the United States to open unconditional negotiations with the opposition in El Salvador;
- suspend Canadian bilateral aid until Honduras renews its neutrality; and
- establish a Canadian embassy in Managua and initiate immediate and sizable humanitarian and bilateral aid.[5]

Their recommendations had little immediate effect. Nevertheless, Canadian nongovernmental organizations (which include trade unions, universities, and development agencies) have played a distinctive role in promoting development in Central America.

The term "NGO" was originally coined by the United Nations. NGOs rely primarily on voluntary funding and labor, although at least 200 receive subsidies from the federal government. Most NGOs concentrate on the long-term development problems of health care, education, and food production. Many are able to respond quickly and effectively to community needs. Their cost-effectiveness in project delivery has drawn praise from cabinet officials and senior public servants. NGOs tend to target specific recipients for support and are able to implement programs with a minimum of bureaucratic red tape.

Until the announced budget cutbacks in 1981, CIDA had continually increased its subsidy support to NGOs working in Central America. Reasons for CIDA's increased support for NGOs included a Western consensus that the large-scale infrastructure aid of the fifties and sixties had failed, and that integrated rural development and other modest community-based projects could be models for a more effective type of development assistance. CIDA established agriculture, energy, and human resources as its policy priorities and called upon community institutions and groups with relevant levels of expertise to help implement these programs.

In practice the most successful NGOs seek policy goals that complement Canadian commercial priorities--hence the importance of "tied aid," discussed in the previous chapter. Ottawa also realizes an excellent public image due to its association with activist NGOs. In addition, NGOs are inexpensive since they are reliant on volunteers or poorly paid workers. The federal government does not have to maintain an expensive bureaucratic staff.[6] Nongovernmental organizations receive matching grants from CIDA at a ratio that is typically nine dollars from CIDA for every dollar from NGOs.

Some of the nongovernmental organizations active in promoting economic and social development in Central America include Care Canada, Oxfam Canada, Inter-Pares, and Horizons for Friendship. Liisa North points out that in 1982-83 there were about fifty Canadian-based agencies involved in over 800 projects throughout Latin America.[7]

CIDA's support of NGOs is laudable; however, there remains the worrisome issue of whether NGOs can retain functional independence from government strings. When NGO policy conflicts with federal government priorities, government interests will prevail, and NGO funding will be at risk. External affairs ministers and their senior bureaucrats have been most attentive to NGO concerns in Central America, but there is no question that when differences of opinion exist and compromise is impossible, government officials hold national security interests to be of paramount importance. The best example of this is the fact that submissions of various NGOs to parliamentary committees on Canadian aid to, or foreign policy in, Central America have done little more than collect dust on library shelves. Various NGOs have recommended cutting off aid to Guatemala, El Salvador, or even Honduras, but no action has followed these requests. Repeated calls for a Canadian embassy in Nicaragua have gone unheeded for reasons cited earlier.

Furthermore, NGO concerns are often dismissed by government actors because of a sense that as public interest groups they cannot have the clout of business associations. If it is a Canadian government priority in Central America to seek ways to promote industrial development and commercial investment, then government officials will only pay lip service to most of the demands of public advocacy NGOs. If NGOs are to have a meaningful policy, impact, however, they might be well advised to band together with like-minded groups. There is evidence to suggest that when NGOs work within large-scale networks they make more of a substantial policy impact because of the media attention they may attract or the votes that they may control.[8]

For example, on June 12-13, 1989, a coalition of nongovernmental aid and human rights organizations called the Inter-agency El Salvador Monitoring Group presented a report to CIDA and other government officials that documented and denounced the harassment of organizations performing humanitarian work in El Salvador. This report received attention in the Canadian mass media and prompted the Department of External Affairs to warn Canadian NGOs involved in projects in El Salvador to avoid traveling there whenever possible.

Unlike nongovernmental organizations, Canadian political parties are ideally placed to influence Canadian foreign policy interests in Central America because of their proximity to the levers of power. New Democratic party (NDP) critics have been prominent in advocating Canadian government support for the Sandinista government in Nicaragua, opposing aid to Guatemala and El Salvador when perceived and real human rights violations exist, and suggesting other measures.

Former NDP external affairs critic Pauline Jewitt stated:

> The NDP . . . has taken and continues to take a very strong position of non-intervention in Central America. It has been particularly critical of U.S. intervention and, above all, U.S. support of the Contras, of the mining of Nicaraguan harbors and the American refusal to have the International Court ruling be binding upon it.[9]

Most of the political parties and interest groups who try to influence government policy come from the political left or, less often, from the center. There are few organized groups in Canada that try to promote policies consistent with those of former president Reagan's administration. Scarcely any groups suggest that Communist insurgents are the primary cause of the region's problems. Here again, a motivating factor for most interest groups is the desire to distinguish Canadian policy from that of the United States, in addition to helping to remedy the social and economic inequality prevalent in the region. One exception to this trend is the conservative, Toronto-based Citizens for Foreign Aid Reform (C-FAR). This group argues that Ottawa should not support governments that are radically opposed to Canadian values. In 1987 their cofounder Paul Fromm: "we would agree with Elliott Abrams, the U.S. Assistant Secretary of State that Canadian aid is shoring up a Marxist regime in Nicaragua."[10]

C-FARs' views are dwarfed by the number of critics who argue that Nicaragua should be given the benefit of the doubt by Canadian government officials. For example, in June 1987, in Toronto, a coalition of forty-seven different groups and 800 protesters called upon the Canadian government to help end the war in Nicaragua by condemning U.S. involvement there, increasing aid and trade with Central America, and opening its doors to refugees. Other demonstrations Canadian government to help end the war in Nicaragua by condemning U.S. involvement there, increasing aid and trade with Central America, and opening its doors to refugees. Other demonstrations with various numbers of protestors have taken place in Ottawa, Vancouver, and Montreal.

As noted, it is unclear whether interest groups in Canada can wield direct influence on Canadian foreign policy in Central America. On one occasion, the 1982 effort by the Task Force on the Churches and Corporate Responsibility succeeded in halting the sale of Canadian aircraft to the repressive regimes in Guatemala and Honduras. This was a rare event, however. John Foster of the Inter-Church Committee on Human Rights, in a discussion with James Rochlin, stated:

> There has been a response to our presence [by the government]. We are taken as a factor. Our information and expertise is important since the government has a lack of resources. We get an audience with the government, but whether we are listened to is another question.[11]

The government has provided several forums for interest group articulation regarding concerns about Canadian government policy. In addition, Ambassador Richard Gorham was appointed by the government to listen to interest groups, business interests, and the mass media, and to explain Ottawa's position in Central America. Increasing numbers of average Canadians have also grown more fascinated with the region. During 1987, for example, 30 to 40 percent of the mail received by Prime Minister Mulroney pertained to Central America.[12]

Among the most active of the institutional groups that monitor Canadian government policy in Central America is the Catholic Church. Canadian bishops, many within the Jesuit order and especially the Inter-Church Committee on Human Rights in Latin America (ICCHRLA), have occasionally been vociferous in criticizing Canadian policy. The ICCHRLA sees its mandate as part of an effort to achieve a "just, participatory and sustainable society."[13] Wherever possible, human rights protection is advocated, and political, social, and economic rights are promoted. To that end, the ICCHRLA has periodically recommended the following measures: the cut-off of aid to repressive regimes in Central America; the investigation of Canadian bank loans to authoritative governments; and the establishment of an international code of corporate conduct for the Canadian government whereby investment, credit, or aid would be offered or withdrawn depending on the human rights record of the nation's government. The Canadian churches argue that the Department of External Affairs, historically, has compartmentalized the promotion of human rights and separates it from political and economic issues. They have argued that "human rights promotion has been effectively separated from practically all other foreign policy issues."[14]

They stress that this has resulted in a weakened Canadian relationship with the region. The churches have voiced support for a Canadian role in the Contadora peace process and the Arias plan. They have been instrumental in pressuring the cabinet to admit more refugees from Central America. They have called upon the Canadian government to pressure the United States to stop aiding repressive regimes in the area, and to cease its trade/aid embargo on Nicaragua. Church representatives have also been active in monitoring various elections in Central America and subsequently discussing their observations with the Department of External Affairs. At times, church officials have had access to electoral constituencies that were unapproachable by government monitors. The United Church of Canada and the Anglican Church of Canada have cooperated in projects to promote reconstruction and development in Nicaragua. They have donated funds and expertise to child welfare programs, to adult education programs, and to efforts to improve the quality of life in rural areas.[15] The activities of Canadian churches in Central America reflect widespread Canadian humanitarian concern within the region. This challenges the narrow view of those who stress that Canada should be concerned only with its national interest.   The churches' outspokenness has forced government officials to consider administering programs on moral grounds, rather than just strategic ones. As noted, this is not to say that religious groups are usually successful, because frequently their demands go unheeded.   However, they increase public awareness and force politicians to consider the electoral consequences of inaction.   In this sense, they have made an important contribution to the Canadian policy initiation process.

The churches of Canada have condemned the U.S. funding of the contra rebels and called upon Canada to use what influence it might have to dissuade the United States from attacking the Sandinista regime militarily or economically. From time to time, they have suggested that Nicaragua be made a "core country" for Canadian development aid, or that a Canadian embassy be established in Managua. The Inter-Church committees have generally been reluctant to criticize the Sandinistas' crackdown on its domestic press or the limitation of its citizens' basic freedoms. Indeed, their only substantial criticism of the Ortega-led government was for its oppressive treatment of its Indian minorities. The churches tend to be most sympathetic to the policy goals of the Nicaraguan government and have even recommended that Canada give compensatory aid "to offset the impact" of the contra attacks.[16] As noted, the effort to curb U.S. support for the contras has been of particular concern to church groups. Before an April 1987 summit between Prime Minister Mulroney and President Reagan, a public letter was sent by the leaders of nine of Canada's most important church denominations, calling for an end to the Nicaraguan civil war and U.S. financial involvement there.

> The cruelty and corruption of the U.S. administration's policy
> of covert action, aid to the Contras and the economic blockade
> of Nicaragua have been exposed . . . the millions of dollars of
> military aid spent each day in El Salvador and Honduras distort
> domestic economies and subvert the dependence of these small
> nations.[17]

This was strong language, and typical of the kind of pressure that the federal government faced from passionately interested groups.   As discussed earlier however, when such humanitarian concerns clashed with the government's perception of the national interest, even if this meant not speaking out on U.S. policy in Central America, the latter option was chosen.

When Secretary of State for External Affairs Joe Clark visited Central America in late 1987, the largest Christian denominations called for Clark to pursue the following policy goals:

1. Speak out publicly against U.S. support for the contras.
2. Increase Canada's aid package to the region and favor those countries with better human rights records, such as Costa Rica and Nicaragua. Link further aid to human rights advancement, compliance with the Contadora peace plan, and economic reforms favoring the poor.
3. Open an embassy in Nicaragua.
4. Call for direct talks between the United States and Nicaragua.
5. Set up a "peace fund" to help defray the costs of meetings, travel, and technical studies associated with creating suggestions for peace.
6. Increase the number of refugees to be admitted to Canada from Central America.

Clark was sympathetic to the calls for increased aid and the promotion of the Contadora peace plan, but he would not go so far as to criticize U.S. policy publicly, nor was a new Central American embassy considered a viable prospect.

In February 1989, on the eve of a visit by President Bush to Ottawa, the Inter-Church Committee on Human Rights in Latin America again wrote to the prime minister. It called on Mulroney to press the new president to seek negotiated political solutions to the Central American conflicts. To that end, the president would be encouraged to endorse the Esquipulas II peace process, initiate direct talks with Nicaragua, end the economic embargo, and normalize relations. In addition, the prime minister was urged to ask President Bush to promote political negotiations between the Salvadorean government and the FMLN insurgents. As before, the prime minister listened politely to the church representatives, but did little of substance, at least publicly.

Soon after, the Inter-Church Committee asked the federal government to stop bilateral aid to Guatemala and El Salvador[18] because of human rights violations there. The government was also urged to monitor closely the deteriorating human rights situation in Honduras.[19] As before, the prime minister was noncommittal, except to say that such a cut-off might hurt the poor the most. Aid to Guatemala and El Salvador had been curtailed, but it was not clear whether this was to punish those countries for their human rights violations or just to protect Canadian aid workers who might otherwise have been sent there. There is merit to this concern, for, as mentioned, several Canadian priests and church workers had been murdered in Guatemala. Thus, while Ottawa was cutting off aid, its local embassies still provided some assistance through mission-administered funds, as did NGOs and Canadian representatives to the International Monetary Fund, the Inter-American Development Bank, and the World Bank. One can argue persuasively then that Canada's suspension of bilateral aid was less damaging than it could have been, given the assistance supplied through other channels.

On the other hand, in February 1986, the government established a standing committee on human rights, as a response to church proposals for an annual parliamentary hearing on the status of human rights-violating countries. However, there is little evidence that the federal government has been responsive to the committee's suggestions with regard to Central America.

According to Matthews, we should not be surprised by this.[20] In a fascinating article he describes the churches as a "counter-consensual" group[21]--that is, a group adhering to values inconsistent with those of the government. The churches view human rights protection as part of a larger effort to promote various political goals. A concern for human rights cannot be purely humanitarian, but is tied to aid-giving and diplomatic relations. The government does not completely ignore the churches, but their goals are so ambitious and inconsistent with Ottawa's perception of the national interest that they are relegated to the margins of political life. By contrast, Matthews argues that corporate interests frequently have more influence with federal authorities because their primary goals of promoting trade and investment are consistent with government policy, whether it be Liberal or Conservative party policy. It is a persuasive argument.

Nevertheless, the churches continue to influence federal government policy in Central America. In November 1989 they sent a high-profile delegation with aid to needy civilians in El Salvador. They also appeared to be successful in convincing government officials to contribute $1 million to their aid program. They were less successful, however, in convincing the Canadian government to urge the United States to end military support to the Salvadorean government, or in getting a government representative to talk directly to the Salvadorean government and the FMLN rebels.

CANADIAN GOVERNMENT POLICY AND CENTRAL AMERICAN REFUGEES

In addition to suggesting strategies for human rights protection in Central America, Canadian church groups also insist that Canadian immigration policymakers be cognizant of the special needs of refugees and Canada's obligations to them.

Canada has long had a reputation as a haven for refugees.[22] Furthermore, it has been a place of permanent settlement, rather than temporary accommodation, for Central Americans. However, its refugee policy had traditionally been conducted on an ad hoc, case-by-case basis rather than by any formal policy.[23]

A 1974 green paper attempted to remedy the situation.[24] It focused on the lack of long-term policy goals or objectives and offered recommendations that became the basis of a new immigration act in 1976 and of subsequent enabling regulations in April 1978. Refugee policy would now be rooted in legal statute. Nevertheless, in the late 1970s and early 1980s, church and labor groups in Canada charged the federal government with not offering Central American refugee claimants the same prompt and generous service that was offered to claimants from other world regions. This was likely due to political and ideological considerations, rather than to discrimination. Various Canadian churches implored the Canadian government to accept thousands of Guatemalan and Salvadorean refugees who could not find sanctuary elsewhere in Central America. As a tentative measure, in March 1981, Canada implemented a limited program enabling Salvadoreans in Canada, who were classified as students or visitors, to remain, temporarily. Nevertheless, in 1981-82, the immigration ministry set aside only 1,000 places for all Latin American refugees. Those eligible for settlement in Canada would include those with family members in Canada, those with a well-founded fear of persecution if sent back to their country of origin, and those unsuited for rural resettlement in Central America due to above-average educational attainments or career background. By 1985 the projected level of places for Latin American and Caribbean refugees doubled to 2,000 mostly skilled professionals who were expected to come from Central America.

One reason for the substantial increase in the number of Central American refugees admitted concerned the plight of a Salvadorean, Victor Regalado, who sought refuge in Canada in January 1982. The Canadian government initially sent him back to the United States from where he faced deportation. His case attracted a great deal of negative publicity in the Canadian press, however, and the government reached an agreement with U.S. customs officials to transfer Regalado back to Canada to face an immigration hearing. It was subsequently revealed that two Canadian cabinet ministers had considered Regalado a security risk for unspecified reasons.

Church groups, trade unions, and the Canadian press protested Regalado's treatment by government officials (he was being held in prison) and by mid-March he was released. The government was thoroughly embarrassed, and serious changes to Canada's immigration policy, including higher levels of refugee acceptance, were ordered.[25]   In mid-1982, a Canadian government fact-finding team toured Central America to assess the need for refugee resettlement, to evaluate Canadian policy in the region, and to study the extent to which Canadian efforts were recognized and applied there. The team concluded that no major resettlement program was necessary. Rather, asylum should be provided to those refugees who would be in physical peril if returned to their native countries.

By the mid-1980s, Central Americans successfully gaining refugee status in Canada continued to increase in number. In 1983-84, for example, 2,810 refugees from El Salvador and 420 refugees from Guatemala were admitted. In 1984-85, 2,344 from El Salvador and 727 from Guatemala successfully gained admittance (out of a global total of 12,000).

A substantial number of those admitted were Salvadoreans who had entered the United States first, but had then been told that they would not be classified as refugees. The position of the Reagan administration was that El Salvador was not a refugee-producing state. Through its consulates in the United States then, Canadian government officials processed and offered entry visas to Salvadoreans who would not have been permitted to stay in the United States.

The 73.1 percent increase in the number of refugees from Guatemala reflected Canada's indignation over the increase in human rights abuses there. Embassy staff in San Jose, Costa Rica, and Guatemala City, Guatemala, were also increased, so that the process whereby refugees could be identified and processed for Canadian settlement was facilitated. In addition, Canada contributed $3 million to the United Nations High Commissioner for Refugees (UNHCR) to help settle refugees in long-term or temporary camps throughout Central America. Working with UNHCR, during 1984 Canada instituted a plan whereby Guatemalans in immediate peril would be sent to Costa Rica for processing and to await entry visas for Canada. Fewer than 100 Guatemalans took advantage of this program, however.

In March 1985 at the 41st session of the United Nations Commission on Human Rights, Canada cosponsored a resolution condemning the human rights situation in Guatemala, and called for improvements. This was not the first time that Canada had taken such a stand, but it was a comparatively rare event. Government policy had consistently favored quiet diplomacy over public denunciation. Also, Canadian government policy was cautious because of a publicly declared wish not to contradict UNHCR objectives in Central America. Officials stressed the desire to settle dislocated individuals in Central America, rather than to move them to distant countries.[26] The government concentrated on admitting to Canada those in immediate danger with little prospect for repatriation. In addition, and as earlier noted, the Canadian government had concentrated its Central American investments in Guatemala, and it was usually reluctant to criticize that country. However, as pressure from domestic groups mounted, and as reports of Guatemalan government atrocities became publicly known, Canada took an increasingly hard-line stance culminating in the government's decision to suspend aid deliveries.[27]

Furthermore, in 1984 Guatemalan refugees to Canada were included in the "political prisoners and operational minorities class" and special measures to facilitate reunification of their families came into effect. Those with close relatives in Canada could now emigrate under relaxed conditions. Those already in Canada could not be sent back. In addition to monitoring the distressing human rights situation in Guatemala, a team of independent Canadian observers judged the November-December 1985 Guatemalan elections to be fair and honest. Interestingly, no official observers were sent to the November 1984 elections in Nicaragua. Canada was not willing to take an action that was likely to irritate the United States, such as sending observers and thereby helping to legitimize the elections. Also, in 1985 Canada resumed its aid to El Salvador, another U.S. ally.

In January 1987 the Department of External Affairs issued a policy statement focusing on its view of Canadian human rights concerns in Central America.[28] With regard to El Salvador, the ministry emphasized its interest in promoting multilateral and bilateral efforts to ameliorate abuses. It announced that aid to El Salvador, which was suspended in 1979, would be resumed. This action was in response to elections in El Salvador in 1984, which Canadian officials considered legitimate, and a devastating earthquake in October 1986, which displaced hundreds. Furthermore, government officials noted reductions in human rights abuses under President Duarte, although some abuses continued and remained reprehensible to Canadians. Nevertheless, Canada would not allow the victims of human rights abuses, often the poorest in society, to be deprived of outside help.

With regard to Nicaragua, Canadian officials were concerned about the suspension of certain basic civil rights under the state of emergency there. They deplored the closing of the newspaper *La Prensa* and the harassment of opposition groups and the church. *La Prensa* has resumed publishing and the harassment no longer exists.

Canada's strongest position has been in regard to human rights violations in Guatemala. Canadian developmental aid to that country was suspended for many years. However, the Cerezo government made major attempts to curtail the abuses of the military, and met with mixed success. Labor and human rights groups began to operate fairly freely. Hundreds of Guatemalan refugees in Mexico returned to their native country as threats to their safety diminished. Nevertheless, persecution of left-wing dissidents and of Indians continued.

THE VOLATILE REFUGEE DETERMINATION ISSUE

In 1986 Canada accepted 3,000 refugees from Central America. The Department of External Affairs recommended that Canada be generous in providing sanctuary to these refugee claimants and that it extend an oral hearing to all of them.[29] Canada's attitude toward refugees did not go unnoticed. In October 1986 the nation was given the United Nations' Fridt Nansen Award in recognition of its work in protecting and assisting refugees. The U.N. High Commissioner for Refugees, Jean-Pierre Hocke, said that Canada deserved the award because of "the humanitarian impulse that lies behind the welcome traditionally extended to refugees." When the United States decided to crack down on illegal aliens there, Canadian immigration officials were forced to test this generosity. From January 1987 to February 10, 1987, for example, 1,884 Salvadoreans and 467 Guatemalans from the United States sought refugee status in Canada, compared with a total of 170 during July-August 1986.[30] Salvadorean and Guatemalan refugees in Canada could work under a minister's visa until their claims were settled. External Affairs Minister Clark stated that "the American position was inappropriate . . . we have greatly deplored the failure of the United States to provide safe haven for people internationally recognized as in need of it."[31]

However, on February 20, 1987, the government announced two bills, C-55 and C-84, which called Canada's goodwill into question, at least according to its critics. These bills were introduced by Immigration Minister Benoit Bouchard to eliminate bogus refugee claimants, clear up the backlog of unprocessed claims, and institute a more efficient and streamlined system. Critics of the legislation charged that genuine refugees would be deported and their sponsors penalized. Those who would be most vulnerable would be Central American refugee claimants fleeing repression in El Salvador and Guatemala. As per the new legislation, refugee claimants arriving at the Canadian border would be temporarily returned to the United States while waiting for their cases to be heard in Canada. Canadian government officials insisted that guarantees had been obtained from U.S. immigration authorities that refugee claimants would not be deported to their countries of origin and would be allowed to return for their hearings in Canada. U.S. officials denied that any such arrangement existed, however, and outlined conditions whereby claimants might be deported. Such conditions might emerge if an alien had a criminal record, was a possible security risk, or was facing a final order of deportation. Clearly, a serious situation was made worse by the mixed signals coming from Canada and the United States.

The Canadian government's new immigration policy was troubling for other reasons as well. The so-called B-1 category of immigrants, which often applied to Guatemalans and Salvadoreans, was abolished. Formerly, citizens of these countries arriving in Canada could not be sent back to their native countries against their will, on ethical grounds. This safeguard was eliminated. In addition, refugee claimants to Canada who were temporarily in the United States could be sent back to the United States if no refugee adjudicator was available to process their claim. This was a frequent occurrence, given the small number of adjudicators. Canadian refugee policies were being portrayed as morally insensitive in much of the nation's press.

Furthermore, in May 1987 the Mulroney government established a new refugee determination process which included:

1. A streamlined process cutting the stages of hearings, inquiries and appeals from eight to three.
2. The completion of claims in under six months rather than the existing system's taking three to five years.
3. The establishment of a nonadversarial refugee board.

Refugee claimants would now have to convince an immigration adjudicator and a refugee board member that their cases had merit before they could be considered by the full refugee board. In addition, claimants would now be required to prove that prior to coming to Canada they had not had an opportunity to make a refugee claim elsewhere. In this regard the United States was used as an example of a "safe" country where refugee claimants might have first tried to claim refugee status.

Opposition critics, church leaders and other NGOs lambasted the government policy, charging it with callousness toward refugee rights, and predicting that access to Canada for legitimate refugees would now be restricted. Since the acceptance rate of Central Americans by the United States was only 2 percent, for example, as opposed to nearly 50 percent in Canada, Canadian bureaucrats would be allowing American officials to deport genuine claimants back to face persecution and possibly death. Other criticisms focused on the increased difficulties in obtaining a hearing before an independent body and a subsequent appeal, if necessary; the fact that the burden of proof had now shifted to refugee claimants; and the greater chance that legitimate refugees would be denied the right to work or attend school in Canada. Taken together, opponents of the Canadian policy worried that access to Canada for Central Americans in the United States would sharply diminish. Indeed, New Democratic party member of parliament Michael Cassidy suggested that Canada should return the Nansen medal "because we will no longer deserve it."[32]

The government's position was that the new immigration policy would stem the flood of phony refugees--not turn away those who were fleeing persecution in their homelands. Officials stressed that the stricter measures were necessary because refugee claims had swelled in 1986-87, creating a major backlog of individual claims. In addition, as other nations tightened their immigration laws, Canada was unable to accept all the refugees who were affected. In fact, Canada's actions compared favorably to those taken in the United States and most European countries. From December 1986 to February 1987, 10,000 refugees, most of whom were from Central America, entered Canada. Most were avoiding U.S. immigration laws. The numbers began to dwindle--to 273 in March and 191 in April--after Canada's new immigration policy went into effect. Hundreds were left stranded in halfway houses and church convents along the border.

In August 1987 it had become clear that Canada's new policy had not escaped the attention of outside observers. The High Commissioner for Refugees at the United Nations in Geneva, Jean-Pierre Hocke, wrote to the Canadian government to say that the refugee bill "could risk exposing bonafide asylum seekers and refugees to forcible return to territories where their lives or freedom would be threatened."[33]

In the House of Commons the next day, Immigration Minister Bouchard insisted that the legislation did not violate the U.N. policy on refugees. Public opinion polls in Canada revealed widespread support for the government's refugee bill, to the extent that it could prevent abuses. The bill was far from universally popular, however. Many religious and other human rights leaders, the federal opposition parties, and a few conservative members of parliament voiced opposition to the government's refugee stance on various grounds including partisanship, fairness, and the possible unconstitutionality of the legislation.

A committee representing various human rights, legal, church, women's, multicultural, and academic organizations appealed to the government for changes to the refugee bill. The appeal stated: "One thing must be understood by all Canadians. . . . If this bill is passed, it is certain that genuine refugees will be deported from Canada to situations where their lives or liberty will be in danger."[34]

The committee said that the system for processing refugees must ensure the following conditions:

1.   All those who claim refugee status have the right to state their case before an independent refugee board.
2.   All decisions must be rendered rapidly.
3.   All government officials must comply with Canada's international obligations under the Geneva convention on refugees.

Critics maintained that the existing legislation did not meet these standards. The government was unmoved by these concerns, however. Its position was strengthened in July 1987, when a boatload of Sikh immigrants seeking refugee status landed in Canada. Government officials stressed that these people, and others from all over the world, would flood Canada's borders unless steps were taken to carefully screen their entry. Many Canadians spoke out in favor of the government's position and the refugee legislation. The immediate result was that Central American immigration to Canada continued to drop.

In September the federal government declared that henceforth, all travelers from Honduras would have to obtain visas before entering Canada. This would help to stem the tide of illegal refugees from that country, the government spokesman declared. Refugee aid groups charged that the new requirements would also prevent genuine refugees from being able to enter Canada. Nevertheless, the government refused to back down, and the refugee bill was subsequently passed into law, with a few modifications, in July 1988. It took effect on January 1, 1989. Church groups pledged to fight it in the courts.

To many critics, the new refugee legislation revealed a harsher government immigration policy. Clearly, Canada would no longer be a nation of first asylum for many refugee applicants. To supporters of the Mulroney strategy, however, the legislation was fair, and more efficient than earlier laws. Bogus refugee claimants would be weeded out and the processing time of refugees would be reduced. The legislation remains controversial at this writing; it continues to be debated in parliament, in the courts, and in the mass media.

It should be stressed that Canadians' interest in human rights issues increased in the 1980s. In a 1985 poll published by Decima Research, only 7 percent of Canadians felt that the Canadian government should make human rights a high priority. By 1987, however, a North-South Institute poll revealed that 68 percent of respondents endorsed Canadian government protests when human rights abuses took place. In addition, 86 percent of Canadians believed that human rights were an important issue for the country.[35] This did not go unnoticed by the federal government, for in December 1987 it announced that it was creating a Crown corporation, the International Center for Human Rights and Democratic Development, to promote development strategies and encourage democratic practice in various countries around the world. (The center was officially established in September 1988.) Furthermore, in October 1987 Canadian government officials, at the meeting of the United Nations High Commission for Refugees (UNHCR) Executive Committee, argued for increased efforts toward more equitable burden-sharing among all states directly or indirectly involved in assisting refugees. Between 1982 and 1987 Canada had admitted 15,877 refugees from Central America, most of whom (11,251) originated in El Salvador. Under special programs for relatives and immediate dependents of refugees, a further 4,444 civilians were granted refugee status in Canada, bringing the five-year total to 20,955.

In late 1988 unprecedented numbers of Nicaraguans (3,564) sought refuge in Canada after escaping the ravages of Hurricane Joan. Many were also seeking a higher economic standard of living. Others sought to avoid mandatory military service. To this point, Nicaraguans did not need visas to enter Canada, but because of the deluge of refugee applicants, new Canadian Immigration Minister Barbara McDougall announced that henceforth, Nicaraguans would need visitors' visas. She argued that such a measure was necessary because "the integrity of our immigration laws must be maintained."[36]

In addition, in March 1989 the government decided to deport two Salvadorean refugee claimants, despite major opposition from such groups as Oxfam Canada, Vigil, and the Inter-Church Committee for Human Rights in Latin America. Spokesmen for these organizations charged that Canada should not send people back to a political environment characterized by repression and violence. Indeed, they maintained that, those deported would be particularly vulnerable to the Salvadorean "death squads." McDougall acknowledged that human rights abuses in El Salvador had increased since the election of the Arena party to government in March, and that Canadian immigration officials would be particularly sensitive to the plight of Salvadorean and Guatemalan refugee applicants. But the Canadian government's "get tough" policy on the matter would stand.

Clearly, the Canadian policy was intended to deter a majority of the potential refugee claimants from seeking entry into Canada. Skilled workers would be strongly favored. Those applying on humanitarian grounds and possessing few skills applicable to the Canadian work force would be at a disadvantage. The Mulroney government stressed that belt-tightening in every department, but especially Employment and Immigration, was necessary. Government officials maintained that Central Americans with access to air travel would continue to arrive at Canadian border points unless steps were taken to curb their interest in resettling in Canada. Between January and June of 1989, 6,522 people worldwide had applied for refugee status in Canada. Of that number, 406 had withdrawn their claims or had them rejected, and of those, 115 were deported. It was estimated that only 15,000 would seek refugee status in Canada by the end of 1989, down from 35,000 in 1988. However, 90 percent of the new claimants would be allowed to settle in Canada.

Canada's new refugee determination process has attracted criticism from a variety of groups. Even though Canadian refugee determination process is more compassionate than those of most other Western industrialized countries, there lies a hint of racism, albeit undebated and even unsuggested. Traditionally, Eastern European immigrants sought refuge in Canada, but in the 1980s people from all over the developing world were applying to be admitted. Furthermore, these applicants were often unskilled and, at least in the short run, unsuited for the demands of the industrialized Canadian work force. Presumably, many Canadians were also concerned about the impact of so many people with different backgrounds on the Canadian social fabric. Only reactionary right-wing groups like Canadians for Foreign Aid Reform (C-FAR) or the Immigration Association of Canada have explicitly expressed such sentiments. However, a substantial minority of Canadians see refugees from the Third World as a long-term burden on society and would prefer to see immigration, when absolutely necessary, from predominantly "white" European countries. They also insist that those admitted should be entrepreneurs who would be prepared to invest capital in Canada and employ Canadians.[37]

In general, it seems clear that Canada's tougher immigration policy reflects a fear that too many bogus refugees are crippling the refugee determination system and taxing the nation's diminishing social service benefits. To many Canadians, these claimants seem to be fleeing their countries for economic reasons, rather than because of genuine concerns about their safety. Undoubtedly there is some truth to this. On the other hand, legitimate refugees from strife-torn El Salvador and Guatemala are discovering that Canada is not the haven that it once was. There is an increased possibility of deportation. Once refugees are safely admitted into the country, discrimination in the work place and elsewhere may also become a problem, in an era of budget cutting and layoffs.

Canada's religious and trade union leaders have been in the forefront of those striving to provide more sanctuaries, reduce bureaucratic tie-ups, and facilitate transitions to Canadian society for Central American refugees. Their influence has been profound, but their task has been made more difficult by the most recent refugee legislation. Particularly unfortunate for those legitimate refugees who must now consider other destinations is the fact that there are so few other places to choose. Most European nations and the United States have stricter immigration laws than does Canada. Honduras, Costa Rica, and Mexico are struggling to accommodate the refugees that they already have.

All Western industrialized nations are facing budget cutbacks of varying magnitudes, and services tailored to the needs of refugees are an easy expense to cut. Nevertheless, immigration pressures are likely to increase in the 1990s. Furthermore, in Canada, as in most nations, there is no evidence to suggest that refugees and immigrants inhibit economic growth. Indeed, they usually enhance it by working diligently and frequently employing Canadian-born citizens. Nevertheless, for reasons of discrimination, and because of the perception that native-born Canadians are vulnerable to job loss, politicians in many countries have created measures designed to reduce immigration. In the Canadian context such actions threaten to limit economic growth, feed existing xenophobic tendencies, and contribute to reduced population increases at a time when Canada has one of the lowest population growths in the world. Ultimately, tough immigration laws contribute to a reduced quality of life for all Canadians.

NOTES

1. It should be acknowledged that certain trade unions and church leaders wrote to the Department of External Affairs in 1978 calling for Canada to break off relations with the repressive Somoza regime in Nicaragua and the Garcia regime in Guatemala. It was the events in 1979 that really captured the attention of Canadian pressure groups, however.

2. Indeed, a small number of Canadian clerics have also been murdered in Guatemala. For a discussion, see Peter McFarlane, *Northern Shadows: Canadians and Central America* (Toronto: Between the Lines, 1989), pp. 179-83.

3. The most prominent Canadian interest groups and the cities in which they are located include: The Inter-Church Committee on Human Rights in Latin America (Toronto); Canadian-Caribbean-Central American Policy Alternatives group (Toronto); Latin American Working Group (Toronto); Canadian Labour Congress (Ottawa); Christian Task Force on Central America (Vancouver); The Canadian Congress of Catholic Bishops (Toronto); Centre de Documentation d'Amérique Latine (Montreal), Canadian Association for Latin America and the Caribbean (Toronto) (since dissolved); Development Education Information and Resource Centre (Halifax); The Marquis Project (Brandon, Manitoba); Tools for Peace (Toronto); Canadian Hispanic Congress (Toronto); Canadian Action for Nicaragua (Toronto); Commission des Droits Humains de Guatemala (Montreal); Toronto Guatemala Solidarity Committee (Toronto); Salvaid (Toronto); The Human Rights Commission of El Salvador (Toronto); National Federation of Salvadorean Workers Unions (Toronto).

4. For example, see the statement by ICCHRLA entitled "An Opportunity for Canadian Action: Canadian Government Policy and the Crisis in Central America," a public statement by the Canadian churches (March 23, 1982).

5. The *Globe and Mail*, (December 24, 1983), as reprinted in *Brief on Canada and Central America* (Toronto: CAPA, March 29, 1984), p. 23.

6. For an excellent discussion of the relationship between CIDA and NGOs, see a booklet published by the Latin American Working Group entitled "Overview of Canadian Aid to Central America: 1980-85," 9:3 (February 1988).

7. For a discussion of this point, see Liisa North, *Negotiations for Peace in Central America*, (Ottawa: CIIPS, September 27-28, 1985). For an excellent discussion of the structure and mandate of Canada's NGOs worldwide, see Tim Brodhead et al., *Bridges of Hope? Canadian Voluntary Agencies and the Third World* (Ottawa: The North-South Institute, 1988).

8. For some examples of this networking see Jutta Teigeler, "Foreign Aid and NGOs," *International Perspectives* (March/April 1988), pp. 21-23.

9. Liisa North, *Negotiations for Peace in Central America*.

10. As quoted in *Maclean's* (Feb. 23, 1987), pp. 26-27.

11.   James Rochlin, "Aspects of Canadian Foreign Policy Towards Central America, 1979-1986," *Journal of Canadian Studies*, 22:4 (Winter 1987-88), p. 17.

12.   *Washington Report on the Hemisphere* (Nov. 9, 1987).

13.   For a full discussion of the church's role and interests in Latin America, see John R. Williams (ed.), *Canadian Churches and Social Justice* (Toronto: Lorimer, 1984), pp. 241-50.   For a more recent, if more limited, discussion, see Peter McFarlane, *Northern Shadows: Canadians and Central America* (Toronto: Between the Lines, 1989), chaps. 11, 12, and 14.

14.   Task Force on the Churches and Corporate Responsibility, "The compartmentalization of the promotion of human rights," a paper presented at the Canadian Caucus on Human Rights (Ottawa, Dec. 8-11, 1983).

15.   For a broad overview of the church's involvement in Nicaragua, see a booklet published by the Latin American Working Group entitled "Overview of Canadian Aid to Central America 1980-85," (February 1988), p. 24.

16.   This point is discussed in a brief by CAPA entitled "From Acquiescence to Action" (Toronto, 1984).

17.   See the public letter from the Inter-Church Committee on Human Rights in Latin America to the prime minister of Canada (Toronto; March 11, 1987).

18.   For a good discussion of the Catholic church's interest in human rights abuses in El Salvador, see Bonnie Greene (ed.) *Canadian Churches and Foreign Policy* (Toronto: Lorimer, 1990), pp. 130-72.

19.   This is of particular interest because the Canadian church has always held a substantial degree of influence in Honduras.   Since the 1950s, Honduras has been a prime target of Canadian church missionary efforts.   The Catholic church built and staffed the Honduran National Seminary and sent many priests and nuns to work in Honduras.   Indeed, in 1984 a Quebec missionary, Raoul Corriveau, was appointed bishop to the Southern Honduras Diocese of Chulateca.

20.   Robert Matthews, "The Christian Churches and Human Rights in Canadian Foreign Policy," *Journal of Canadian Studies* 24:1 (Spring 1989), pp. 5-31.

21.   This is a term borrowed from Cranford Pratt, "Dominant Class Theory and Canadian Foreign Policy: The Case of the Counter-Consensus," *International Journal* 39:1 (Winter 1983-84), pp. 127-29.

22.   For a discussion of a notable and despicable exception--Canada's reluctance to admit European Jews during World War II--see Harold

Troper and Irving Abella, *None Is Too Many* (Toronto: Lester and Orpen Dennys Ltd., 1982).

23. For a discussion of Canada's ad hoc immigration policy until 1978, see Freda Hawkins, *Canada and Immigration: Public Policy and Public Concern*, 2d ed. (Montreal: McGill-Queen's University Press, 1988); or Gerald Dirk's "A Policy within a Policy: The Identification and Admission of Refugees to Canada," *Canadian Journal of Political Science* 17:2 (June 1984), pp. 279-307.

24. Canadian Department of Manpower and Immigration, *A Report of the Canadian Immigration and Population Study*, 4 vols. (Ottawa: Information Canada, 1974).

25. For a more complete discussion of the Regalado episode and subsequent developments, see Peter McFarlane, *Northern Shadows*, pp. 199-203.

26. See the statement by the minister for employment and immigration to this effect in the House of Commons, *Debates* (November 5, 1981), pp. 12, 534-35.

27. Canada's condemnation of Guatemalan human rights violations during the early 1980s, and related issues, are discussed by Steven Baranyi, "Canadian Foreign Policy Towards Central America, 1980-84: Independence, Limited Public Influence, and State Leadership," *Canadian Journal of Latin American and Caribbean Studies*, 10:19 (1985), pp. 23-57.

28. The statement was entitled "Consultations in preparation for the 43rd session of the U.N. Commission on Human Rights, Jan. 28-29, 1987."

29. See *Canada's International Relations,* published by the Department of External Affairs (Ottawa, 1986).

30. Susan Delacourt, "Refugee Claimants pouring into Canada from U.S.," *Globe and Mail* (February 12, 1987), p. A-4.

31. Ibid, p. A-4.

32. Christopher Neal, "Critics Slam Planned Refugee Curb," *Ottawa Citizen* (May 6, 1987), pp. A1-A2.

33. "U.N. Criticizes Canada for Refugee Bill," *Montreal Gazette* (August 15, 1987), p. A-1.

34. "Refugee Bill Fundamentally Flawed, Prominent Citizens Say," *Montreal Gazette* (September 1987).

35. The North-South Institute, *Review '87, Outlook '88* (Ottawa, 1988), p. 11.

36. As quoted in the *Montreal Gazette* (November 29, 1988).

37. For a discussion of the underlying racism associated with this issue, see "Phone-ins, Polls Bristle with Anti-Immigration Feeling," *Globe*

and Mail (March 6, 1987); or the poll revealing that only 27 percent of Canadians think that "most people who now apply as refugees are legitimate," *Toronto Star* (June 3, 1987).

Conclusion

The 1980s have been characterized by a new Canadian interest in Central America. Once at the bottom of Canada's foreign policy priorities, it has now become a major area of interest. Canadian non-governmental organizations, policy-makers, the mass media and the public have discovered an enormous reservoir of interest for what had long been regarded as an American concern.

Several explanations for this turnaround are evident. First, former Prime Minister Trudeau's emphasis on North-South concerns inspired a measure of interest in the early 1980s. Second, a desire to distinguish Canadian from American foreign policy inspired some concern for the region. Perhaps a sense that Canadians saw themselves as dependent on the U.S., much like Central Americans, promoted a common Canadian-Central American identity. The presence of a small number of Central Americans living permanently in Canada might also have had some effect.

Most important, however, was a perception that Canada could make a legitimate difference in Central America. Canadians believed that their development aid, peacekeepers and advice could be useful. They sensed that Canada could help to ameliorate the region's poverty and instability. It remains to be seen how realistic this perception is, but this cannot detract from the fact that many Canadians now demand that their government pursue a purposeful strategy in Central America.

As noted earlier in this study, Canadian officials have diverged from their American counterparts only in their relations with Nicaragua. Canada had not recognized the U.S. embargo of Nicaragua under the Sandinista government. They had provided a substantial amount of developmental and emergency aid to that country. They had pursued limited commercial opportunities with the Sandinista government and allowed a Nicaraguan trade office to open in Toronto. Canada also provided election observers and policy advice to Nicaragua. All of these policy strategies met with widespread support from every sector of Canadian society. The United States took no action to contravene the Canadian policy, nor should any have been expected, based on past experience.

The Canadian government is thus likely to pursue the following strategies in Central America. First, it will seek to exert influence through the OAS. It will soon discover however that the largest hemispheric organization is regarded as largely unimportant and illegitimate by the veteran members of the organization. As a result, they will seek influence through other multilateral organizations (United Nations, Inter-American Development Bank) and bilateral institutions.

The Mulroney government will investigate various commercial opportunities in Central America, but may likely discover that the regions' underdevelopment and instability mitigate against a substantial level of business involvement. A more promising area of Canadian involvement might be as a donor of development aid and advice. There is evidence to suggest that some Central American leaders are aware of Canada's contribution. Certainly this aspect of Canada's involvement has met with popular approval at home.

Canada has provided military troops and supplies under the rubric of the United Nations. It is not clear how integral these contributions to peace and political stability in the region will be, but there is no doubt that Canadians are supportive of the peace process. Indeed, the aggressive lobbying of various church groups, trade unions and other NGOs suggests that many Canadians would like to be more active in the region. Their particular interest, of course, is to protect and promote human rights in Central America. It is hoped that Canada's fairly admirable human rights record, notwithstanding its periodic violation of the rights of aboriginal Canadians or the existence of certain language abuses in Quebec and elsewhere, would serve as a model for the fledgling democracies of Central America.

Overall, it can be safely argued that Canada's recent interest and support of the Central American peace process is an admirable development. Whether Canada's influence will make a difference remains to be seen. But the Canadian interest in Central America is an indication that its concerns have finally extended beyond its more familiar interests in the United States and Western Europe. Perhaps this is a sign that Canada is finally taking a more global focus. If so, the Canadian government may become a more determined and effective player on the world stage. On the other hand, it should not be forgotten that Canadian foreign policymakers must understand the realities of realpolitik. Canada will not take an action that might hinder its vital interests with the United States, notwithstanding the absence of a history of policy linkage. Canadian decision-makers must also recognize that for all of their goodwill towards Central America, as a middle power there are limits to what can be accomplished. The Canadian public may have high hopes for their government's policy in Central America, but they must understand that there are limits to their nations' foreign policy independence. These high expectations will pose difficult challenges for Canadian policymakers, who will be forced to walk a fine line between meeting the high aspirations of their constituents while simultaneously pursuing a realistic foreign policy agenda.

Appendix A: Excerpts from the Draft Contadora Treaty

CHAPTER III
COMMITMENTS WITH REGARD TO SECURITY MATTERS

In conformity with their obligations under international law and in accordance with the objective of laying the foundation for effective and lasting peace, the Parties assume commitments with regard to security matters relating to the prohibition of international military manoeuvres; the cessation of the arms build-up; the dismantling of military foreign bases, schools or other installations; the withdrawal of foreign military advisers and other foreign elements participating in military or security activities; the prohibition of the traffic in arms; the cessation of support for irregular forces; the denial of encouragement or support for acts of terrorism, subversion or sabotage; and lastly, the establishment of a regional system of direct communication.

To that end, the Parties undertake to take specific action in accordance with the following:

Section 1. COMMITMENTS WITH REGARD TO MILITARY MANOEUVRES

16. To comply with the following provisions as regards the holding of national military manoeuvres, with effect from the signing of this Act;

    (a) When national military manoeuvres are held in areas less than 30 kilometres from the territory of another State, the appropriate prior notification to the other States Parties and the Verification and Control Commission, mentioned in Part II of this Act, shall be made at least 30 days beforehand.

    (b) The notification shall contain the following information:

        (1) Name;

        (2) Purpose;

        (3) Participating troops, units and forces;

        (4) Area where the manoeuvre is scheduled;

(5) Programme and timetable;

(6) Equipment and weapons to be used.

(c) Invitations shall be issued to observers from neighbouring States Parties.

17. To comply with the following provisions as regards the holding of international military manoeuvres.

1. From the entry into force of the Act and for a period of 90 days, the holding of international military manoeuvres involving the presence in their respective territories of armed forces belonging to States from outside the Central American region shall be suspended.

2. After the 90 days, the Parties may, by mutual agreement and taking into account the recommendations of the Verification and Control Commission, extend the suspension until such time as the maximum limits for armaments and troop strength are reached, in accordance with the provisions of paragraph 19 of this Chapter. If no agreement is reached on extending the suspension, international military manoeuvres shall be subject, during this period, to the following regulations:

(a) The Parties shall ensure that manoeuvres involve no form of intimidation against a Central American State or any other State;

(b) They shall give at least 30 days' notice of the holding of manoeuvres to the States Parties and to the Verification and Control Commission referred to in Part II of this Act. The notification shall contain the following information:

(1) Name;

(2) Purpose;

(3) Participating States;

(4) Participating troops, units and forces;

(5) Area where the manoeuvre is scheduled;

(6) Programme and timetable;

(7) Equipment and weapons to be used.

(c) They shall not be held within a 50 kilometre belt adjacent to the territory of a State which is not participating, unless that State gives its express consent;

(d) The Parties shall limit manoeuvres to one a year; it shall last not longer than 15 days;

(e) They shall limit to 3,000 the total number of military troops participating in a manoeuvre. Under no circumstances shall the number of troops of other States exceed the number of nationals participating in a manoeuvre;

(f) Observers from the States Parties shall be invited;

(g) A State Party which believes that there has been a violation of the above provisions may resort to the Verification and Control Commission.

3. Once the maximum limits for armaments and troop strength have been reached in accordance with the provisions of paragraph 19 of this Chapter, the holding of international military manoeuvres involving the participation of States from outside the Central American regional shall be prohibited.

4. From the entry into force of this Act, the holding of international manoeuvres with the participation exclusively of Central American States in their respective territories shall be subject to the following provisions:

   (a) Participating States shall give at least 45 days' notice of the holding of manoeuvres to the States Parties and to the Verification and Control Commission referred to in Part II of this Act. The notification shall contain the following information:

       (1) Name;

       (2) Purpose;

       (3) Participating States;

       (4) Participating troops, units and forces;

       (5) Area where the manoeuvre is scheduled;

       (6) Programme and timetable;

       (7) Equipment and weapons to be used.

   (b) the manoeuvres shall not be held within a 50 kilometre belt adjacent to the territory of a State that is not participating, unless that State gives its express consent;

   (c) The conduct of manoeuvres shall be limited to 30 days a year. If several manoeuvres are held each year, each manoeuvre shall last not longer than 15 days;

   (d) They shall limit to 4,000 the total number of military troops participating in manoeuvres;

   (e) Obsereverers from the States Parties shall be invited;

   (f) A State Party which believes that there has been a violation of the above provisions may resort to the Verification and Control Commission.

5. Commitments with regard to international military manoeuvres shall be subject to the provisions of paragraph 19 of this Chapter.

Section 2. COMMITMENTS WITH REGARD TO ARMAMENTS AND TROOP STRENGTH

18. To halt the arms race in all its forms and begin immediately negotiations permitting the establishment of maximum limits for armaments and the number of troops under arms, as well as their control and reduction, with the object of establishing a reasonable balance of forces in the area.

19. On the basis of the foregoing, the Parties agree on the following implementation of stages:

FIRST STAGE

(a) The Parties undertake not to acquire, after the entry into force of the Act, any more military *matériel*, with the exception of replenishment supplies, ammunition and spare parts needed to keep existing *matériel* in operation, and not to increase their military forces, pending the establishment of the maximum limits for military development within the time-limit stipulated for the second stage.

(b) The Parties undertake to submit simultaneously to the Verification and Control Commission their respective current inventories of weapons, military installations and troops under arms within 15 days of the entry into force of this Act.

The inventories shall be prepared in accordance with the definitions and basic criteria contained in the annex to this Act;

(c) Within 60 days of the entry into force of this Act, the Verification and Control Commission shall conclude the technical studies and shall suggest to the States Parties, without prejudice to any negotiations which they have agreed to initiate, the maximum limits for their military development, in accordance with the basic criteria laid down in paragraph 20 of this section and in accordance with the respective timetables for reduction and dismantling.

SECOND STAGE

After a period of 60 days from the entry into force of this Act, the Parties shall establish within the following 30 days:

(a) Maximum limits for the types of weapons classified in the annex to this Act, as well as timetables for their reduction.

(b) Maximum limits for troops and military installations which each party may have, as well as timetables for their reduction or dismantling.

(c) If the Parties do not reach agreement on the above-mentioned maximum limits and timetables within such period, those suggested by the Verification and Control Commission in its technical studies shall apply provisionally, with the prior consent of the Parties. The Parties shall set by mutual agreement a new time-limit for the negotiation and establishment of the above-mentioned limits.

Should the Parties fail to reach agreement on maximum limits, they shall suspend execution of the commitments with regard to international military manoeuvres, foreign military bases and installations and foreign military advisers for which time-limits have been set in the Act, except in cases where the Parties agree otherwise.

The maximum limits referred to in subparagraphs (a), (b) and (c) and the timetables shall be regarded as an integral part of this Act and shall have the same legally binding force from the day following expiry of the 30 days established for the second stage or the day following their establishment by agreement among the Parties.

Unless the parties agree otherwise, under subparagraph (c) the maximum agreed limits shall be reached 180 days after the entry into force of the Act or in a period established by the Parties.

20. In order to satisfy the requirements of peace, stability, security and economic and social development of the countries of the region and in order to establish maximum limits for the military development of the Central American States and to control and reduce their military levels, the Parties will agree on a table of values that will consider the following basic criteria and in which all armaments will be subject to control and reduction:

   (1) Security needs and defence capacity of each Central American State;

   (2) Size of its territory and population;

   (3) Length and characteristics of its borders;

   (4) Military spending in relation to gross domestic product (GDP);

   (5) Military budget in relation to public spending and other social indicators;

   (6) Military technology, relative combat capability, troops, quality and quantity of installations and military resources;

   (7) Armaments subject to control, armaments subject to reduction;

   (8) Foreign military presence and foreign advisers in each Central American State.

21. Not to introduce new weapons sytems that alter the quality or quantity of current inventories of war *materiél*.

22. Not to introduce, possess or use lethal chemical weapons or biological, radiological or other weapons which may be deemed to be excessively injurious or to have indiscriminate effects.

23. Not to permit the transit through, stationing, or mobilization in, or any other form of utilization of their territories by foreign armed forces whose actions could mean a threat to the independence, sovereignty and territorial integrity of any Central American State.

24. To initiate constitutional procedures so as to be in a position to sign, ratify or accede to treaties and other international agreements on disarmament, if they have not already done so.

Section 3. COMMITMENTS WITH REGARD TO FOREIGN MILITARY BASES

25. To close down any foreign military bases, schools or installations in their respective territories, as defined in paragraphs 11, 12 and 13 of the annex, within 180 days of the signing of this Act. For that purpose, the parties undertake to submit simultaneously to the Verification and Control Commission, within 15 days of the signing of this Act, a list of such foreign military bases, schools or installations, which shall be prepared in accordance with the criteria set forth in the above-mentioned paragraphs of the annex.

26. Not to authorize in their respective territories the establishment of foreign bases, schools or other installations of a military nature.

Section 4. COMMITMENTS WITH REGARD TO FOREIGN MILITARY ADVISERS

27. To submit to the Verification and Control Commission a list of any foreign military advisers or other foreign elements participating in military, paramilitary and security

activities in their territory, within 15 days of the signing of this Act. In the preparation of the list, account shall be taken of the definitions set forth in paragraph 14 of the annex.

28. To withdraw, within a period of not more than 180 days from the signing of this Act and in accordance with the studies and recommendations of the Verification and Control Commission, any foreign military advisers and other foreign elements likely to participate in military, paramilitary and security activities.

29. As for advisers performing technical functions related to the installation and maintenance of military equipment, a control register shall be maintained in accordance with the terms laid down in the respective contracts or agreements. On the basis of that register, the Verification and Control Commission shall propose to the Parties reasonable limits on the number of such advisers, within the time-limit established in paragraph 27 above. The agreed limits shall form an integral part of the Act.

Section 5.   COMMITMENTS WITH REGARD TO THE TRAFFIC IN ARMS

30. To stop the illegal flow of arms, as defined in paragraph 15 of the annex, towards persons, organizations, irregular forces or armed bands trying to destabilize the Governments of the States Parties.

31. To establish for that purpose control mechanisms at airports, landing strips, harbours, terminals and border crossings, on roads, air routes, sea lanes and waterways, and at any other point or in any other area likely to be used for the traffic in arms.

32. On the basis of presumption or established facts, to report any violations to the Verification and Control Commission, with sufficient evidence to enable it to carry out the necessary investigation and submit such conclusions and recommendations as it may consider useful.

Section 6.   COMMITMENTS WITH REGARD TO THE PROHIBITION OF SUPPORT FOR IRREGULAR FORCES

33. To refrain from giving any political, military, financial or other support to individuals, groups, irregular forces or armed bands advocating the overthrow or destabilization of other Governments, and to prevent, by all means at their disposal, the use of their territory for attacks on another state or for the organization of attacks, acts of sabotage, kidnappings or criminal activities in the territory of another State.

34. To exercise strict control over their respective borders, with a view to preventing their own territory from being used to carry out any military actions against a neighbouring State.

35. To deny the use of and dismantle installations, equipment and facilities providing logistical support or serving operational functions in their territory, if the latter is used for acts against neighbouring Governments.

36. To disarm and remove from the border area any group or irregular force identified as being responsible for acts against a neighbouring State. Once the irregular forces have been disbanded, to proceed, with the financial and logistical support for international organizations and Governments interested in bringing peace to Central America, to relocate them or return then to their respective countries, in accordance with the conditions laid down by the Governments concerned.

37. On the basis of presumption or established facts, to report any violations to the
     Verification and Control Commission, with sufficient evidence to enable it to carry
     out the necessary investigation and submit such conclusions and recommendations as
     it may consider useful.

Section 7. COMMITMENTS WITH REGARD TO TERRORISM, SUBVERSION OR SABOTAGE

38. To refrain from giving political, military, financial or any other support for acts of
     subversion, terrorism or sabotage intended to destabilize or overthrow Governments
     of the region.

39. To refrain from organizing, instigating or participating in acts of terrorism, subversion
     or sabotage in another Stage, or acquiescing in organized activities within their
     territory directed towards the commission of such criminal acts.

40. To abide by the following treaties and international agreements:

     (a) The Convention for the Suppression of Unlawful Seizure of Aircraft, 1970;

     (b) The Convention to prevent and punish the acts of terrorism taking the form of
          crimes against persons and related extortion that are of international
          significance, 1971;

     (c) The Convention for the Suppression of Unlawful Acts against the Safety of Civil
          Aviation, 1971;

     (d) The Convention on the Prevention and Punishment of Crimes against
          Internationally Protected Persons, including Diplomatic Agents, 1973;

     (e) The International Convention against the Taking of Hostages, 1979.

41. To initiate constitutional procedures so as to be in a position to sign, ratify or accede
     to the treaties and international agreements referred to in the preceding paragraph, if
     they have not already done so.

42. To prevent in their respective territories the planning or commission of criminal acts
     against other States or the nationals of such States by terrorist groups or
     organizations. To that end, they shall strengthen co-operation between the competent
     migration offices and police departments and between the corresponding civilian
     authorities.

43. On the basis of presumption or established facts, to report any violations to the
     Verification and Control Commission, with sufficient evidence to enable it to carry
     out the necessary investigation and submit such conclusions and recommendations as
     it may consider useful.

Section 8. COMMITMENTS WITH REGARD TO DIRECT COMMUNICATIONS SYSTEMS

44. To establish a regional communications system which guarantees timely liaison
     between the competent government, civilian and military authorities, and with the
     Verification and Control Commission, with a view to preventing incidents.

45. To establish joint security commissions in order to prevent incidents and settle disputes between neighbouring States.

PART II

COMMITMENTS WITH REGARD TO EXECUTION AND FOLLOW-UP

1. The Ministers for Foreign Affairs of the Central American States shall receive the opinions, reports and recommendations presented by the execution and follow-up mechanisms provided for in this Part II and shall take by consensus and without delay the appropriate decisions to ensure full compliance with the commitments entered into in the Act. For the purposes of this Act, consensus means the absence of any express opposition that would constitute an obstacle to the adoption of a decision under consideration and in which all the States Parties are to participate. Any dispute shall be subject to the procedures provided for in this Act.

2. In order to ensure the execution and follow-up of the commitments contained in this Act, the Parties decide to establish the following mechanisms:

   A. *Ad Hoc* Committee for Evaluation and Follow-up of Commitments concerning Political Matters and Refugees and Displaced Persons;

   B. Verification and Control Commission for Security Matters; and

   C. *Ad Hoc* Committee for Evaluation and Follow-up of Commitments concerning Economic and Social Matters.

3. The mechanisms established in the Act shall have the following composition, structure and functions;

   A. *Ad Hoc* Committee for Evaluation and Follow-up of Commitments concerning Political Matters and Refugees and Displaced Persons.

      (a) Composition

         The Committee shall be composed of five (5) persons of recognized competence and impartiality, proposed by the Contadora Group and accepted by common agreement by the Parties. The members of the Committee must be of a nationality different from those of the Parties. The Committee shall have a technical and administrative secretariat responsible for its ongoing operation.

      (b) Functions

         The Committee shall consider the reports which the Parties undertake to submit annually on the ways in which they have proceeded to implement the commitments with regard to national reconciliation, human rights, electoral processes and refugees.

         In addition, the Committee shall receive the communications on these subjects transmitted for its information by organizations or individuals which might contribute data useful for the fulfillment of its mandate.

         The Committee shall elicit the information which it deems relevant; to that end, the Party to which the communication refers shall permit the members of the Committee to enter its territory and shall accord them the necessary facilities.

The Committee shall prepare an annual report and such special reports as it deems necessary on compliance with the commitments, which shall include conclusions and recommendations when appropriate.

The Committee shall send its reports to the Parties and to the Governments of the Contadora Group. When the period established by the rules for the submission of observations by the States Parties has expired, the Committee shall prepare final reports, which shall be public unless the Committee itself decides otherwise.

(c) Rules of procedure

The Committee shall draw up its own rules of procedure, which it shall make known to the Parties.

(d) The Committee shall be established at the time of entry into force of the Act.

B. Verification and Control Commission for Security Matters

(a) Composition

The Commission shall be composed of four commissioners, representing four States of recognized impartiality having a genuine interest in contributing to the solution of the Central American crisis, proposed by the Contadora Group and accepted by the Parties.

A Latin American Executive Secretary with technical and administrative duties, proposed by the Contadora Group and accepted by common agreement by the Parties, who shall be responsible for the ongoing operation of the Commission.

(b) Functions

For the performance of its functions, the Commission shall have an International Corps of Inspectors, provided by the member States of the Commission and co-ordinated by a Director of Operations.

The International Corps of Inspectors shall carry out the functions assigned to it by the Commission, according to the procedures that the Commission determines or establishes in its rules of procedure.

The International Corps of Inspectors shall have at its disposal all the human and material resources that the Commission decides to assign to it in order to ensure strict observance of the commitments on security matters. Its actions shall be prompt and thorough.

The Parties undertake to give the Commission all the co-operation it needs to facilitate and perform its task.

For the purpose of co-operating in the performance of the functions of the Commission, the latter shall have an Advisory Committee consisting of one representative from each Central American State and having the following duties:

1. To serve as a liaison body between the Verification and Control Commission and the Parties.

2. To help in the fulfillment of the duties assigned to the Verification and Control Commission.

3. To co-operate, at the request of the Commission, in the speedy resolution of incidents or disputes.

—   The Commission may invite a representative of the Secretary-General of the United Nations and a representative of the Secretary-General of the Organization of American States to participate in its meetings as observers.

—   The Commission may establish auxiliary bodies and seek the assistance and collaboration of any Mixed Commissions that may exist.

(c) Functions of the Commission

The function of the Commission shall be to ensure compliance with the commitments assumed concerning to security matters. To that end it shall:

—   Verify that the commitments concerning military manoeuvres provided for in this Act are complied with.

—   Ascertain that no more military *matériel* is acquired and that military forces are not increased, in accordance with the provisions of paragraph 19 (a) of Chapter III of Part I of this Act.

—   Receive simultaneously from the Parties their respective current inventories of armaments and military installations and troops under arms, in accordance with the provisions of subparagraph (b) of the FIRST STAGE in Paragraph 19 of Part I, Chapter III, of this Act.

—   Carry out the technical studies provided for in subparagraph (c) of the FIRST STAGE in paragraph 19 of Part I, Chapter III, of this Act.

—   Ascertain that the Parties comply fully with the maximum limits agreed to or provisionally in effect for the various categories of armaments, military installations and troops under arms and with the reduction timetables agreed to or provisionally in effect.

—   Ascertain that the replenishment supplies, ammunition, spare parts and replacement equipment acquired are compatible with the inventories and registers submitted previously by the Parties and with the limits and timetables agreed to or provisionally in effect.

—   Verify that no new weapon systems are introduced which qualitatively or quantitatively alter current inventories of war *matériel*, and that weapons prohibited in this Act are neither introduced nor used.

—   Establish a register of all weapons transactions carried out by the Parties, including donations and any transfer of war *matériel*.

— Verify fulfillment of the commitment by the States Parties to initiate and complete the constitutional procedures for signing, ratifying or acceding to the treaties and other international agreements on disarmament and follow-up actions directed to that end.

— Receive simultaneously from the Parties the list of foreign military bases, schools and installations and verify their dismantlement, in accordance with the provisions of this Act.

— Receive the census of foreign military advisers and other foreign elements participating in military and security activities and verify their withdrawal in accordance with the recommendations of the Verification and Control Commission.

— Verify compliance with this Act in respect of traffic in arms and consider any reports of non-compliance. For that purpose the following criteria shall be taken into account:

   (1) Origin of the arms traffic: port or airport of embarkation of the weapons, munitions, equipment or other military supplies intended for the Central American region.

   (2) Personnel involved: persons, groups or organizations participating in the organization and conduct of the traffic in arms, including the participation of Governments or their representatives.

   (3) Type of weapon, munitions, equipment or other military supplies; category and calibre of weapons; country in which they were manufactured; country of origin; and the quantities of each type of weapon, munitions, equipment or other military supplies.

   (4) Extra-regional means of transport: land, maritime or air transport, including nationality.

   (5) Extra-regional transport routes: indicating the traffic routes used, including stops or intermediate destinations.

   (6) Place where weapons, munitions, equipment and other military supplies are stored.

   (7) Intra-regional traffic areas and routes: description of the areas and routes; participation of governmental or other sectors in or consent to the conduct of the traffic in arms; frequency of use of these areas and routes.

   (8) Intra-regional means of transport: determination of the means of transport used; ownership of these means; facilities provided by Governments, governmental and other sectors; and other means of delivery.

   (9) Receiving unit or unit for which the arms are destined: determination of the persons, groups or organizations to whom the arms traffic is destined.

— Verify compliance with this Act with regard to irregular forces and the non-use of their own territory in destabilizing actions against another State, and consider any report in that connection.

To that purpose, the following criteria should be taken into account:

(1) Installations means, bases, camps or logistic and operational support facilities for irregular forces, including command centres, radiocommunications centres and radio transmitters.

(2) Determination of propaganda activities or political material, economic or military support for actions directed against any State of the region.

(3) Identification of persons, groups and governmental sectors involved in such actions.

— Verify compliance with the commitments concerning terrorism, subversion and sabotage contained in this Act.

— The Commission and the States Parties may request, as they deem appropriate, the assistance of the International Committee of the Red Cross in helping to solve humanitarian problems affecting the Central American countries.

(d) Rules and procedures

— The Commission shall receive any duly substantiated report concerning violations of the security commitments assumed under this Act, shall communicate it to the Parties involved and shall initiate such investigation as it deems appropriate.

— It shall also be empowered to carry out, on its own initiative the investigations it deems appropriate.

— The Commission shall carry out its investigations by making on-site inspections, gathering testimony and using any other procedure which it deems necessary for the performance of its functions.

— Without prejudice to its quarterly and special reports, the Commission shall, in the event of any reports of violations or of non-compliance with the security commitments of this Act, prepare a report containing recommendations addressed to the Parties involved.

— The Commission shall be accorded every facility and prompt and full co-operation by the Parties for the appropriate performance of its functions. It shall also ensure the confidentiality of all information elicited or received in the course of its investigations.

— The Commission shall transmit its reports and recommendations to the States Parties and to the Governments of the Contadora Group on a confidential basis. It may make them public when it considers that that would contribute to full compliance with the commitments contained in the Act.

(d) Rules of procedure

　– After the Commission is established, it shall draw up its own rules of procedure in consultation with the States Parties.

(e) Duration of the mandate of the Commissioners

— The representatives of the member States of the Commission shall have an initial mandate of two years, extendable by common agreement among the Parties, and the States participating in the Commission.

(f) Establishment

— The Commission shall be established at the time when the Act is signed.

C. *Ad Hoc* Committee for Evaluation and Follow-up of Commitments concerning Economic and Social Matters.

(a) Composition

— For the purposes of this Act, the Meeting of Ministers for Economic Affairs of Central America shall constitute the *Ad Hoc* Committee for Evaluation and Follow-up of Commitments concerning Economic and Social Matters.

— The Committee shall have a technical and administrative secretariat responsible for its ongoing operation; this function shall be assumed by the Secretariat of Central American Economic Integration (SIECA).

(b) Functions

— The Committee shall receive the annual reports of the Parties concerning progress in complying with the commitments concerning economic and social matters.

— The Committee shall make periodic evaluations of the progress made in complying with the commitments concerning economic and social matters, using for that purpose the information produced by the Parties and by the competent international and regional organizations.

— The Committee shall present, in its periodic reports, proposals for strengthening regional co-operation and promoting development plans, with particular emphasis on the aspects mentioned in the commitments contained in this Act.

4. Financing of the Execution and Follow-up Mechanisms

(a) The Execution and Follow-up Mechanisms referred to in Part II of the Act shall be financed through a Fund for Peace in Central America.

(b) The resources for that Fund shall be obtained in the form of equal contributions by the States Parties and additional contributions obtained from other States, international organizations or other sources, which may be managed by the Central American States with the collaboration of the Contadora Group.

Appendix B: Esquipulas II Agreement

PREAMBLE

We, the Presidents of the Republics of Guatemala, El Salvador, Honduras, Nicaragua and Costa Rica, meeting at Guatemala City on 6 and 7 August, encouraged by the far-sighted and unfailing determination of the Contadora Group and the Support Group to achieve peace, strengthened by the steady support of all the Governments and peoples of the world, their main international organisations and, in particular, the European Economic Community and His Holiness John Paul II, drawing inspiration from the Esquipulas I Summit Meeting and having some come together in Guatemala to discuss the peace plan presented by the Government of Costa Rica, have agreed as follows:

To take up fully the historical challenge of forging a peaceful destiny for Central America;

To commit ourselves to the struggle for peace and the elimination of war;

To make dialogue prevail over violence and reason over hatred;

To dedicate these peace efforts to the young people of Central America whose legitimate aspirations to peace and social justice, freedom and reconciliation have been frustrated for many generations;

To take the Central American Parliament as the symbol of the freedom and independence of the reconciliation to which we aspire in Central America.

We ask the international community to respect and assist our efforts. We have our own approaches to peace and development but we need help in making them a reality. We ask for a international response which will guarantee development so that the peace we are seeking can be a lasting one. We reiterate firmly that peace and development are inseparable.

We thank President Vinicio Cerezo Arévalo and the noble people of Guatemala for having hosted this meeting. The generosity of the President and people of Guatemala were decisive in creating the climate in which the peace agreements were adopted.

PROCEDURE FOR THE ESTABLISHMENT OF A FIRM AND LASTING PEACE IN CENTRAL AMERICA

The Governments of the Republics of Costa Rica, El Salvador, Guatemala, Honduras and Nicaragua, determined to achieve the principles and purposes of the Charter of the United Nations, the Charter of the Organization of American States, the Document of Objectives, the Caraballeda Message for Peace, Security and Democracy in Central America, the Guatemala Declaration, the Punta del Este Communiqué, the Panama Message, the Esquipulas Declaration and the draft Contadora Act of 6 June 1986 on Peace and Co-operation in Central America, have agreed on the following procedure for the establishment of a firm and lasting peace in Central America.

1. NATIONAL RECONCILIATION

(a) Dialogue

Wherever deep divisions have taken place within society, the Governments agreed to urgently undertake actions of national reconciliation which permit popular participation, with full guarantees, in genuine democratic political processes on the basis of justice, freedom and democracy and, to that end, to create mechanisms permitting a dialogue with opposition groups in accordance with the law.

To this end, the Governments in question shall initiate a dialogue with all the domestic political opposition groups which have laid down their arms and those which have availed themselves of the amnesty.

(b) Amnesty

In each Central American country, except those where the International Verification and Follow-up Commission determines this to be unnecessary, amnesty decrees shall be issued which establish all necessary provisions guaranteeing the inviolability of life, freedom in all its forms, property and security of person of those of whom such decrees are applicable. Simultaneously with the issue of amnesty decrees, the irregular forces of the countries in question shall release anyone that they are holding prisoner.

(c) National Reconciliation Commission

To verify fulfilment of the commitments with regard to amnesty, a cease-fire, democratization and free elections entered into by the five Central American Governments in signing this document, a National Reconciliation Commission shall be set up in each country, responsible for verifying genuine implementation of the process of national reconciliation and also unrestricted respect for all the civil and political rights of Central American citizens guaranteed in this document.

The National Reconciliation Commission shall be composed of: a representative of the executive branch and his alternate; a representative and an alternate proposed by the Conference of Bishops and chosen by the Government from a list of three bishops. This list shall be submitted within 15 days following receipt of the formal invitation. Governments shall make this invitation within five working days following the signing of this document. The same procedure of proposing three candidates shall be used to choose a representative and an alternate representative of legally registered opposition political parties. The list of three candidates shall be submitted within the same period as indicated above. Each Central American Government shall also choose an eminent citizen belonging to neither the Government nor the government party, and his alternate, to serve on the Commission. The agreement or decree setting up the corresponding National Commission shall be communicated immediately to the other Central American Governments.

2. APPEAL FOR AN END TO HOSTILITIES

The Governments make an urgent appeal that, in those States of the region where irregular or insurgent groups are currently active, agreement be reached to end hostilities. The Governments of those States undertake to take all necessary steps, in accordance with the constitution, to bring about a genuine cease-fire.

3. DEMOCRATIZATION

The Governments undertake to promote an authentic democratic process that is pluralistic and participatory, which entails the promotion of social justice and respect for human rights, the sovereignty and territorial integrity of States and the right of every nation to choose, freely and without outside interference of any kind, its own economic, political and social system. They shall adopt, in a way that can be verified, measures conducive to the establishment and, where appropriate, improvement of democratic, representative and pluralistic systems that will guarantee the organization of political parties and effective popular participation in the decision-making process and ensure that the various currents of opinion have free access to fair and regular elections based on the full observance of citizens' rights. In order to ensure good faith in the implementation of this process of democratization, it shall be understood that:

(a)   There must be complete freedom of television, radio and the press. This complete freedom shall include freedom for all ideological groups to launch and operate communication media and to operate them without prior censorship;

(b)   Complete pluralism of political parties must be established. Political groupings shall, in this connection, have broad access to the communication media and full enjoyment of the rights of association and the power to hold public demonstrations in unrestricted exercise of the right to publicize their ideas orally, in writing and on television, and members of political parties shall enjoy freedom of movement in campaigning for political support;

(c)   Likewise, those Central American Governments which are currently imposing a state of siege or emergency shall revoke it, ensuring that a state of law exists in which all constitutional guarantees are fully enforced.

4. FREE ELECTIONS

Once the conditions inherent in any democracy have been created, free, pluralistic and fair elections shall be held.

As a joint expression by the Central American States of their desire for reconciliation and lasting peace for their peoples, elections will be held for the Central American Parliament proposed in the Esquipulas Declaration of May 25, 1986.

In the above connection, the Presidents expressed their willingness to move ahead with the organization of the Parliament. To that end, the Preparatory Commission for the Central American Parliament shall complete its deliberations and submit the corresponding draft treaty to the Central American Presidents within 150 days.

Elections shall be held simultaneously in all the countries of Central America in the first six months of 1988, at a date to be agreed in due course by the Presidents of the Central American States. They shall be subject to supervision by the corresponding electoral bodies, and the Governments concerned undertake to invite the Organization of American States, the United Nations and the Governments of third States to send observers to verify the electoral process has been governed by the strictest rules of equal access for all political parties to the communication media and by ample opportunities for organizing public demonstrations and any other type of political propaganda.

With a view to enabling the elections to the Central American Parliament to be held within the period indicated, the treaty establishing the Parliament shall be submitted for approval or ratification in the five countries.

Once the elections for the Central American Parliament have been held, equally free and democratic elections for the appointment of popular representatives to municipalities, congress, the legislative assembly and the office of the President of the Republic shall be held in each country, with international observers and the same guarantees, within the established time-limits and subject to time tables to be proposed in accordance with each country's current constitution.

5. TERMINATION OF AID FOR IRREGULAR FORCES AND INSURRECTIONIST MOVEMENTS

The Governments of the five Central American States shall request Governments of the region and Governments from outside the region which are providing either overt or covert military, logistical, financial or propaganda support, in the form of men, weapons, munitions and equipment, to irregular forces or insurrectionist movements to terminate such aid; this is vital if a stable and lasting peace is to be attained in the region.

The above does not cover aid for the repatriation or, failing that, the relocation and necessary assistance with reintegration into normal life of former members of such groups or forces. The Central Americanism. These requests shall be made pursuant to the provisions of the Document of Objectives which calls for eliminating the traffic in arms, whether within the region or from outside it, intended for persons, organizations or groups seeking to destabilize the Governments of Central American countries.

6. NON-USE OF TERRITORY TO ATTACK OTHER STATES

The five countries signing this document reiterate their commitment to prevent the use of their own territory by persons, organizations or groups seeking to destabilize the Governments of Central American countries and to refuse to provide them with or allow them to receive military and logistical support.

7. NEGOTIATIONS ON SECURITY, VERIFICATION AND THE CONTROL AND LIMITATION OF WEAPONS

The Governments of the five Central American States, with the Contadora Group acting as mediator, shall continue negotiating on the points outstanding in the draft Contadora Act on Peace and Co-operation in Central America with regard to security, verification and control.

These negotiations shall also cover measures for disarming irregular forces prepared to avail themselves of amnesty decrees.

8. REFUGEES AND DISPLACED PERSONS

The Central American Governments undertake to attend, as a matter of urgency, to the flows of refugees and displaced persons caused by the crisis in the region, providing them with protection and assistance, particularly in the areas of health, education, work and safety, and to facilitate their repatriation, resettlement or relocation provided that this is voluntary and carried out on an individual basis.

They also undertake to seek assistance from the international community for Central American refugees and displaced persons, to be provided either directly, through bilateral or multilateral agreements, or indirectly, through the Office of the United Nations High Commissioner for Refugees (UNHCR) and other organizations and agencies.

9. CO-OPERATION, DEMOCRACY AND FREEDOM FOR PEACE AND DEVELOPMENT

In the climate of freedom guaranteed by democracy, the Central American countries shall adopt such agreements as will help to speed up development, in order to make their societies more egalitarian and free from misery.

The strengthening of democracy entails creating a system of economic and social well-being and justice. To achieve these goals, the Governments shall jointly seek special economic assistance from the international community.

10. INTERNATIONAL VERIFICATION AND FOLLOW-UP

(a) International Verification and Follow-up Commission

An International Verification and Follow-up Commission shall be established consisting of the Secretary-General of the Organization of American States, or his representative, the Secretary-General of the United Nations, or his representative, and the Ministers for Foreign Affairs of Central America, the Contadora Group and the Support Group. This Commission shall be responsible for verifying and monitoring fulfilment of the commitments set forth in this document.

(b) Support and facilities for reconciliation and verification and follow-up bodies

In order to reinforce the efforts of the International Verification and Follow-up Commission, the Governments of the five Central American States shall issue statements of support for its work. All nations interested in promoting the cause of freedom, democracy and peace in Central America may adhere to these statements.

The five Governments shall provide all necessary facilities for the proper conduct of the verification and follow-up functions of the National Reconciliation Commission in each country and the International Verification and Follow-up Commission.

11. TIMETABLE FOR FULFILMENT OF COMMITMENTS

Within a period of 15 days from the signing of this document, the Central American Ministers for Foreign Affairs shall meet as an Executive Commission to regulate, encourage and facilitate compliance with the agreements contained in this document and to organize working commissions so that, as of that date, the processes leading to fulfilment of the agreed commitments within the stipulated periods can be set in motion by means of consultations, negotiations and any other mechanisms which are deemed necessary.

Ninety days after the signing of this document, the commitments with regard to amnesty, a cease-fire, democratization, termination of aid to irregular forces or insurrectionist movements, and the non-use of territory to attack other States, as defined in this document, shall enter into force simultaneously and be made public.

One hundred and twenty days after the signing of this document, the International Verification and Follow-up Commission shall review the progress made in complying with the agreements set forth in this document.

FINAL PROVISIONS

The elements set forth in this document form a harmonious and indivisible whole. By signing it, the Central American States accept in good faith the obligation to comply simultaneously with what has been agreed within the established time-limits.

We, the Presidents of the five Central American States, having the political will to respond to our peoples' desire for peace, sign this document at Guatemala City on 7 August, 1987.

(Signed) OSCAR ARIAS SANCHEZ
President
Republic of Costa Rica

(Signed) JOSE NAPOLEON DUARTE
President
Republic of El Salvador

(Signed) VINICIO CEREZO AREVALO
President
Republic of Guatemala

(Signed) JOSE AZCONA HOYO
President
Republic of Honduras

(Signed) DANIEL ORTEGA SAAVEDRA
President
Republic of Nicaragua

(Official United Nations Translation)

Selected Bibliography

Bagley, Bruce Michael. "Contadora: The Failure of Diplomacy." In Abraham Lowenthal (ed.), *Latin America and Caribbean Contemporary Record*. New York: Holmes and Meier, 1987.

------ (ed.). Contadora and the Diplomacy of Peace in Central America. Boulder: Westview Press, 1987.

------ and Juan Gabriel Tokatlian. "Contadora: The Limits of Negotiations." Unpublished paper for the Latin American Studies Program of the School of Advanced International Studies, Johns Hopkins University. Washington, D.C.: 1986.

Baranyi, Steven. "Canadian Foreign Policy Towards Central America, 1980-84: Independence, Limited Public Influence, and State Leadership." *Canadian Journal of Latin American and Caribbean Studies*, 10:19 (1985), pp. 23-57.

Bauman, Everett A. *The Strengths and Weaknesses of Contadora as Regional Diplomacy in the Caribbean Basin*. Unpublished working paper for the Latin American program, Woodrow Wilson International Center for Scholars, 1985.

Bell, George. "Canada and the OAS: Going around the Buoy Again?" In Brian MacDonald (ed.), *Canada, the Caribbean and Central America*. Toronto: Canadian Institute of Strategic Studies, 1986, pp. 87-108.

Best, Edward. *U.S. Policy and Regional Security in Central America*. New York: St. Martin's Press, 1987.

Blachman, Morris, William LeoGrande, and Kenneth Sharpe (eds.). *Confronting Revolution: Security through Diplomacy in Central America*. New York: Pantheon, 1988.

Black, George. *Garrison Guatemala*. London: Zed Books, 1984, p. 6.

Bricker, Calvin (ed.). *Central America and Peacekeeping: A Workshop Report*. Toronto: CISS, 1986.

Brumbaugh, Chalmers. *Costa Rica: The Making of a Livable Society*. Unpublished Ph.D. dissertation, University of Wisconsin, 1985.

Bruneau, Thomas. "Canada and Latin America: Background."   In *Canada, the United States, and Latin America: Independence and Accommodation*. Conference report.   Washington, D.C., Latin American Program, Woodrow Wilson International Center for Scholars, April 1984, pp. 1-11.

------, Jan J. Torgensen, and J. O. Ramsay. *CIDA: The Organization of Canadian Overseas Assistance* 24, Centre for Developing Area Studies, McGill University. Montreal: October 1978.

Burns, E. Bradford. "Nicaragua: Paving a Separate Path." *In These Times* (September 10-16, 1986).

------. *At War in Nicaragua: The Reagan Doctrine and the Politics of Nostalgia*. New York: Harper and Row, 1987, p. 115.

Canadian Department of Manpower and Immigration. *A Report of the Canadian Immigration and Population Study*. 4 vols. Ottawa: Information Canada, 1974.

Czerny, Michael, and Tim Draimin. "A Secret Foreign Policy: Canada and Central America." Pamphlet published by CAPA. Toronto: Winter 1985.

Dale, Stephen. "Abetting Uncivil Warfare." *Now* (September 25 - October 1, 1986).

Department of External Affairs. *Canada's International Relations*. Ottawa: 1986.

Dewitt, David, and John Kirton. *Canada as a Principal Power*. Toronto: John Wiley, 1983.

Dirks, Gerald. "A Policy within a Policy: The Identification and Admission of Refugees to Canada." *Canadian Journal of Political Science* 17:2 (June 1984), pp. 279-307.

Dosman, Edgar. "Hemispheric Relations in the 1980's: A Perspective from Canada." *Journal of Canadian Studies* 19:4 (Winter 1985), pp. 42-60.

Draimin, Tim. "Canadian Foreign Policy in El Salvador." In Liisa North (ed.), *Bitter Grounds*. Toronto: Between the Lines Press, 1981, pp. 99-100.

------. *Canada and Central America: An Overview of Business and Governmental Relations*. Toronto: CAPA, 1982.

------. *Canada's Policy Toward Central America*. Pamphlet distributed by CAPA. Toronto: February 1983.

Fagan, Richard. *Forging Peace: The Challenge of Central America*. New York: Basil Blackwell, 1987.

Falcoff, Mark, and Robert Royal. *The Continuing Crisis: U.S. Policy in Central America and the Caribbean*. Lanham, MD: UPA, 1987.

Findling, John E. *Close Neighbors, Distant Friends: United States Central American Relations*. Westport, CT: Westview, 1987.

Graham, John. "Shaping Stability in Central America," in John Holmes and John Kirton (eds.), *Canada and The New Internationalism*. Toronto: University of Toronto Press, 1988.

Haglund, David. "Missing Link: Canada's Security Interests and the Central American Crisis." *International Journal* 43:4 (Autumn 1987), pp. 789-820

Hawkins, Freda. *Canada and Immigration: Public Policy and Public Concern*. 2d ed. Montreal: McGill-Queen's University Press, 1988.

Keenleyside, Terence A. "Foreign Aid and Human Rights." *International Perspectives* (March/April 1987), pp. 15-18.

Kornbluh, Peter. *The Price of Intervention: Reagan's Wars Against the Sandinistas*. Washington, D.C.: IPS, 1987.

Latin American Working Group. "Taking sides: Canadian Aid to El Salvador." *LAWG Letter* 10:1 (August 1987).

------. "Overview of Canadian Aid to Central America: 1980-85." 9:3 (February 1988).

------. "Paved with Good Intentions: Canadian Aid to Honduras. *LAWG Letter* 44 (February 1989).

Leiken, Robert S., and Barry Ruben (eds.). *The Central American Crises Reader*. New York: Summit Books, 1987.

Lemco, Jonathan. "Canadian Foreign Policy Interests in Central America: Some Current Issues." *Journal of Inter-American Studies and World Affairs* 28:3 (Summer 1986), pp. 119-146.

------. "The Myth of Canadian-American Harmony." *Atlantic Community Quarterly* (Spring 1987), pp. 91-97.

LeoGrande, William. "Rollback or Containment? The United States, Nicaragua, and the Search for Peace in Central America." *International Security* 11:2 (Fall 1986), pp. 89-120.

Leonard, Julie, and Tim Draimin. *Canadian Links to the Militarization of the Caribbean and Central America*. Toronto: CAPA, May 1985.

Lowenthal, Abraham F. *Partners in Conflict: The United States and Latin America*. Baltimore: Johns Hopkins University Press, 1987.

MacEachen, Allan (Canadian Secretary of State for External Affairs). "Address to the 38th Session of the United Nations General Assembly." New York: September 27, 1983.

MacFarlane, Peter. *Northern Shadows: Canadians and Central America*. Toronto: Between the Lines Press, 1989.

Martin, Lawrence. *The Presidents and the Prime Ministers*. New York: Doubleday, 1982.

Matthews, Robert. "The Christian Churches and Human Rights in Canadian Foreign Policy." *Journal of Canadian Studies* 24:1 (Spring 1989), pp. 5-31.

Molineu, Harold. *U.S. Policy toward Latin America: From Regionalism to Globalism*. Boulder, CO: Westview, 1986.

Mount, Graham, and Edelgard Mahant. "Review of Recent Literature on Canadian-Latin American Relations." *Journal of Inter-American Studies and World Affairs* 27:2 (Summer 1985), pp. 127-151.

Murphy, Brian K. "The Pan-American Game: Canada and Central America." *Canadian Forum* (February/March 1988).

Murray, D. R. "The Bilateral Road: Canada and Latin America in the 1980s." *International Journal* 37 (Winter 1981-82), pp. 108-131.

Naylor, Tom. *The History of Canadian Business 1867-1914*. 2. Toronto: Lorimer, 1975.

North, Liisa. *Negotiations for Peace in Central America: A Conference Report*. 1. Ottawa: Canadian Institute for International Peace and Security, 1985.

Nossal, Kim Richard. "Mixed Motives Revisited: Canada's Interest in Development Assistance." *Canadian Journal of Political Science* 21:1 (March 1988), pp. 35-56.

Pastor, Robert A. *Condemned to Repetition: The United States and Nicaragua*. Princeton: Princeton University Press, 1987.

Pratt, Cranford. "Dominant Class Theory and Canadian Foreign Policy: The Case of the Counter-Consensus." *International Journal* 39:1 (Winter 1983-84), pp. 127-129.

------. "Canada: An Eroding and Limited Internationalism." In Cranford Pratt (ed.), Internationalism Under Strain: The North-South Policies of Canada, The Netherlands, Norway and Sweden, Toronto: University of Toronto Press (1989), pp. 24-69.

Queen's Printer. *Supporting the Five: Canada and the Central American Peace Process*. Ottawa, July 5, 1988.

Rochlin, James. "Aspects of Canadian Foreign Policy Towards Central America, 1979-1986. *Journal of Canadian Studies* 22:4 (Winter 1987-88), pp. 5-26.

Rogers, Benjamin. "The Extent, Focus and Changes of Canadian Public Interest in Latin America: 1967-1976." Report prepared for the Historical Division of the Department of External Affairs. Ottawa: March 1977.

Sims, Harold Dana, and Vilma Petrash. "The Contadora Peace Process." *Conflict Quarterly* 7:4 (Fall 1987), pp. 5-28.

Tackaberry, John. "Getting Development Right." *International Perspectives* (July/August 1987), pp. 12-14.

Teigeler, Jutta. "Foreign Aid and NGOs." *International Perspectives* (March/April 1988), pp. 21-23.

Thomson, Bob. *Canadian Aid and Trade Relations With Nicaragua.* Toronto: CAPA, November 1984.

Walker, Thomas W. (ed). *Reagan Versus the Sandinistas: The Undeclared War on Nicaragua.* Boulder, CO: Westview, 1987.

Wiarda, Howard J. (ed.). *Rift and Revolution: The Central American Imbroglio.* Washington, D.C.: AEI, 1984.

Index

ABOUT THE AUTHOR

JONATHAN LEMCO, a native of Montreal, is a Senior Fellow at the National Planning Association and an Adjunct Professor at The Johns Hopkins University Paul Nitze School of Advanced International Studies. He is the author of three books and many scholarly articles exploring Canadian foreign and domestic policy, political development in modernizing countries, and comparative federalism.

DUE DATE

MAY 1 1 2006

Printed
in USA